IMAGES
of America

BLOUNT COUNTY

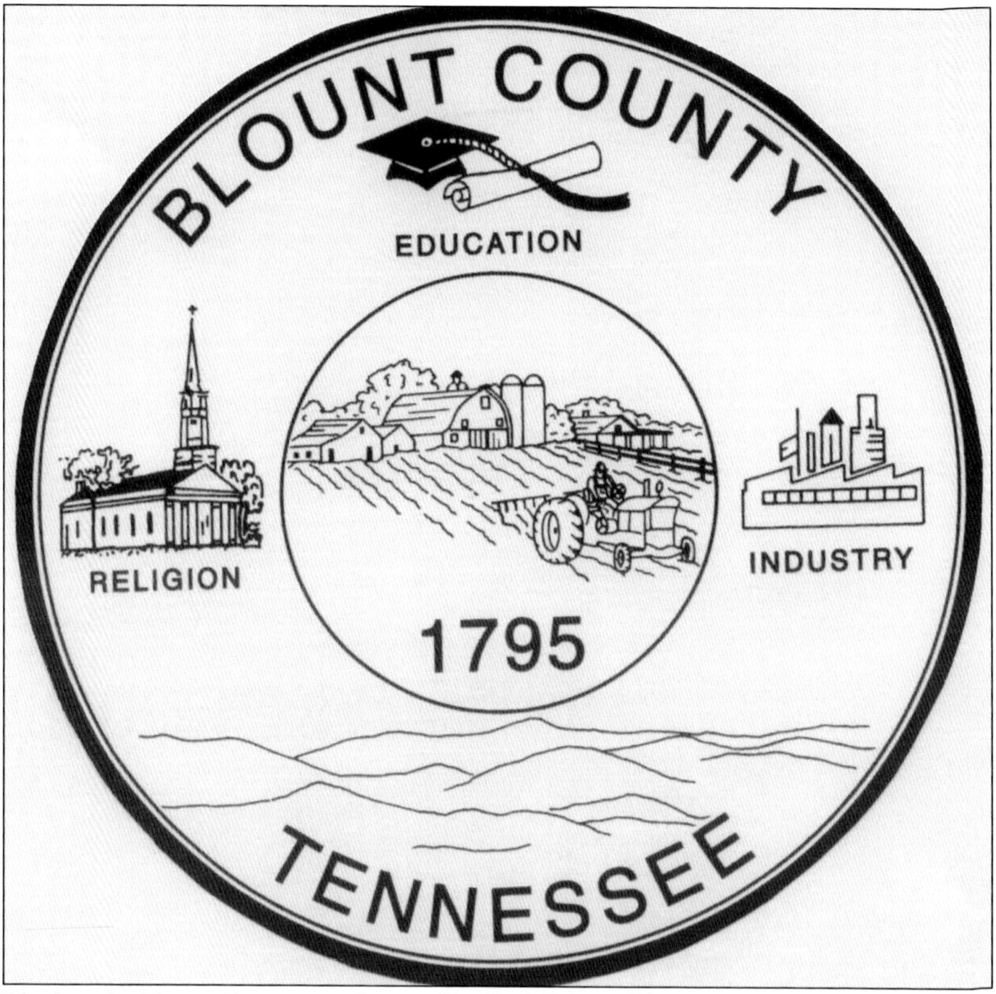

The logo for Blount County was designed by Paul Bales, a Blount County native and retired major accounts executive with the *Daily Times*, Maryville. Bales included the date of the county's founding, 1795, and the facets of life for its residents: religion, education, industry, agriculture, and the Great Smoky Mountains. The logo was the inspiration for the chapters of this book. (Courtesy of Paul Bales.)

On the Cover: This photograph of workers at the Aluminum Company of America (Alcoa, Inc.) was probably taken around 1925. Ernest Avery "Abe" Braden (out of frame) was first employed at the fabricating plant in 1925 at about the age of 27. The aluminum company purchased farmlands north of Maryville for the location of its plants, with the first reduction units, or the South Plant, beginning in 1914. The West Fabricating Plant began in 1920, and the North Plant began in 1939 and was operational in 1942. Alcoa, Inc., continues to be one of Blount County's largest employers. (Courtesy of Ron and Debbie Teffeteller; Martha Birchfield collection.)

IMAGES
of America

Blount County

Linda Braden Albert and
B. Kenneth Cornett

ARCADIA
PUBLISHING

ISBN 978-0-7385-8571-0

Published by Arcadia Publishing
Charleston, South Carolina

Printed in the United States of America

Library of Congress Control Number: 2009939708

For all general information contact Arcadia Publishing at:
Telephone 843-853-2070
Fax 843-853-0044
E-mail sales@arcadiapublishing.com
For customer service and orders:
Toll-Free 1-888-313-2665

Visit us on the Internet at www.arcadiapublishing.com

To all of those who came before and left within us
a hunger to know our roots and preserve our history

Contents

Acknowledgments

The authors are indebted to all those who contributed their precious photographs to be used in this book. We offer a special thanks to Max Crotser, publisher of the *Daily Times,* who allowed us to use whatever we needed from the newspaper's files; to Daryl Sullivan, photo editor at the *Daily Times,* for his technical advice; and to editor Dean Stone, whose own passion for history is well known through his series of books, *Snapshots of Blount County History,* and his column, *Bits of Stone.* We also wish to thank Kathy Pagles, director of the Blount County Public Library, for allowing us to copy photographs from the library's collections, including those of W. O. Garner, Adele McKenzie, and Edwin Best. Historians Lorene Smith and Betty Best, as well as other individuals too numerous to mention but who are credited with the photographs they contributed, were invaluable in providing images and background information.

The majority of the proceeds from the sale of this book will go to the Blount County Historical Museum, the Blount County Genealogical and Historical Society, and the Cades Cove Preservation Association.

INTRODUCTION

This book will showcase a brief bit of the history of Blount County, the 10th county formed in the state of Tennessee. It was carved out of Knox County in 1795 and was named for William Blount, the governor of the Territory South of the River Ohio. Maryville is the county seat and was named for Blount's wife, Mary Grainger Blount.

We, the people of Blount County, live in the shadow of the Great Smoky Mountains, one of the most popular tourist destinations in the United States. We also live in the shadow of history—a long, varied progression of the past that leads from the pioneer settlement of Cades Cove to churches planted here before the county was even formed; to the beginnings of lumber, rail, aluminum, and other industries; to a land once torn asunder by the Civil War. *Blount County* will revisit those gracious homes and the crude cabins where our ancestors lived, raised their families, and died, to be buried beneath the red clay from which they drew their living.

We will see some of the schools, houses of worship, and places of business and industry. We will learn about an 1802 home that stood proudly for more than two centuries until it was consumed by fire in 2008; a late-18th-century stone house reputed to have stood in three states and which survived a cannonball or two from the Civil War; and the historic schoolhouse where Sam Houston taught before he went on to be the governor of Tennessee and, later, of Texas. We will get a glimpse of the leisure activities, as well: picnics on the river, church socials, family reunions, and touring the countryside in a newfangled contraption called an automobile. We will remember the days when families worked the land, providing their own meat, vegetables, and fruits.

History is also preserved in the faces of the ones who came before, in photographs lovingly kept and proudly displayed. In this book, we will see some of these people who populated Blount County in the 19th and early 20th centuries—rich man, poor man, beggar, thief. They are all a part of us, no matter what their circumstances of life. In their faces, we see our own.

Many of the images published in *Blount County* have not been available in other publications, and some are from publications with a very limited circulation. They are borrowed from private collections of longtime Blount families, including those with ties to Cades Cove, the most popular destination in the country's most-visited park, the Great Smoky Mountains National Park. Others are from the holdings of the Blount County Public Library.

What we will find is that we have a better understanding of ourselves and of our culture as we take a look at the past. Hopefully readers will have a greater appreciation for the historic preservation efforts in Blount County through the Blount County Historical Museum, the Cades Cove/Thompson-Brown House Museum, the Sam Houston Historic Schoolhouse and Museum, the Blount County Historic Trust, the Blount County Genealogical and Historical Society, and African Americans in Appalachia and Blount County (AAABC), all in Maryville, and the Great Smoky Mountains Heritage Center and Little River Railroad and Lumber Company Museum in Townsend.

When we know where we have come from, we will have a much better idea of where we are going.

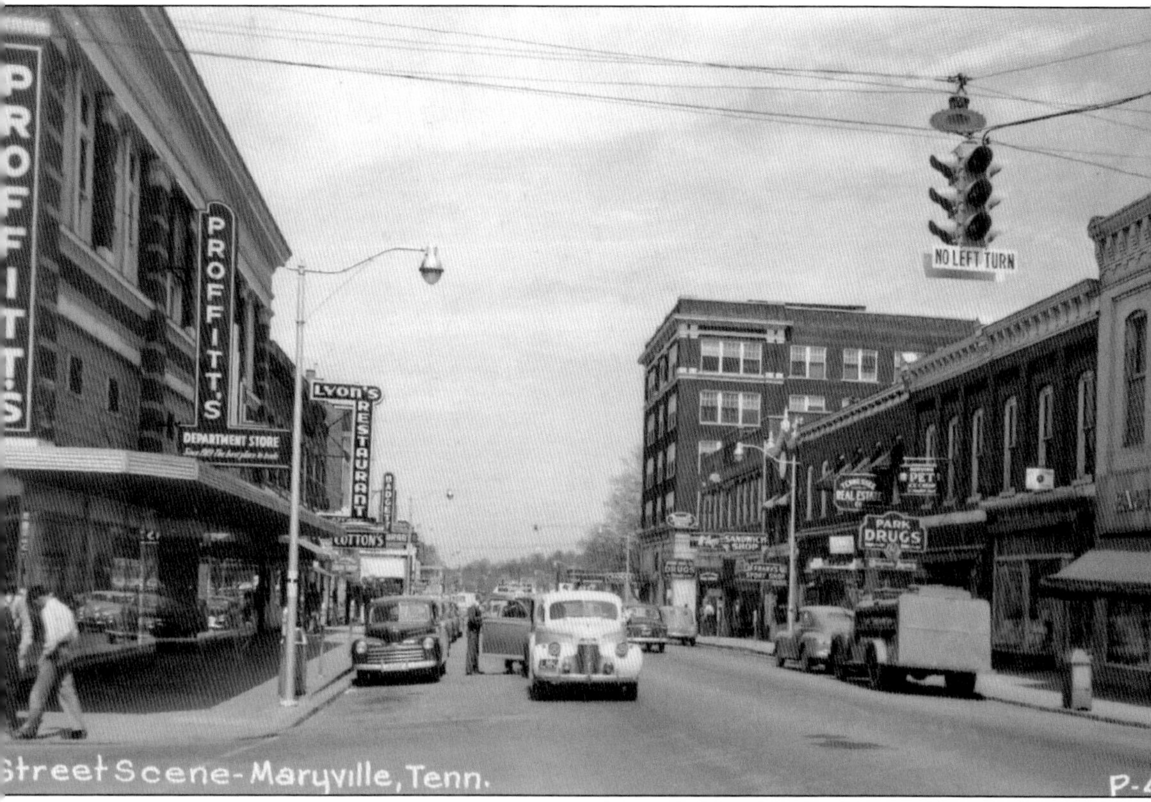

Downtown Maryville is shown in this real-photo postcard from around 1940, taken from the intersection of Main Street, now Broadway Avenue, at Cusick Road looking east. The Blount National Bank Building, known now as Preservation Plaza, is the tallest structure on the right. (Courtesy of B. Kenneth Cornett.)

One

Religion and Faith

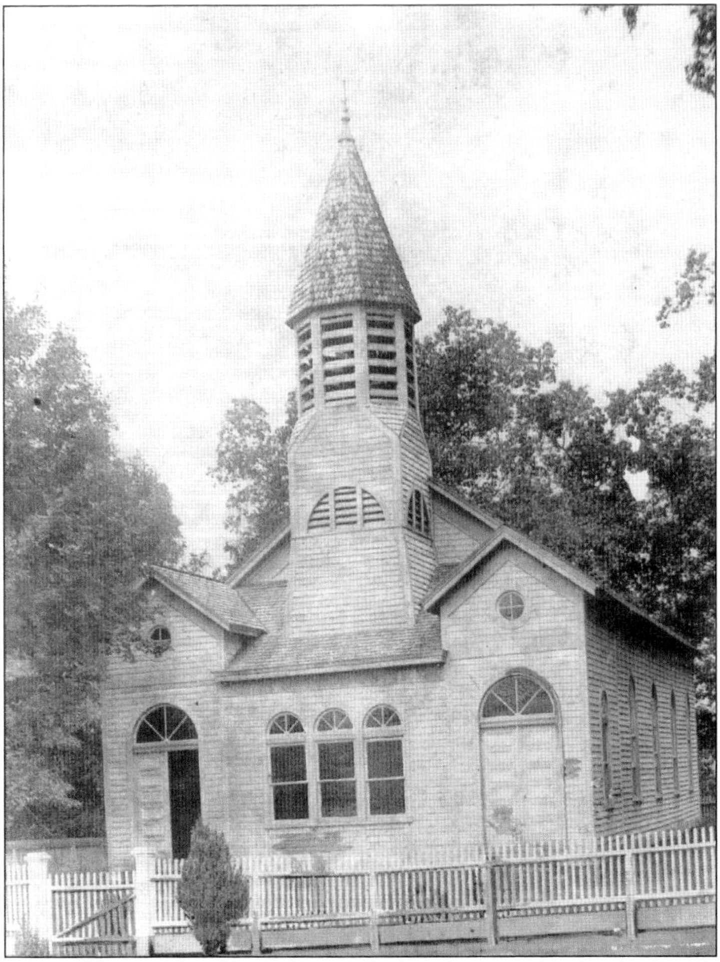

Eusebia Presbyterian Church, shown here, and New Providence Presbyterian Church were both established by Rev. Archibald Scott in 1786. Gideon Blackburn was the first pastor, serving both churches from 1794 until 1810. Until Eusebia's first church building was completed, the congregation met at Robert McTeer's Fort, the site of the first fort, the first school, and the first polling place in Blount County. The frame church pictured here was built in the early 1800s. (Courtesy of B. Kenneth Cornett.)

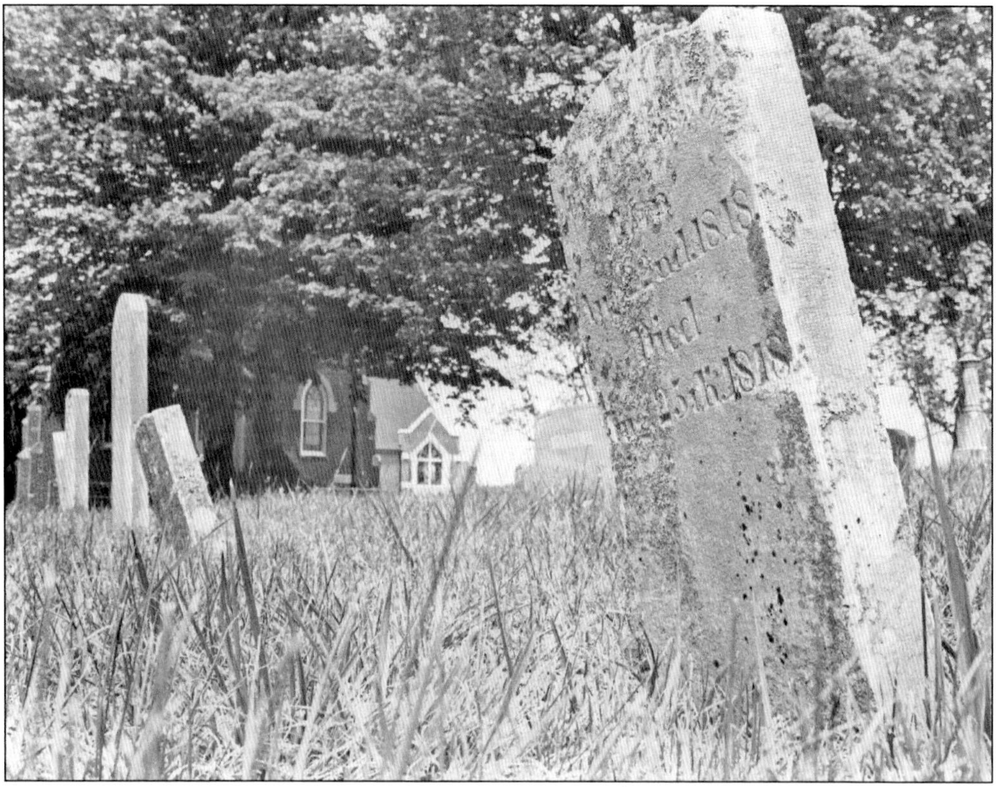

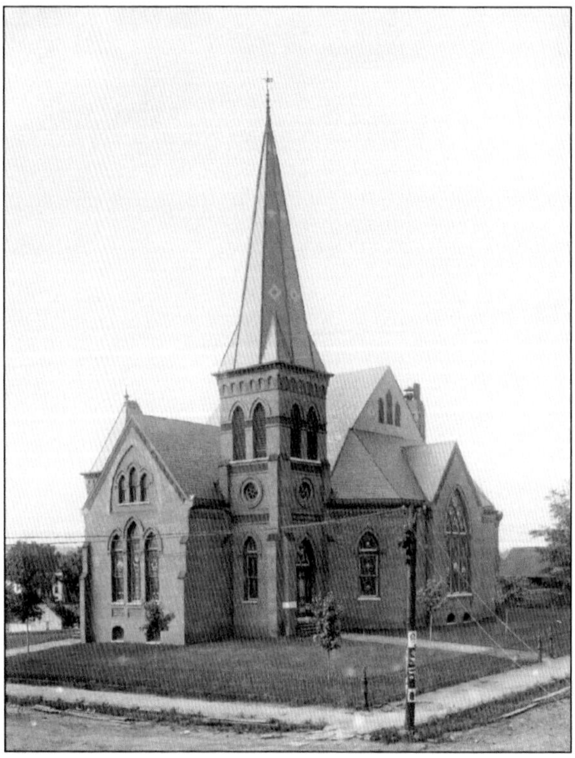

The cemetery at Eusebia Presbyterian Church contains many old gravestones such as this one. The highest concentration of Revolutionary War veterans in Tennessee, at least 15 known, is buried here. (Courtesy of the *Daily Times*.)

New Providence Presbyterian Church was established by Rev. Archibald Scott in 1786, near Craig's Fort at Maryville. Its first pastor, Gideon Blackburn, built a cabin for himself and a log church to house the congregation near what is now the intersection of Cate Street and Broadway Avenue. A stone building replaced the log cabin in 1829 and was torn down in 1852 when a brick structure was erected. The church pictured here was built in 1892 at College and Main (Broadway) Streets, at a cost of $14,211.76. (Courtesy of the Blount County Public Library, Adele McKenzie collection.)

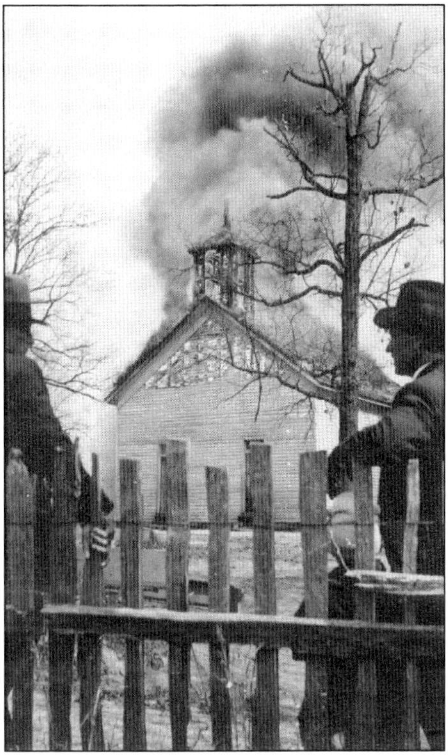

The Methodist Episcopal Church at Pleasant Hill was organized just after the Civil War at Peck's Chapel with about 35 charter members. In 1885, an acre of ground was given to the church by Jesse Whetsell, and four more acres were purchased later. The building shown at right was destroyed by fire in March 1919, and in May 1921, the brick veneer church shown below was dedicated. It cost about $5,500 to build and was clear of all indebtedness when dedicated. The occasion below was the 1950 funeral of Nancy Teffeteller. (Both, courtesy of Ron and Debbie Teffeteller, Martha Birchfield collection.)

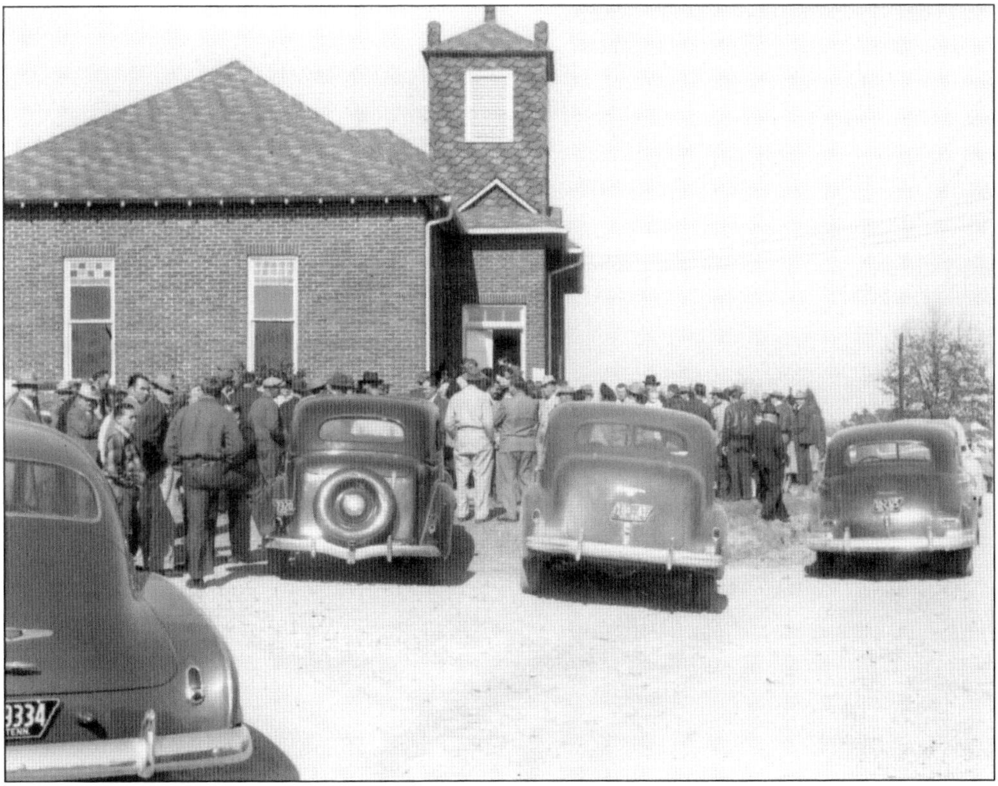

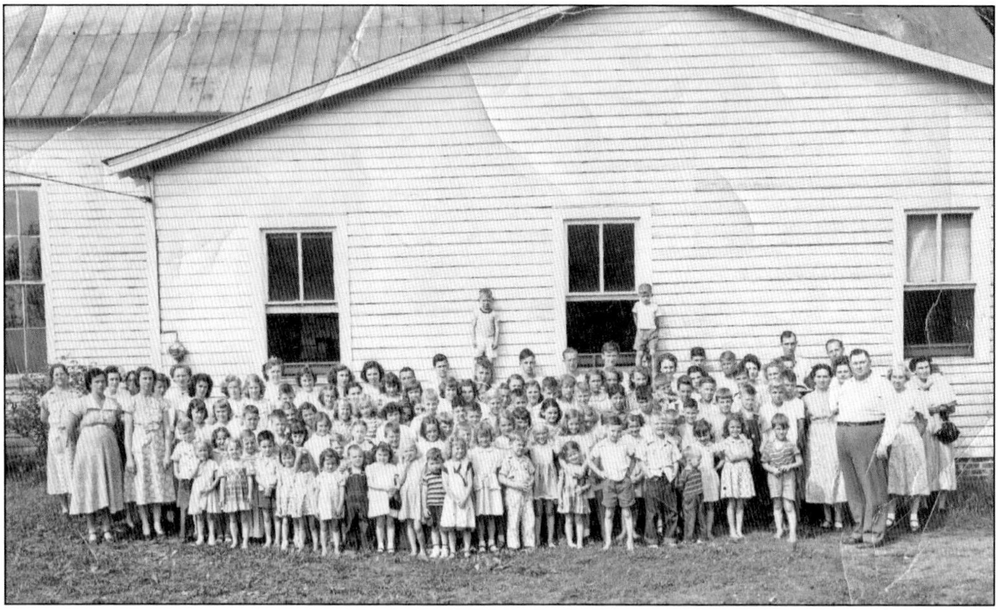

A group of children poses for a photograph at Piney Grove Baptist Church in 1950, when John H. Hipshire was the church pastor. He served from February 1950 until October 1951. The church's first house of worship was a deserted still house, which was moved from the nearby mountain to the old brush arbor where the church was organized in September 1873, near Old Piney Grove Baptist. The church moved to its present location on Blockhouse Road in 1891. (Courtesy of Javonna Manning.)

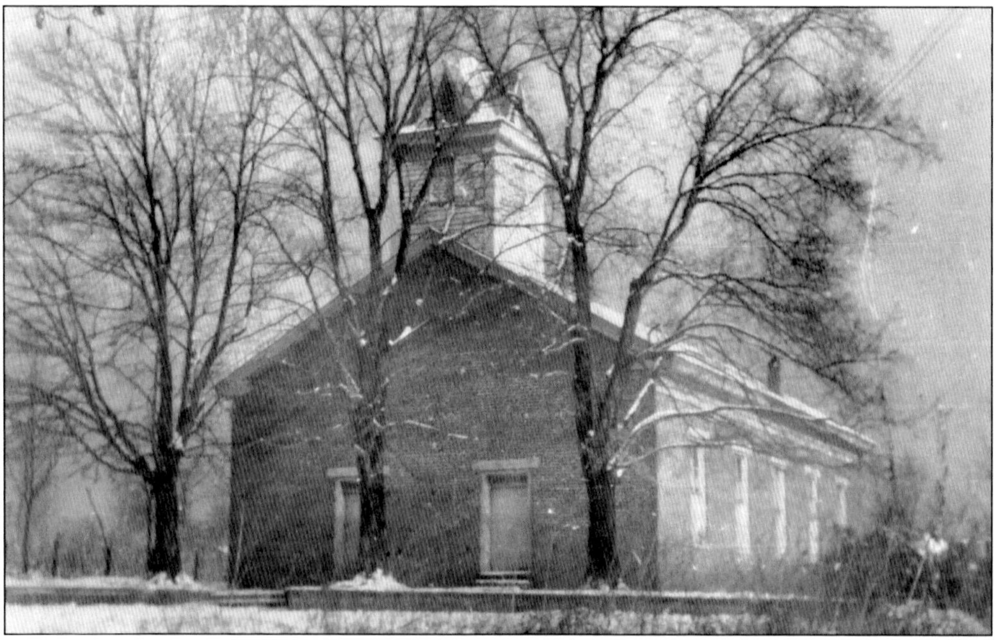

The original location of Louisville Methodist Church, built in 1853, is now the bottom of Fort Loudoun Lake. The name was changed to St. Mark's in 1942 when the church moved across Louisville Road due to construction of Fort Loudoun Dam and the lake that was to come. The original building was disassembled brick by brick and rebuilt at the present location. (Courtesy of Kathleen McCammon.)

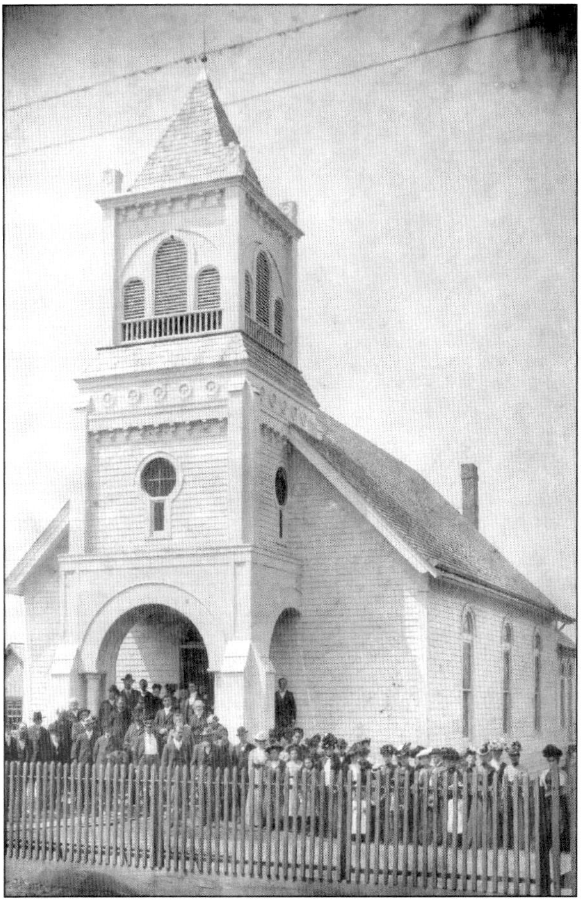

First Baptist Church of Maryville was organized on March 29, 1871, in the Blount County Courthouse with 17 charter members, as a result of a Sunday school offered a few years earlier by Dr. Ben A. Morton at his home. In 1876, a small frame building was constructed on High Street. That building is shown at right in 1905. (Courtesy of the Blount County Public Library, Adele McKenzie collection.)

The second structure serving the congregation of First Baptist Church of Maryville was built in 1914 behind the High Street church, facing Ellis Avenue. A four-story educational building was added in 1949. The church moved to its present location on West Lamar Alexander Parkway in 1957. Second Baptist Church, organized in July 1958, purchased the Ellis Avenue site and met there for a few years. Several businesses currently occupy the building. (Courtesy of B. Kenneth Cornett.)

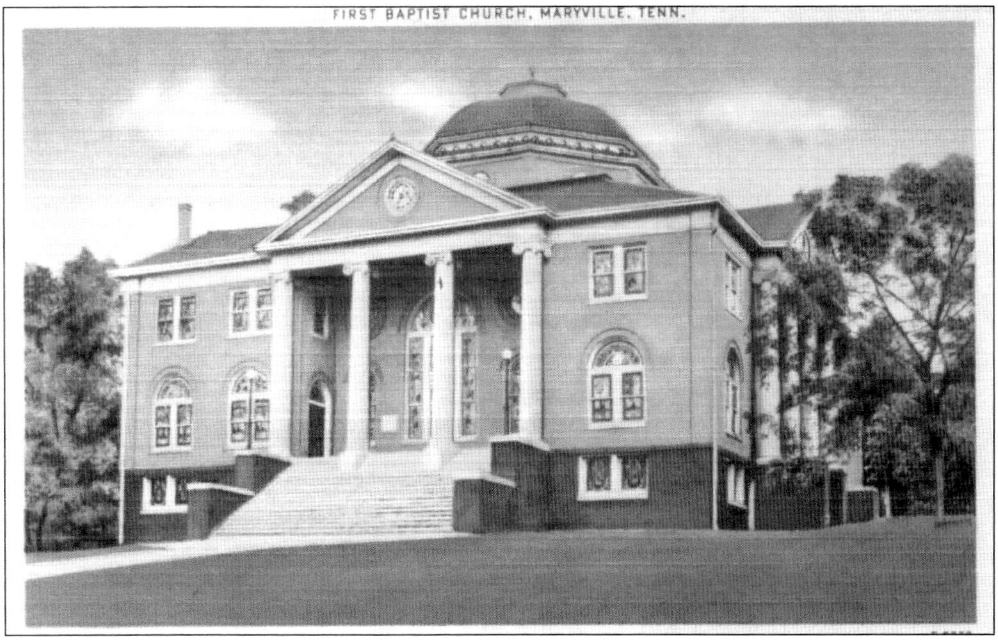

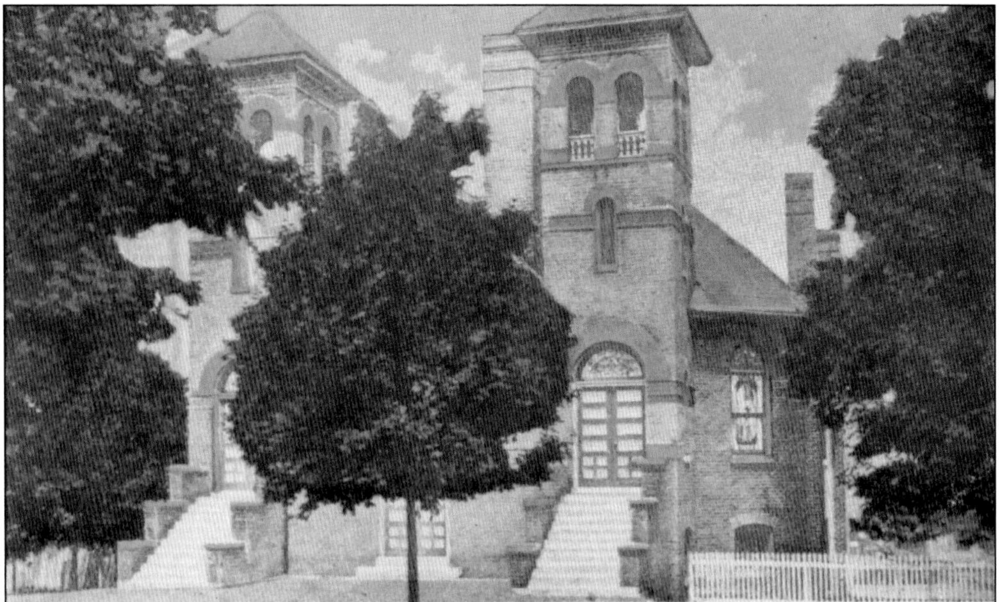

M. E. Church South, Maryville, Tenn.

M. E. Church, Maryville, Tenn.

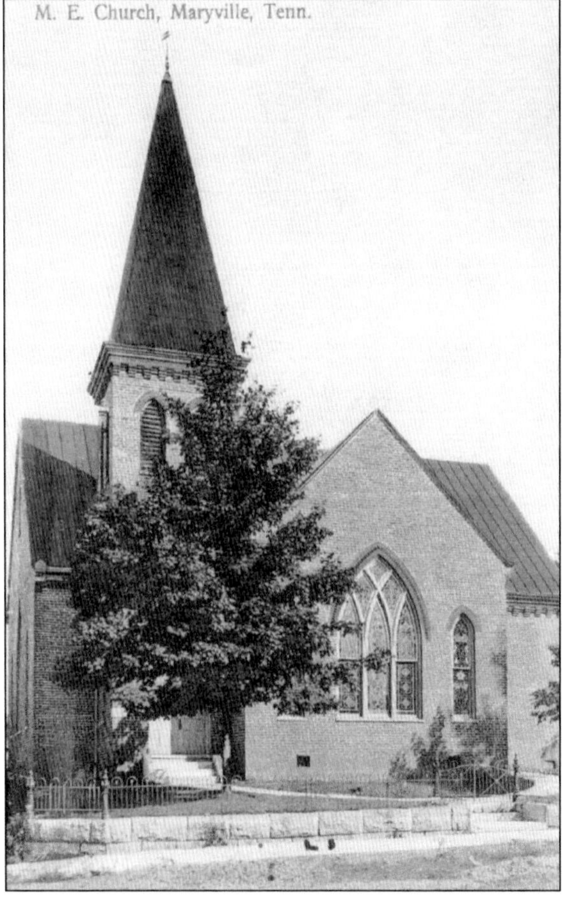

The M. E. (Methodist Episcopal) Church South in Maryville (pictured above) had its beginnings with the early Methodist circuit riders. Mount Gilead Methodist Episcopal Church was organized sometime after 1804, and by 1819, a small wooden structure was built on "Methodist Hill," near the present-day Olympia Townhouses, Maryville. By 1860, this larger structure was built at the corner of Church and Norwood Streets. The Methodist Church split due to divided loyalties from the Civil War, and those with Southern (Confederate) sympathies attended the M. E. Church South. The third building (at left) was constructed in 1899 at the corner of Patton and Main (Broadway) Streets. The church, now called Broadway United Methodist, has been added to and renovated several times since 1928. (Both, courtesy of B. Kenneth Cornett.)

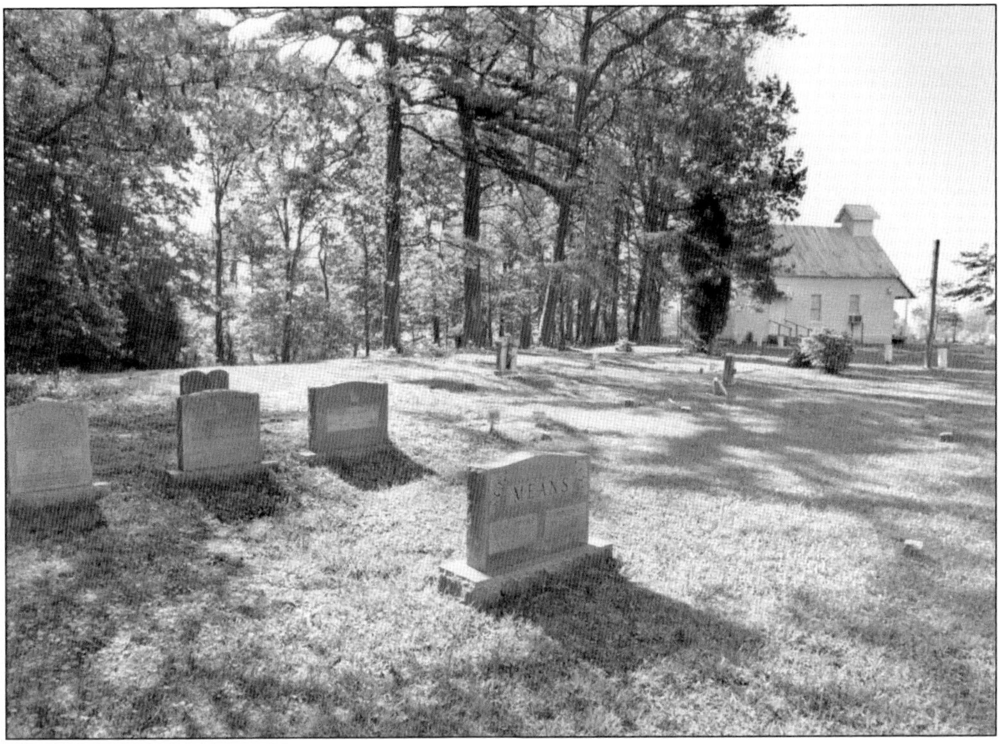

The date of construction of the first Wilder's Chapel African Methodist Episcopal Church, on Amerine Road, is unknown, but burials in the cemetery go back to the early 1890s. The building, shown above in this 1995 photograph, was constructed in 1910. This church will be moved to the Great Smoky Mountains Heritage Center, Townsend, to preserve it for future generations. (Courtesy of the *Daily Times*.)

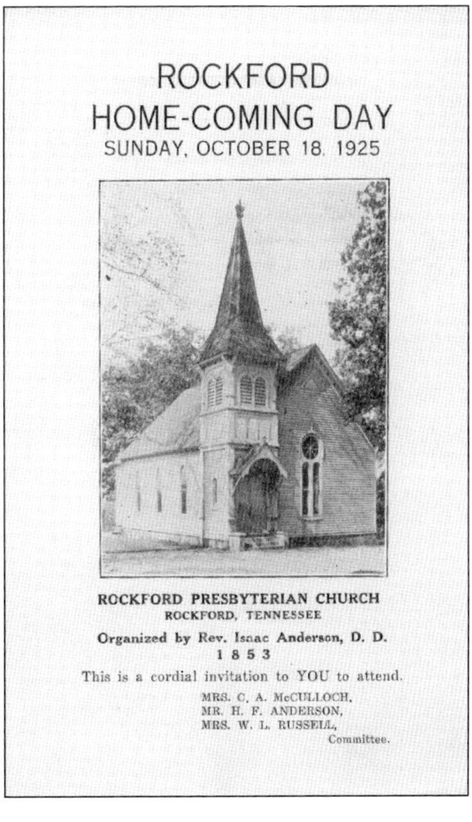

ROCKFORD
HOME-COMING DAY
SUNDAY, OCTOBER 18, 1925

ROCKFORD PRESBYTERIAN CHURCH
ROCKFORD, TENNESSEE
Organized by Rev. Isaac Anderson, D. D.
1 8 5 3
This is a cordial invitation to YOU to attend.
MRS. C. A. McCULLOCH,
MR. H. F. ANDERSON,
MRS. W. L. RUSSELL,
Committee.

This "Rockford Home-Coming Day" program, dated October 18, 1925, is from Rockford Presbyterian Church in Rockford. The church was organized in 1853 by Rev. Isaac Anderson, founder of Maryville College. The program indicates that Rev. E. W. Hall provided preaching every first and third Sunday. The church is no longer in existence. (Courtesy of B. Kenneth Cornett.)

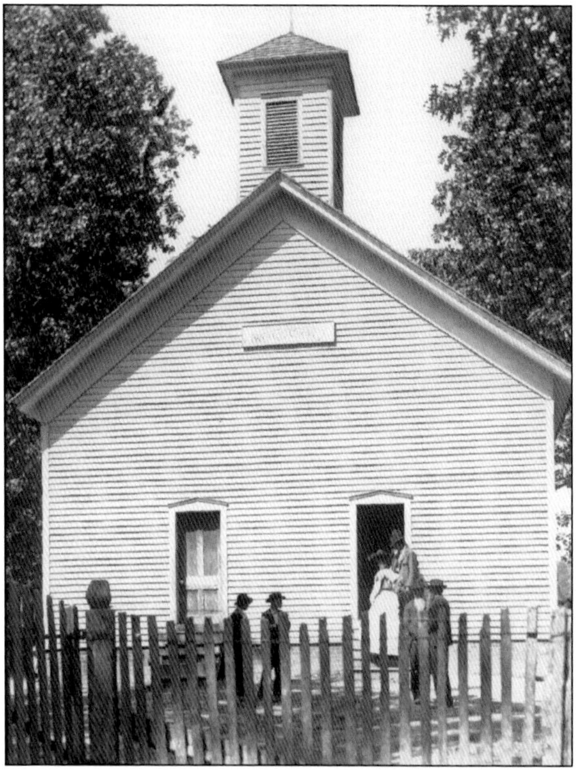

In 1842, Alexander Cook provided a tract of land for camp meetings in the Mint community, and in 1848, a church was built in sight of what is now Carpenter's Campground United Methodist Church. A few years later, the church was moved to its present location. For a short time, it was called Wesley Chapel. (Courtesy of the Blount County Public Library, Adele McKenzie collection.)

In this *c.* 1920 photograph, the children of Carpenter's Campground United Methodist Church are shown in their best Sunday finery. It is only speculation, but the children may have been dressed in their Easter outfits and enjoying an Easter egg hunt in the cemetery. (Courtesy of the Blount County Public Library, Adele McKenzie collection.)

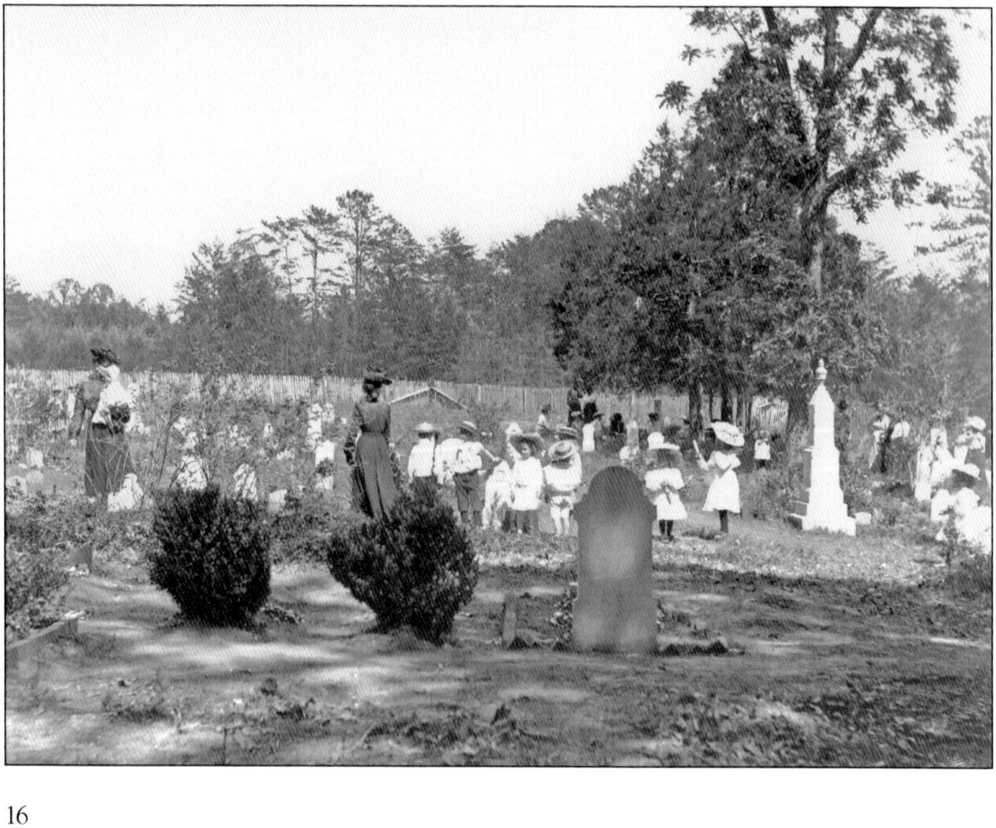

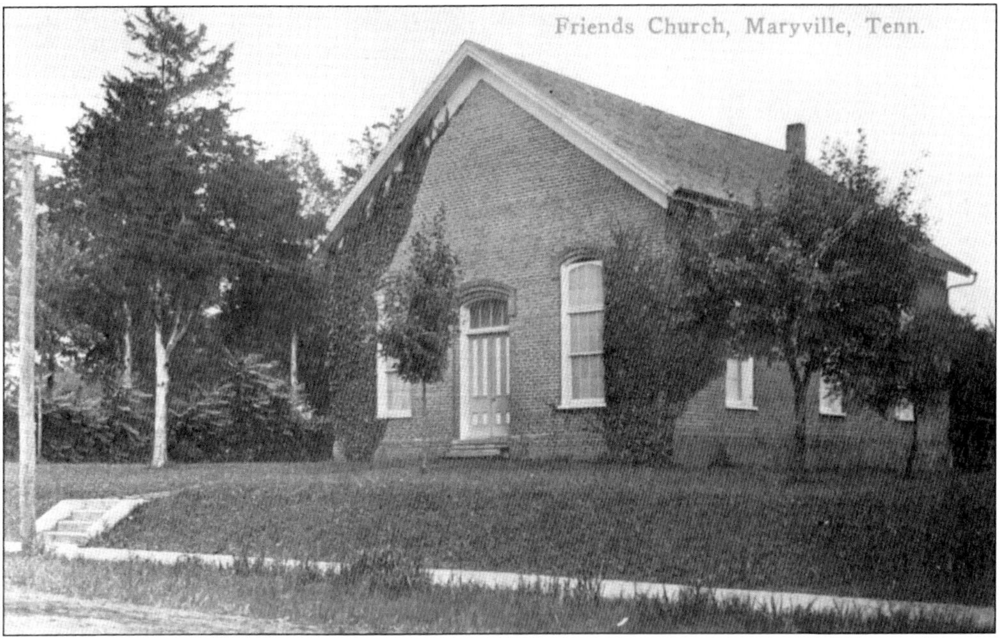

The Maryville Friends Meeting House on Main Street (Broadway), Maryville, was constructed by the Society of Friends, or Quakers, in 1871–1872 at a cost of $2,869.95. It closed in June 1935 and was sold in 1946 to St. Andrew's Episcopal Church. The cemetery adjoining the church lot is the New Providence Presbyterian Cemetery. The Maryville Friends Cemetery is on Lamar Alexander Parkway near North Houston Street, Maryville. (Courtesy of B. Kenneth Cornett.)

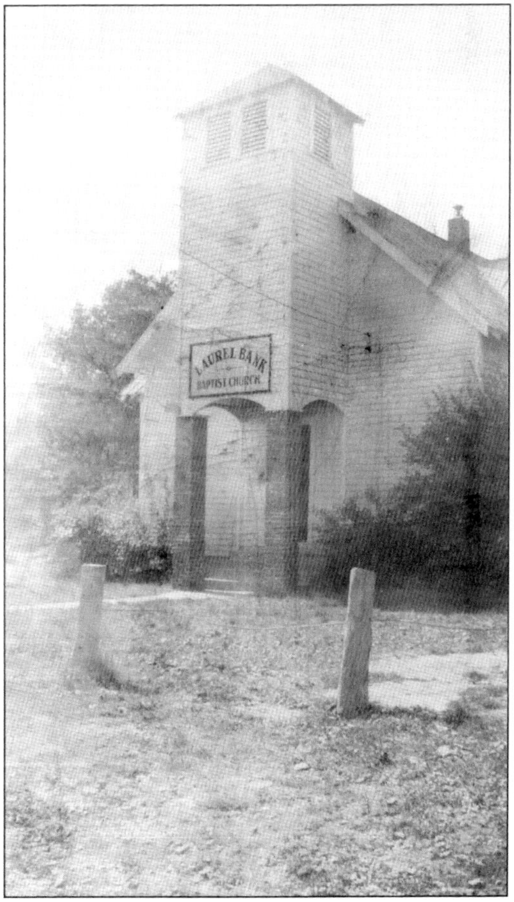

Laurel Bank Baptist Church on County Farm Road had a deed in 1866 to build a church and was admitted to the Chilhowee Baptist Association in 1872. The church fell on hard times in the early 1900s but was reorganized in 1933. On the back of this photograph was written, "Merry Christmas from the Rev. Paul Reneau Family." Reneau was church pastor from May to December 1940 and from January 1943 through March 1944. (Courtesy of Paul Bales.)

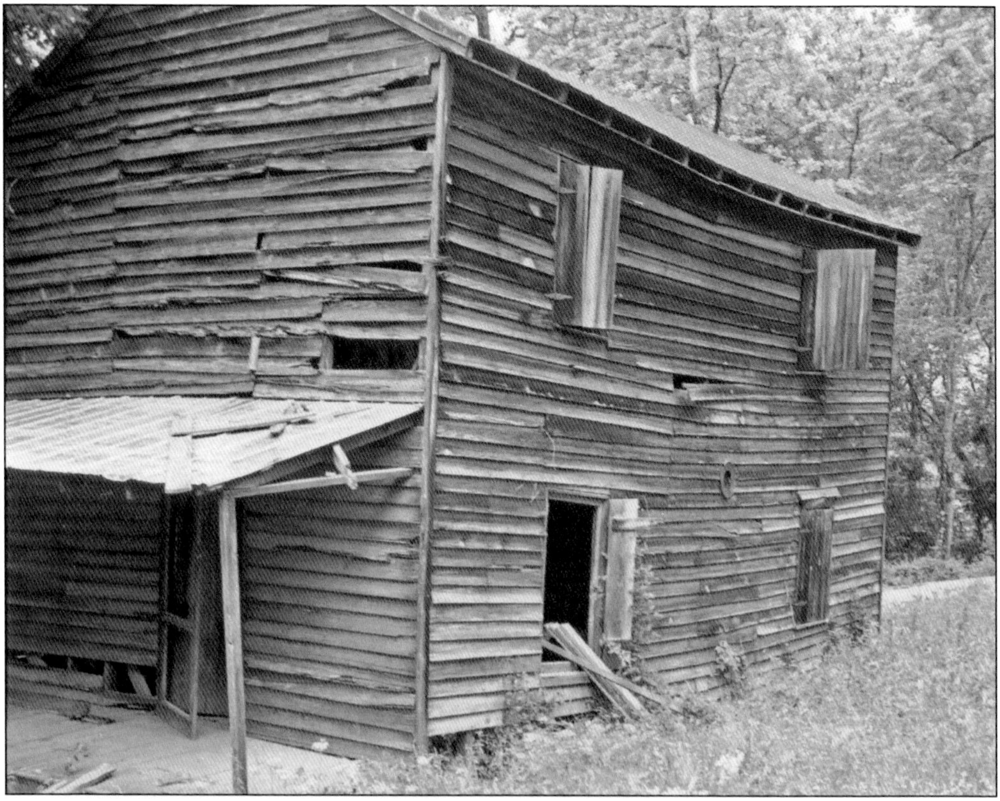

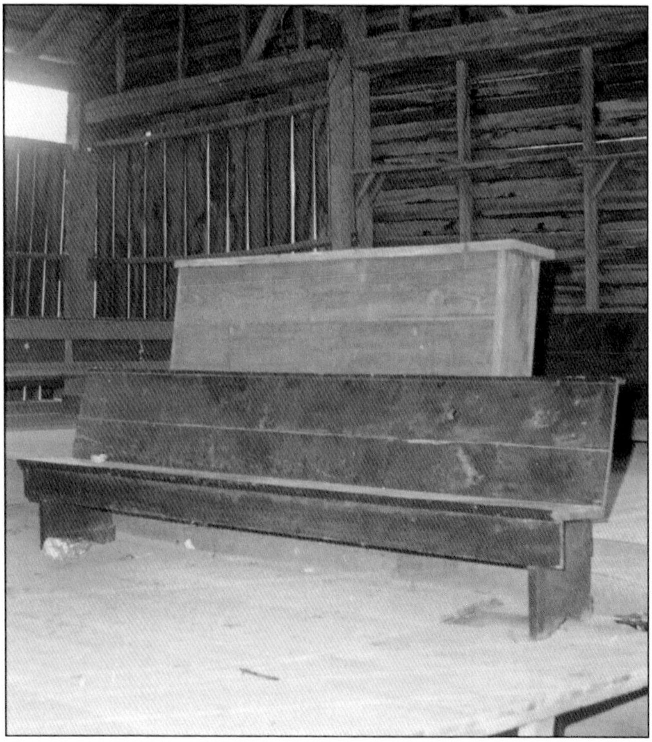

The National Campground near Greenback, a 5-acre tract that now lies in Loudon County but was originally a part of Blount County, was established in 1873 by a nondenominational group of men and women in an effort to bring together friends and neighbors divided by the Civil War. The first services were held in tents or brush arbors. The old preacher's camp house, shown above, is no longer standing, but the tabernacle shed, built in 1874, is still in use today. The pulpit and kneeling bench inside the tabernacle shed are shown at left. The National Campground was placed on the National Register of Historic Places in 1972. (Both, courtesy of B. Kenneth Cornett.)

Piney Level Baptist Church, shown at right around 1921, was formed from Crooked Creek Baptist, which appeared in records in 1825 and split about 1832. Piney Level may have formed about that time but remained unorganized until 1883. The first church was a one-room building of hewn logs and lumber, and underwent many changes as the congregation grew. In 1971, land was donated for a larger facility, which was built in 1976. (Courtesy of Linda Braden Albert, Helen Coulter collection.)

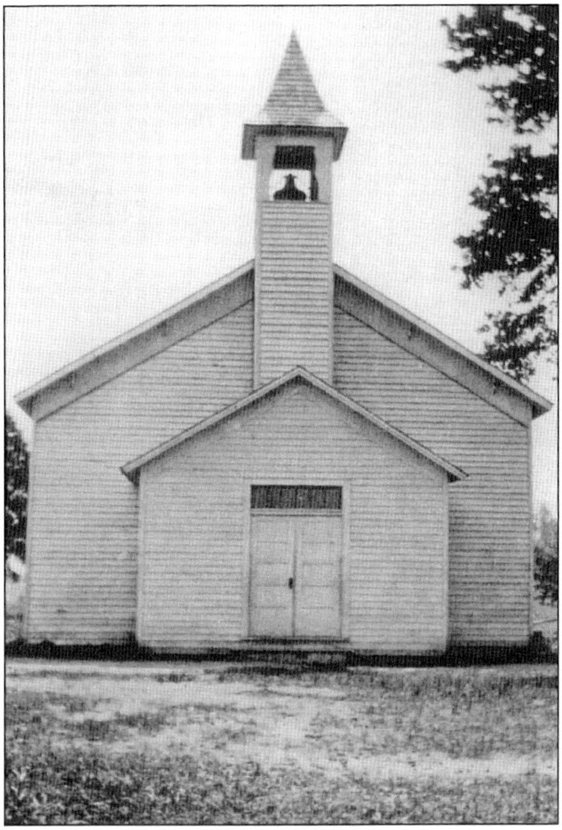

Victory Baptist Church was organized in 1950 with 14 charter members as Blount County's first independent missionary Baptist church. Services were held in this remodeled automobile garage at the corner of Boardman Avenue and Montvale Road, Maryville. The congregation quickly grew to about 600 members in the 1960s due to offering a countywide bus ministry. The present building, across Montvale Road from the garage, was erected in 1962. (Courtesy of B. Kenneth Cornett.)

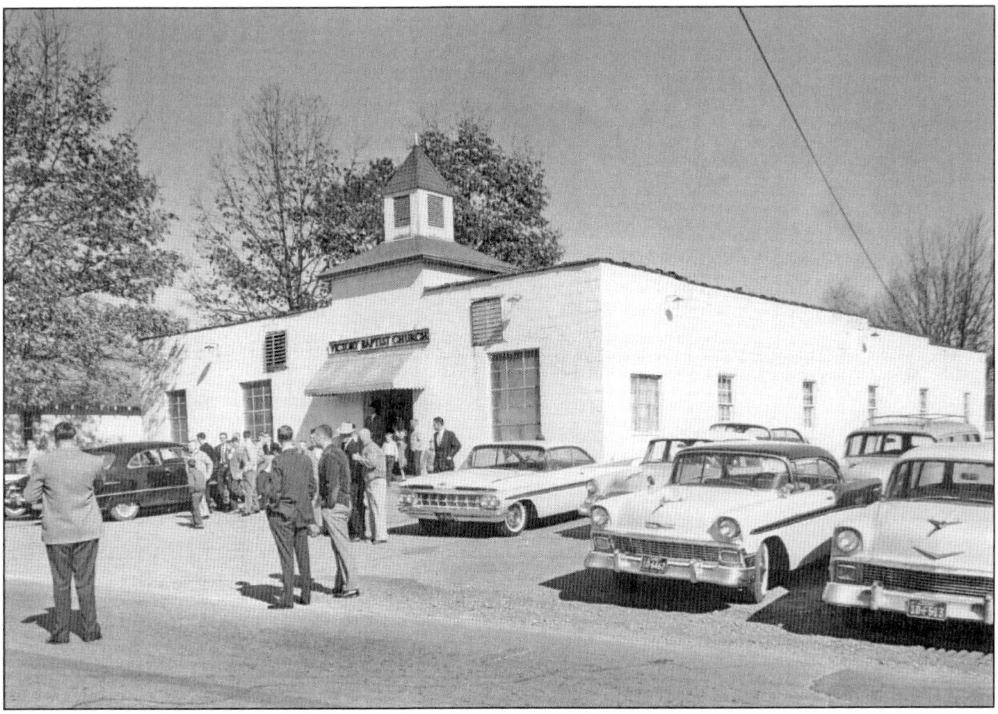

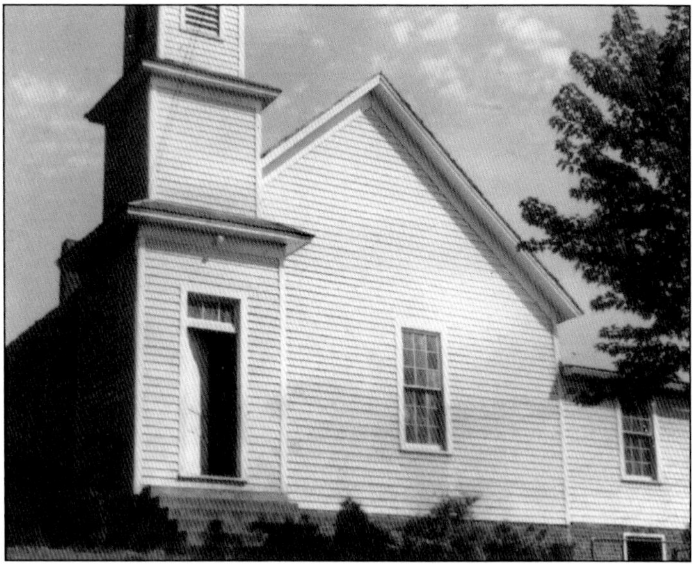

Fairview United Methodist Church had its beginnings in 1913 as a result of a revival meeting conducted by Methodist ministers John and Preston Sanders at the Antioch Primitive Baptist Church. The first building, shown here, was started by members of the newly formed congregation in 1914 with materials and labor donated by the members and the Fairview community. (Courtesy of Fairview United Methodist Church.)

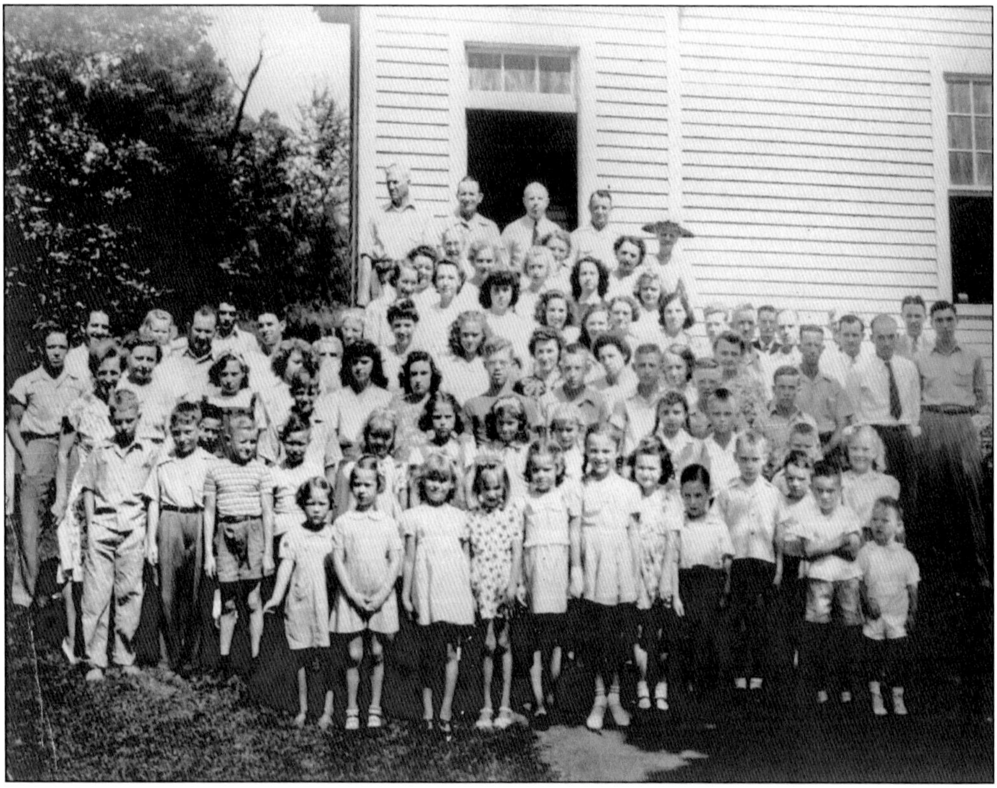

An early congregation at Fairview United Methodist Church gathered in front of the first building for a photograph. The adjacent site was purchased in 1948 by the women of the church, and the second building commenced on Labor Day 1949. Fairview's current, much larger facility is located across Old Niles Ferry Road from the original site. (Courtesy of Fairview United Methodist Church.)

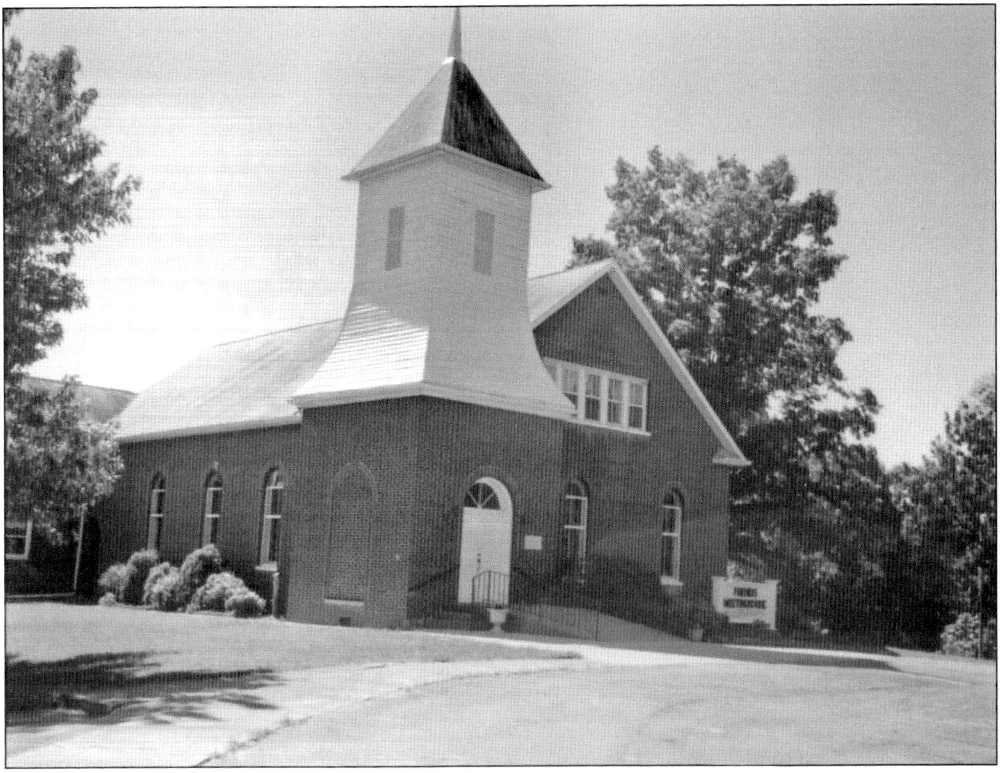

The Friends (Quaker) Meeting in Friendsville was officially organized about 1808, and the deed to the church lot was made by Aaron Hackney and James Moore in 1822. Before and during the Civil War, members of the meeting were active in manumission and the Underground Railroad. (Courtesy of Linda Braden Albert.)

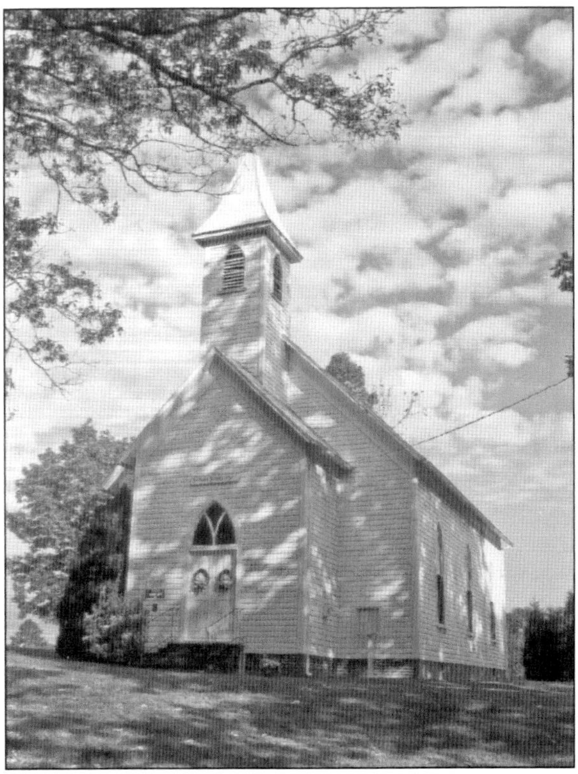

Bethlehem Methodist Church was organized in 1886 to serve the Ellejoy Community and Old Chilhowee area known as the "Knobs." Rev. Wayne Campbell was pastor when the congregation disbanded about 1966. Several Civil War veterans are buried in the adjacent cemetery. The church and cemetery were placed on the National Register of Historic Places in 1986. The church is used occasionally for decoration on Mother's Day, funerals, and weddings. (Courtesy of B. Kenneth Cornett.)

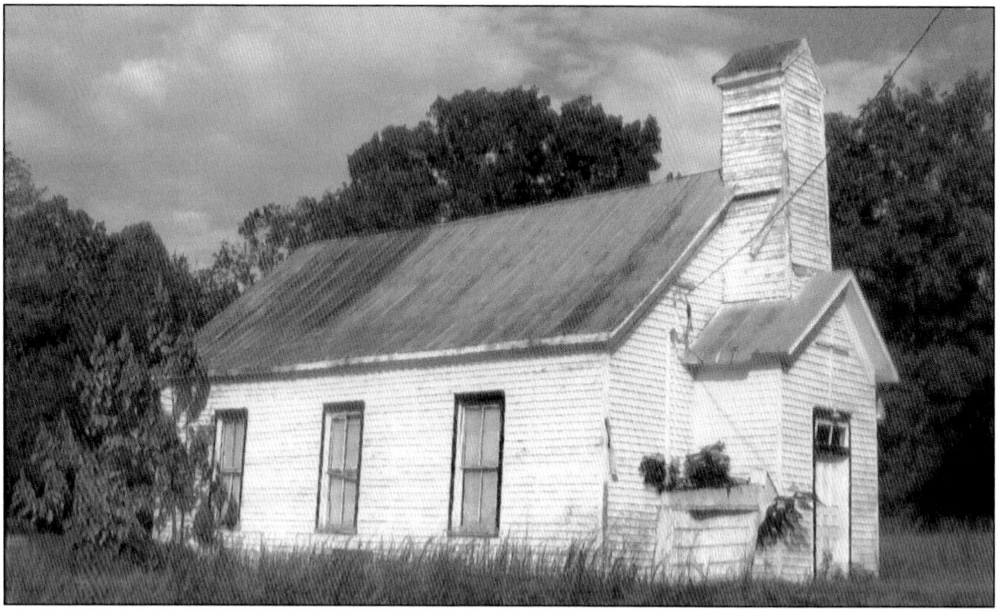

Union Temple AME (African Methodist Episcopal) Church was organized about 1875 by the Holland, Inman, and Sharp families for black residents of the Oakview community. A total of 138 graves, including 31 marked only with fieldstones, are in the cemetery directly behind the church. The church, located at the intersection of Pea Ridge and Temple Roads, is now owned by Crossroads Missionary Baptist Church. (Courtesy of B. Kenneth Cornett.)

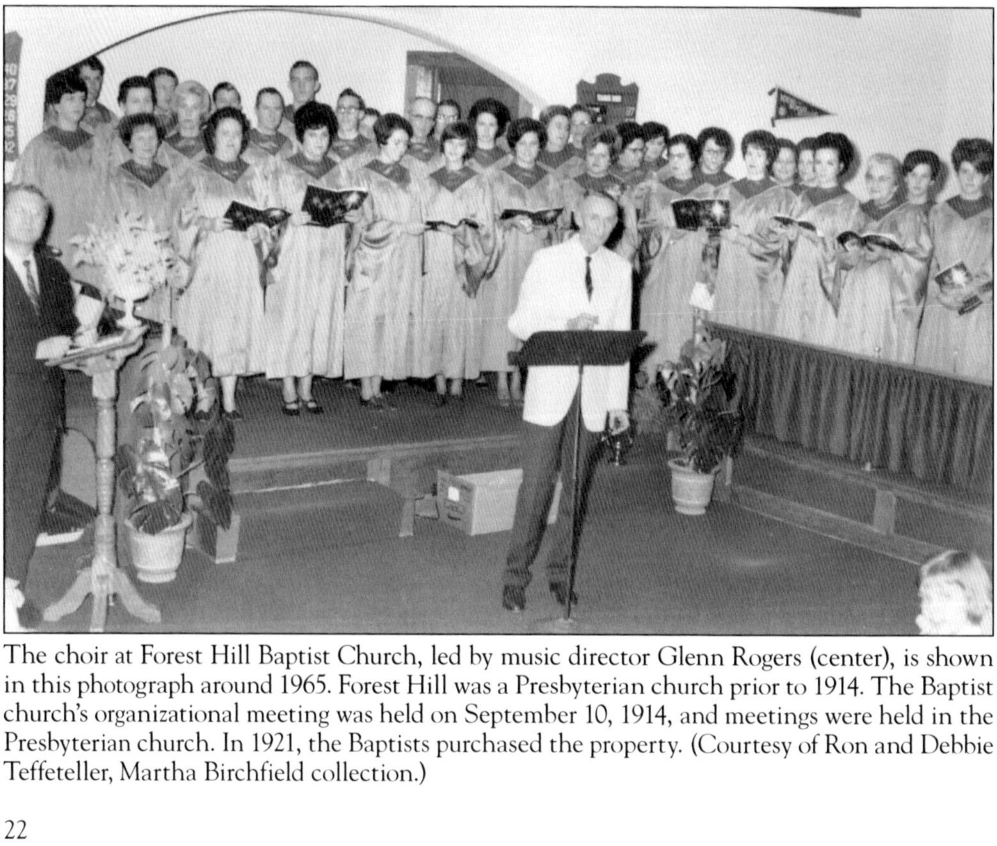

The choir at Forest Hill Baptist Church, led by music director Glenn Rogers (center), is shown in this photograph around 1965. Forest Hill was a Presbyterian church prior to 1914. The Baptist church's organizational meeting was held on September 10, 1914, and meetings were held in the Presbyterian church. In 1921, the Baptists purchased the property. (Courtesy of Ron and Debbie Teffeteller, Martha Birchfield collection.)

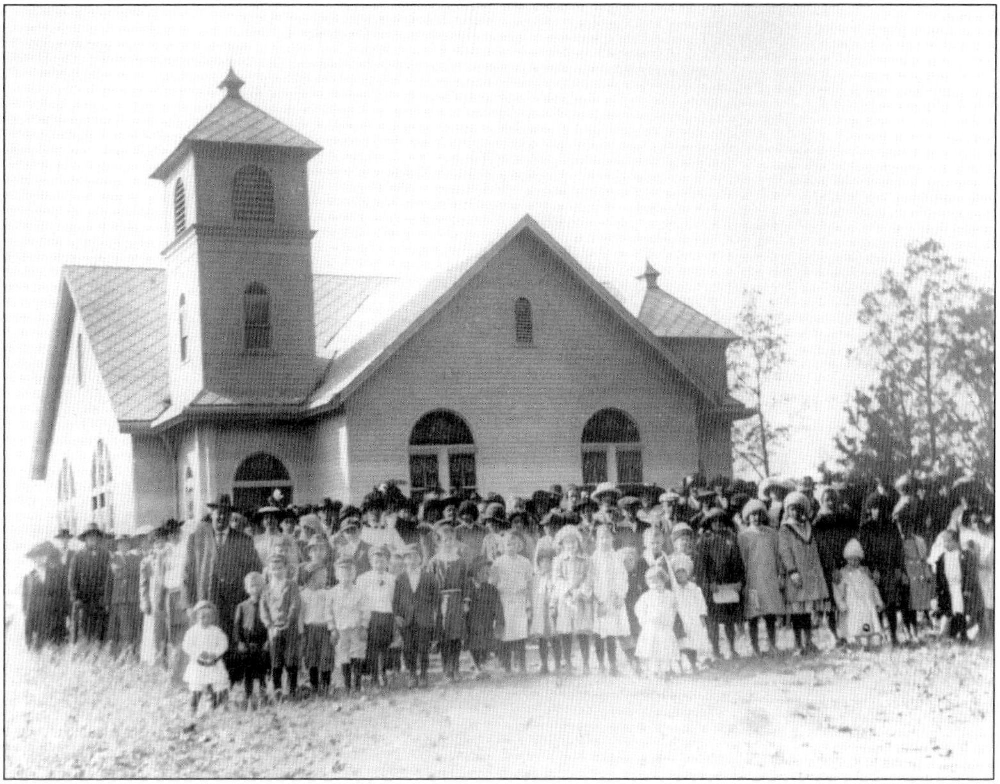

The congregation of Pleasant Grove Baptist Church stands in front of the building around 1911. Pleasant Grove formed in 1832 after Crooked Creek Church divided and 14 members returned to the mother church in Miller's Cove, along with the pastor. The remaining 16 members named themselves Pleasant Grove Baptist Church. (Courtesy of Margaret Davis Coulter.)

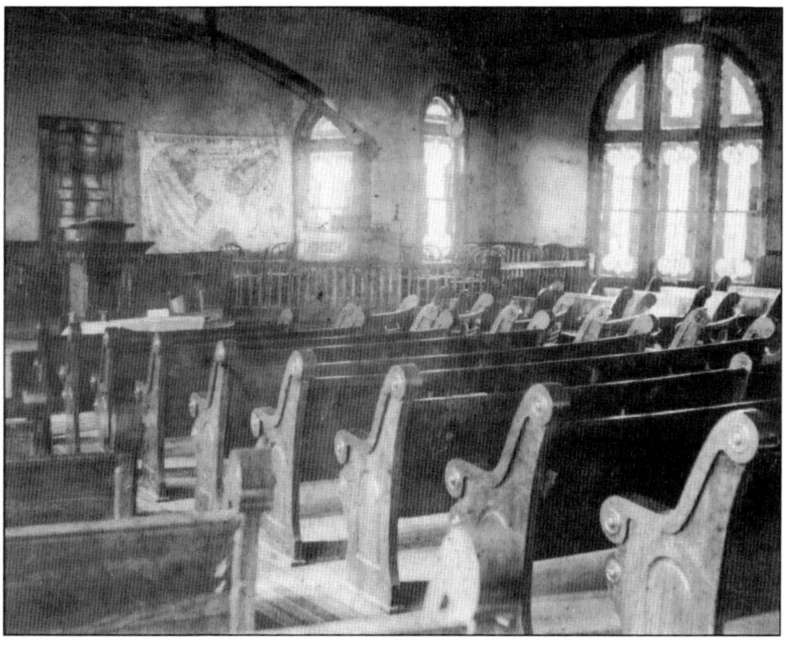

The interior of Pleasant Grove Baptist Church is shown here around 1911. These pews are still used by Pleasant Grove's congregation today. (Courtesy of Margaret Davis Coulter.)

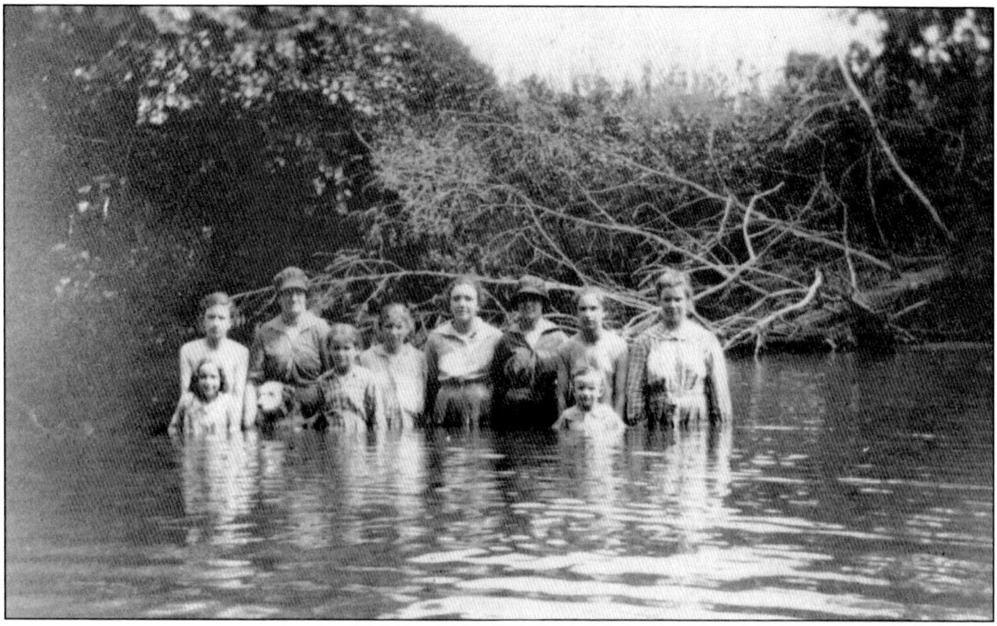

Several of the women of Pleasant Grove Baptist Church stand in Little River near the Coulter's Bridge, where the church held its river baptisms. The church continues to offer a river baptism annually for those who choose to be baptized there, rather than in the church baptistery. (Courtesy of Margaret Davis Coulter.)

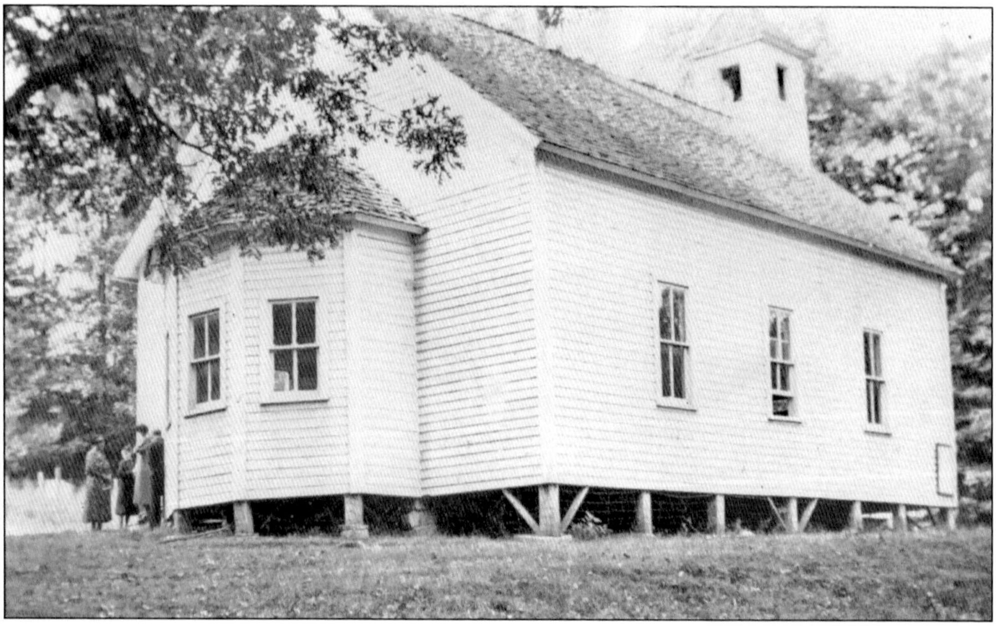

Cades Cove Missionary Baptist Church was the second building for the Missionary Baptist congregation of Cades Cove. It was built in 1915 at the foot of Cades Cove Mountain, where Rich Mountain Road accessed the cove road. Materials were salvaged from Hyatt Hill Baptist Church (see page 25) for the building, which is maintained by the Great Smoky Mountain National Park Service today. Cove descendants occasionally use the facility for services. (Courtesy of Leon Myers.)

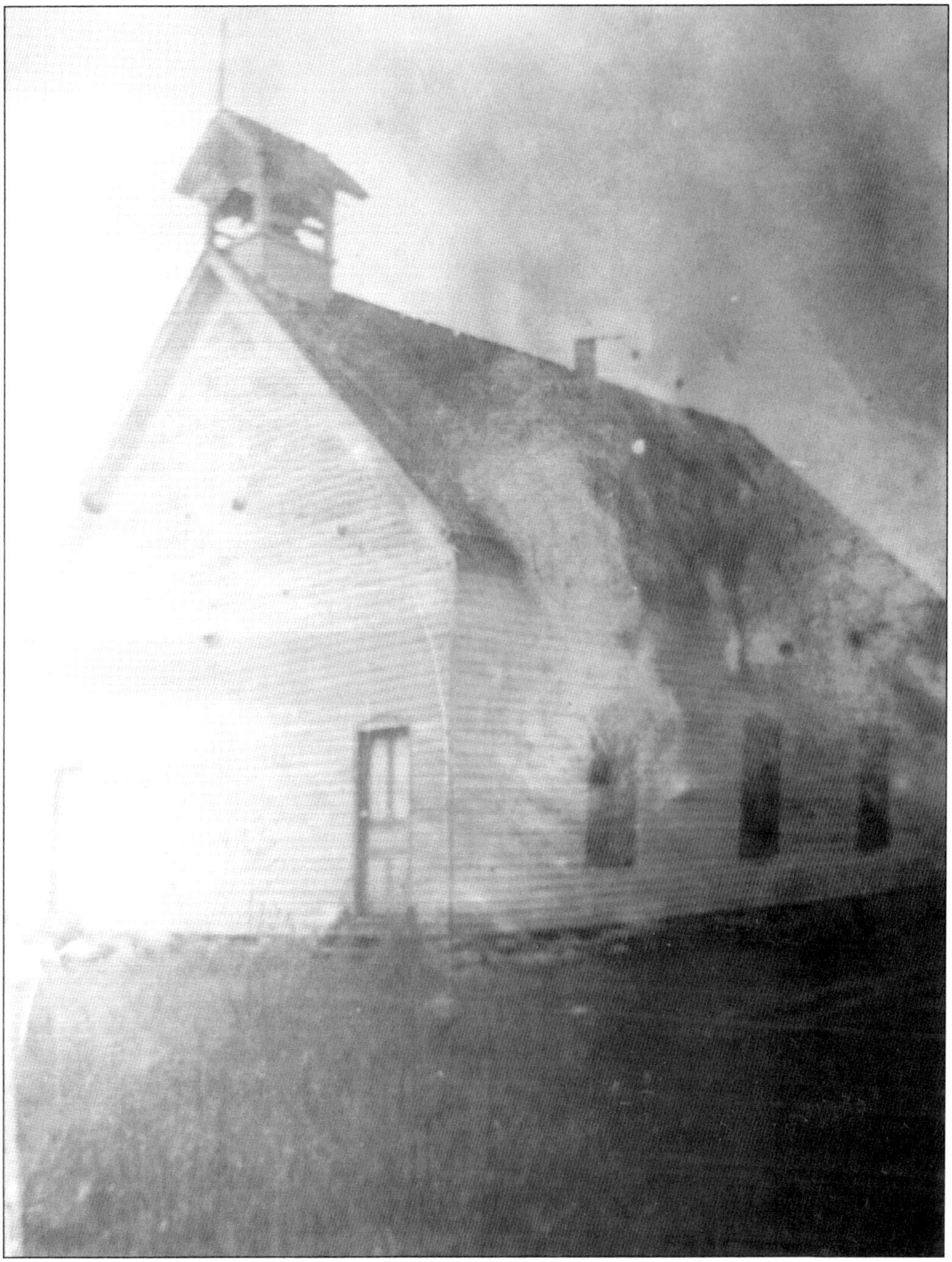

Thirteen former members of the Cades Cove Primitive Baptist Church organized the Missionary Baptist Church in 1839. Members met at various locations until Hyatt Hill Baptist Church, shown here, was built in 1895 on a knoll just west of Hyatt Lane in Cades Cove, near the home of Shadrack Hyatt. This building was used until 1915, when the Missionary Baptist Church (see page 24) was constructed using materials salvaged from Hyatt Hill Baptist Church. (Courtesy of Leon Myers.)

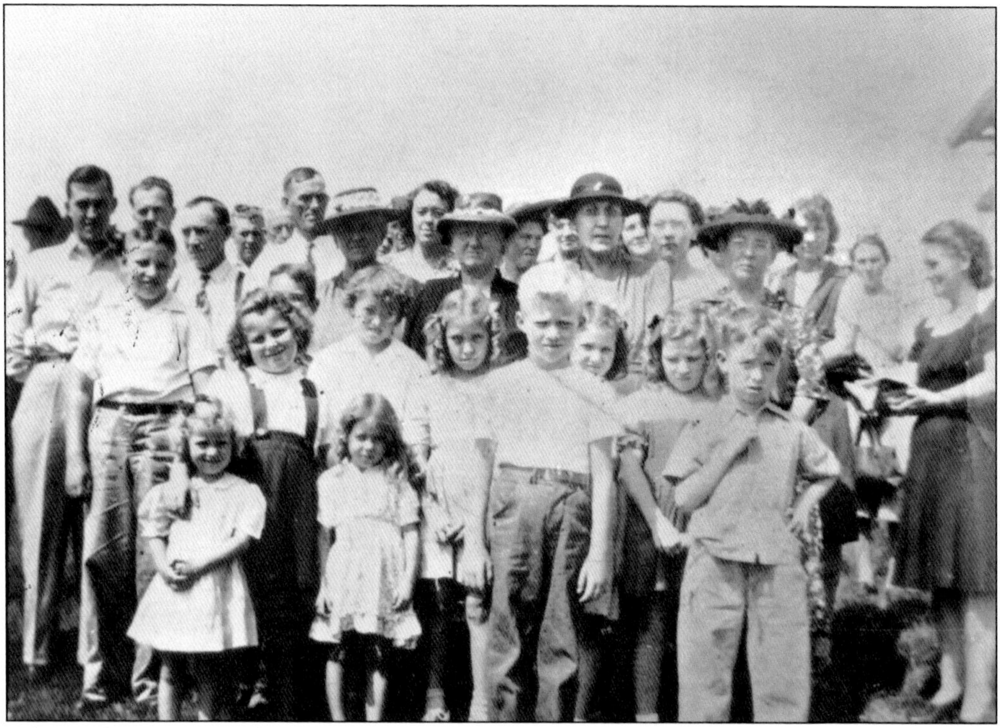

After Cades Cove was absorbed into Great Smoky Mountains National Park, the congregation of the Missionary Baptist Church formed Cades Cove Memorial Baptist Church near Maryville. On October 7, 1945, a group met at the home of Ed and Flo Schlangen to organize. In this early photograph, Flo Schlangen is shown at the far right in front of the home where the membership held services. Pastor Johnny Tipton is the tallest man standing at the back, behind the lady with the hat. (Courtesy of Leon Myers.)

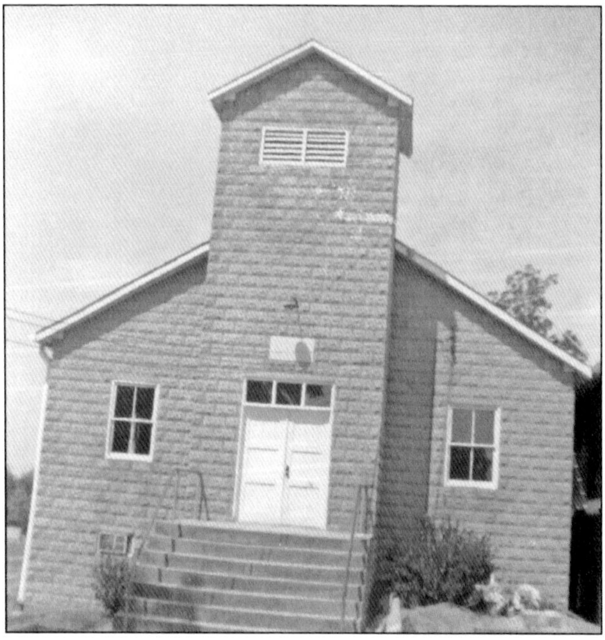

Cades Cove Memorial Baptist Church's first building, constructed in 1947, was the gray stone church shown here in 1967. The church is now called Cades Cove Baptist Fellowship and meets in a much larger, redbrick facility in the same location on Duncan Road, Maryville. (Courtesy of Leon Myers.)

Two

EDUCATION

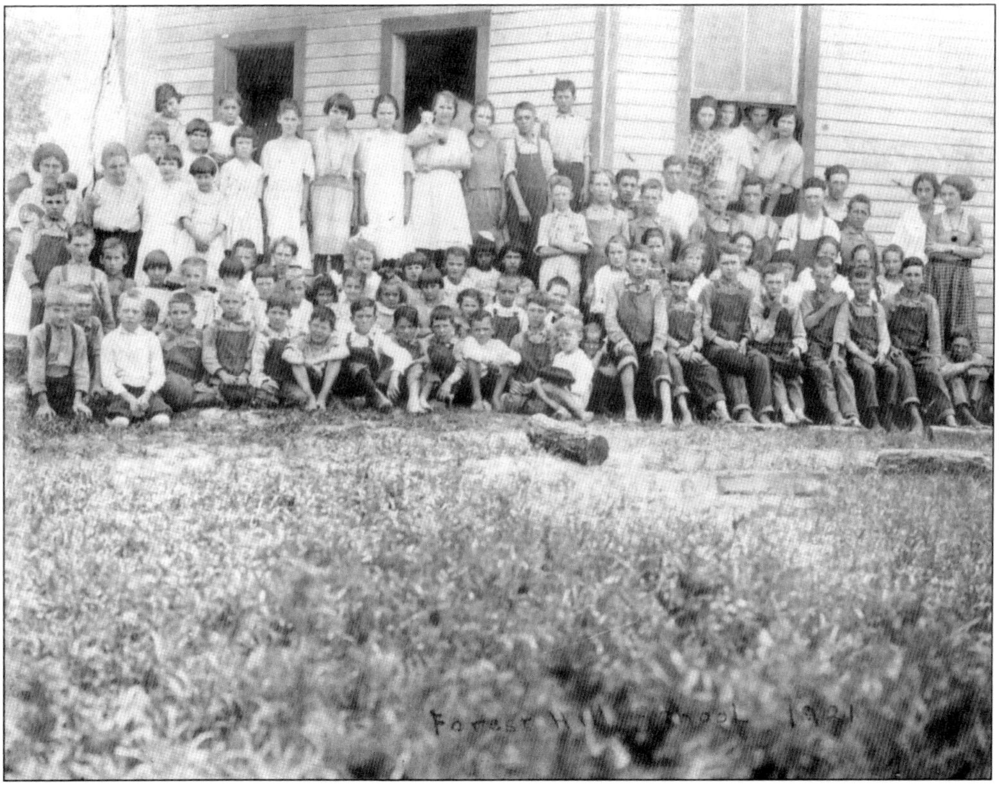

Forest Hill School students are shown in this 1921 photograph. Mildred McCammon and Mae Cook were the teachers. The two-room frame structure shown here was destroyed by fire a few years after the photograph was taken. The school was located near Forest Hill Baptist Church, and students were allowed to leave school and attend revival services. (Courtesy of Linda Braden Albert.)

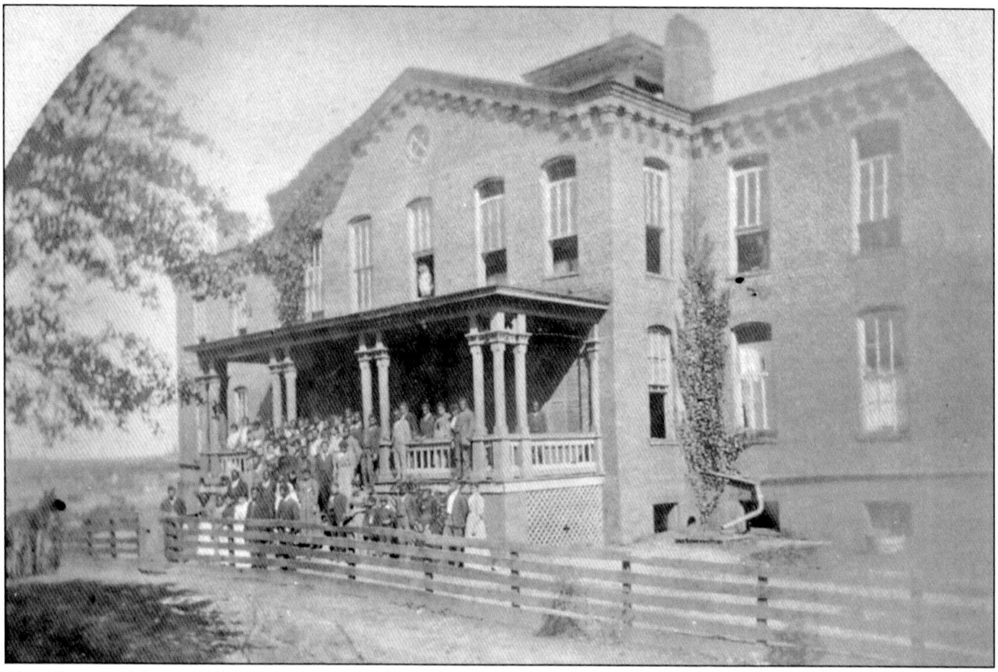

Freedmen's Normal Institute started in a log building in 1867 at the present site of St. Paul AME Zion Church on Main Street (Broadway) in Maryville to train black men and women as teachers for the African American population. A three-story brick building (shown below), funded primarily by the Quakers, or Friends, of New England, commenced in 1872 at the site of present-day Maryville High School. Yardley Warner, a Quaker from the New England Meeting, was the first principal of the school, followed by William P. Hastings in January 1874. Hastings's daughter Letitia and her husband, W. O. Garner, later directed the school until its closure in 1901. (Both, courtesy of the Blount County Historical Museum.)

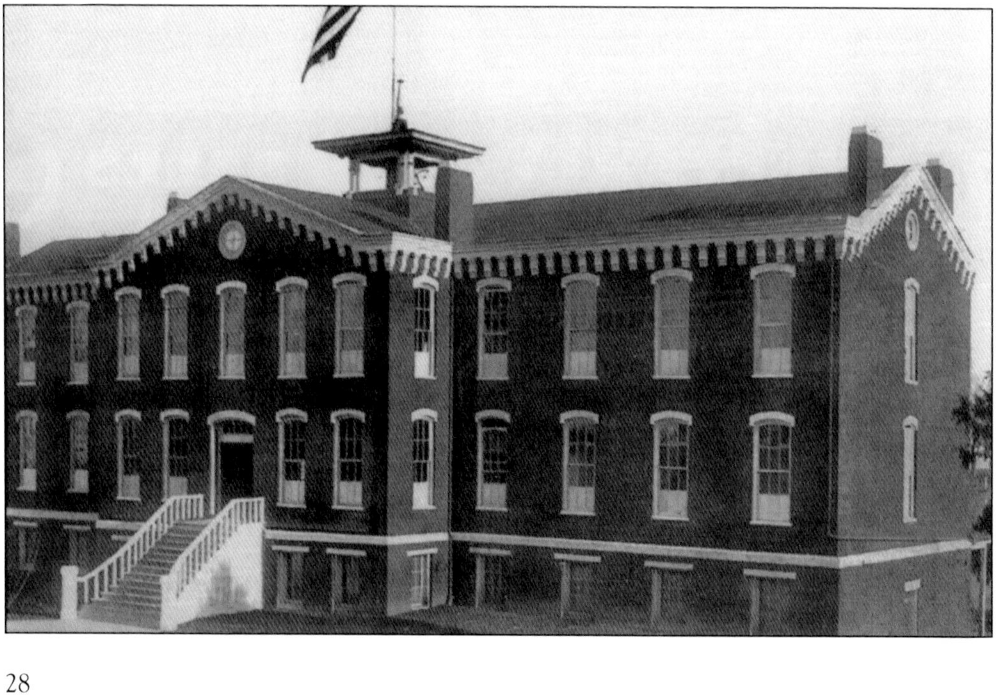

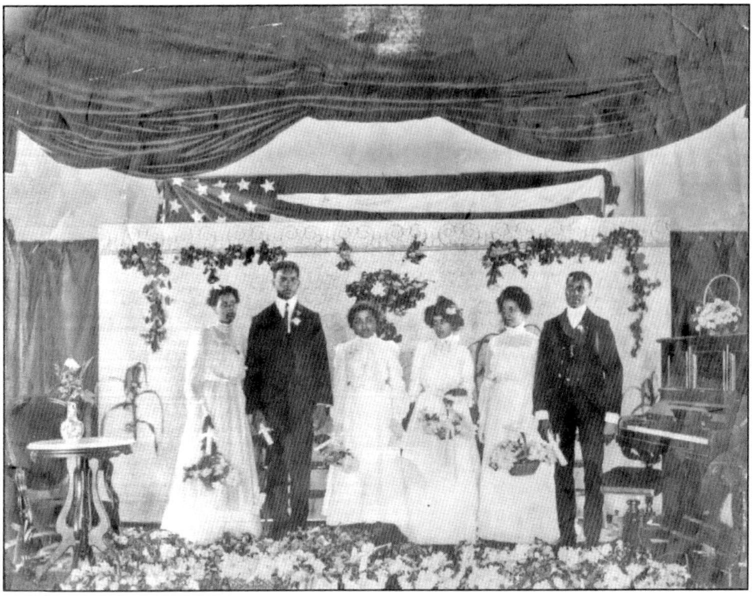

Graduates of Freedmen's Normal Institute stand on the school's stage. The school was founded to train black men and women as teachers for the African American population. It operated from 1867 to 1901. (Courtesy of the Blount County Historical Museum.)

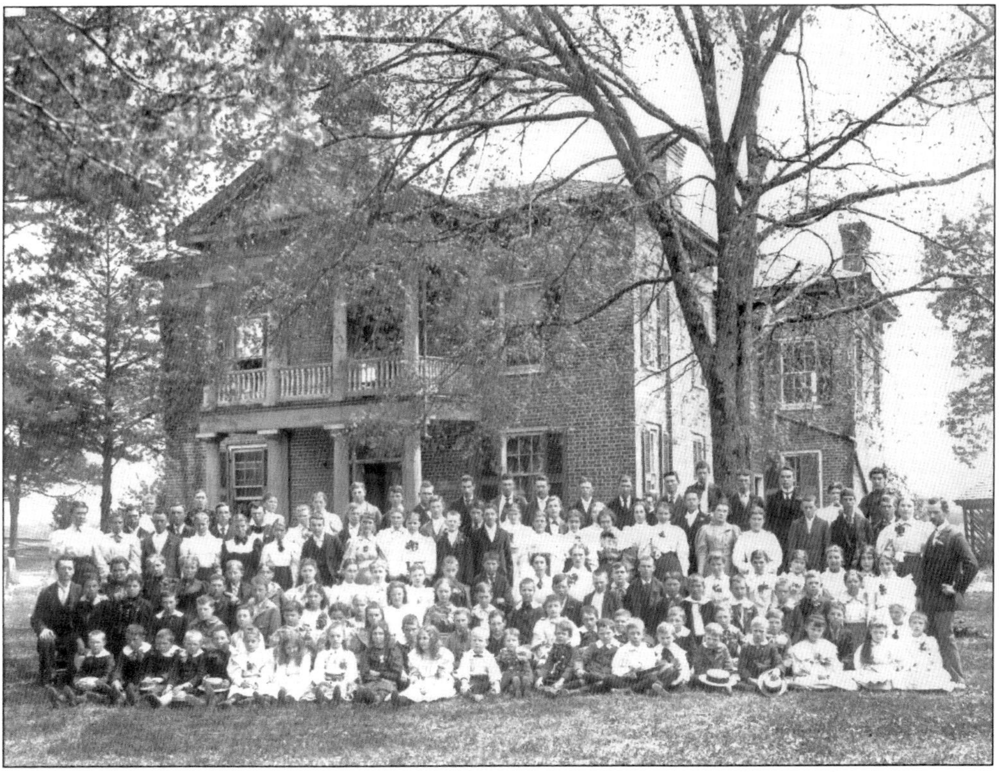

A class at Friends Normal and Preparatory School is shown here around 1895. The structure was built around 1830 as the home of Dr. Samuel Pride. It served as the headquarters for Gen. William T. Sherman in December 1863. In 1878, the building became the Friends Normal and Preparatory School, which operated until 1901. Pride Mansion was dismantled about 1910, and the Westside School was erected. (Courtesy of the Blount County Public Library, Adele McKenzie collection.)

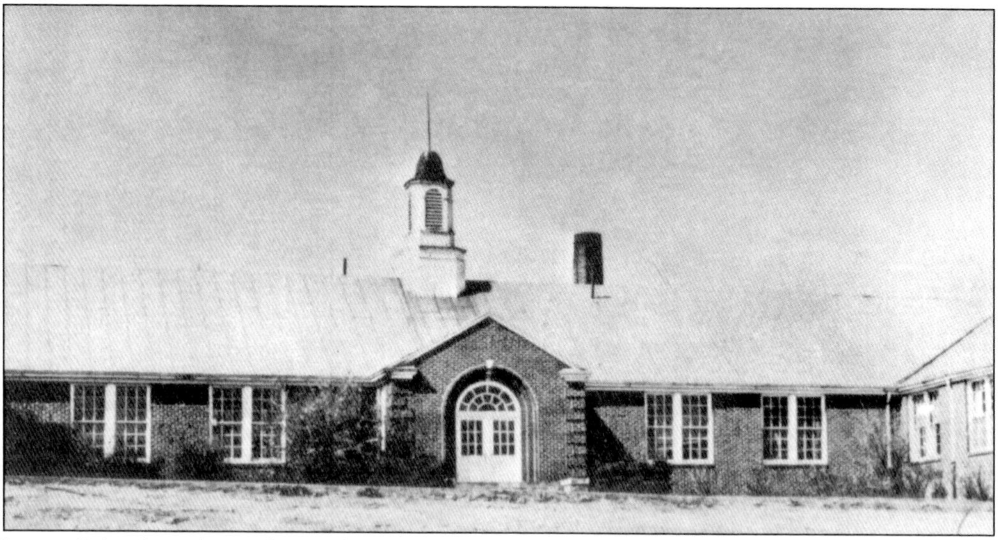

Lanier School was located near the intersection of Lanier and Brick Mill Roads and was named for poet Sydney Lanier, who spent time with his grandfather at Montvale Springs Hotel. The first building, a square redbrick structure, was completed in 1922, and the high school building pictured here opened in 1936. The high school was torn down and replaced by a modern elementary facility in 1988. (Courtesy of Betty Boone Best.)

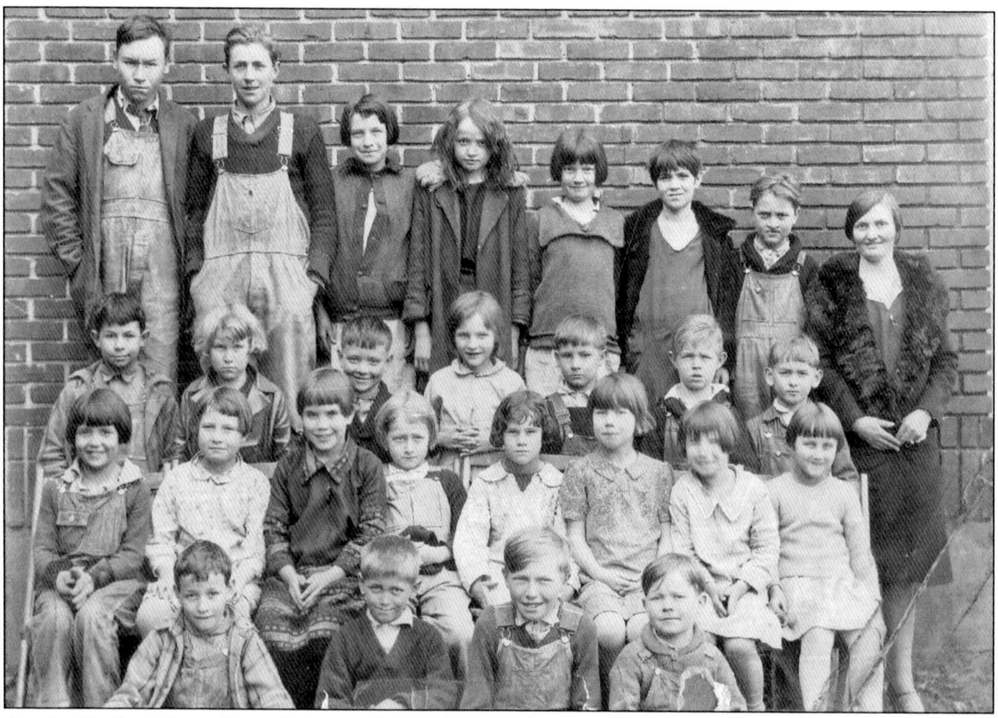

Angie Caylor Myers (far right) was the teacher of this multiage, 1930 class at Townsend School. At that time, schools in outlying areas did not have libraries, and at least once a month, Myers rode the White Star Lines bus to Maryville to check out library books from the Blount County Schools Circulating Library. Around 1950, Elsie Burrell, school supervisor, established elementary school libraries. (Courtesy of Marilyn Myers Byrd.)

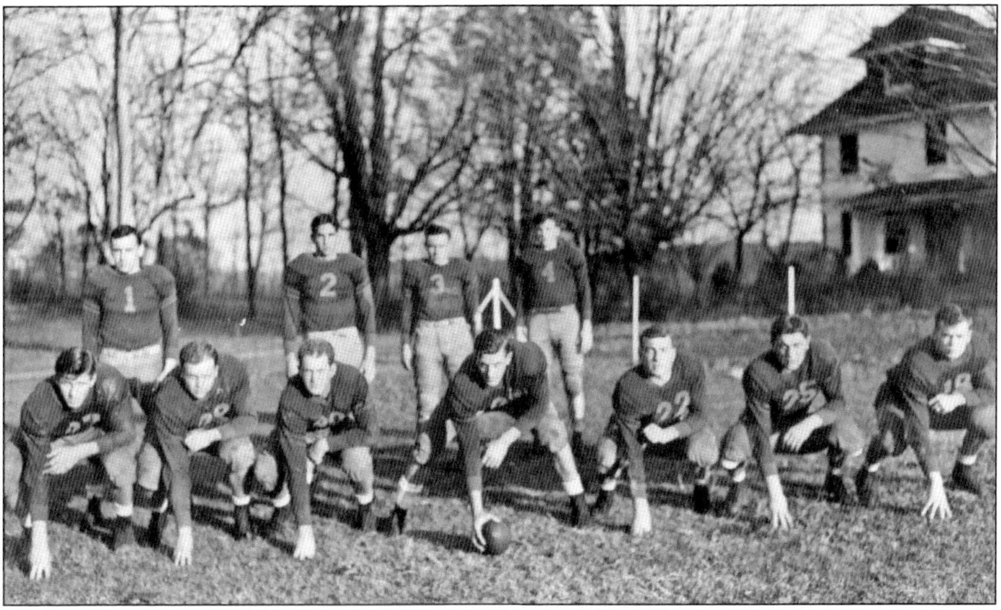

Maryville College's football team of 1946 was undefeated and participated in that year's Citrus Bowl, which is now called the Tangerine Bowl. The players are, from left to right, (first row) Howard Davis, Marvin Mitchell, Ronald "Cotton" Easter, Pie Garner, Bill Proffitt, and two unidentified; (second row) Herschel Merriman, King Berrong, unidentified, and Leon Berrong. (Courtesy of Ed Mitchell.)

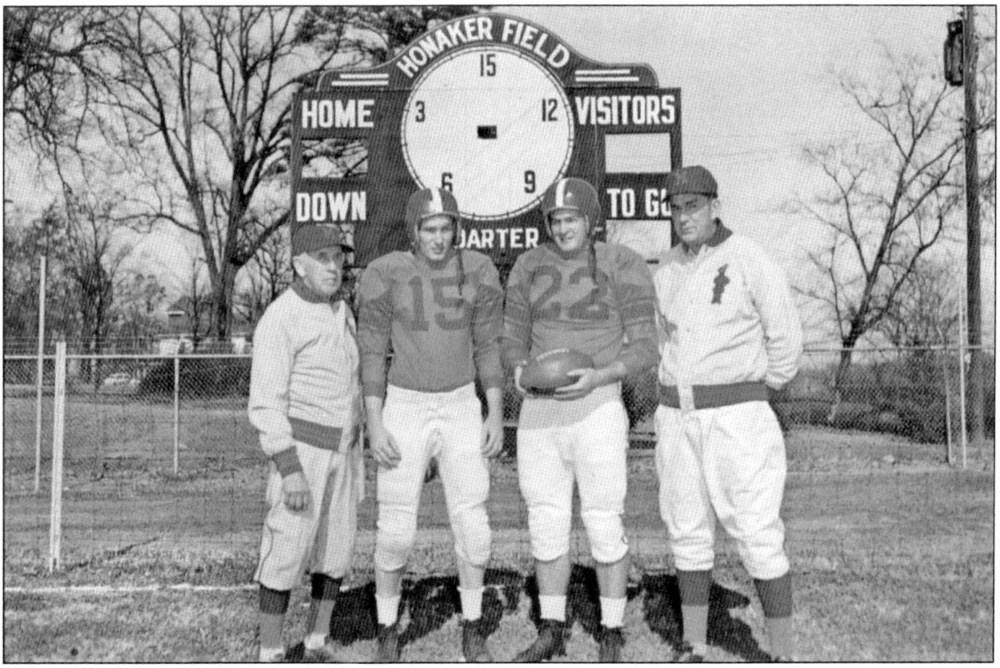

Maryville College coaching staff of 1944 included Lombe Honaker (far left) and J. D. Davis (far right). Ted Wilson, number 15, (second from left) was one of the co-captains. They are seen standing in front of the scoreboard in this postcard, which includes the football schedule for that year on the back. (Courtesy of B. Kenneth Cornett.)

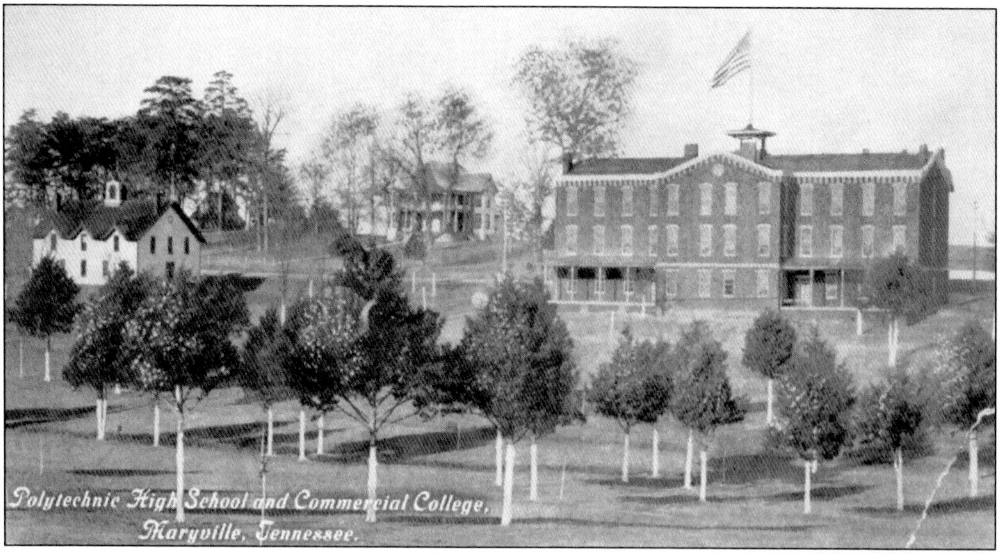

Maryville Polytechnic School began in 1901 as Maryville Business College, a private school operated by C. W. "Bill Joe" Henry on Main Street (Broadway) in Maryville. The school grew, and in 1904, Henry acquired the Freedman's Institute property. He changed the name to Blount County High School and added high school curriculum to his business courses. The name changed to Polytechnic High School and Commercial College in 1908 and, in 1909, to Maryville Polytechnic School. The doors closed in 1926, and Maryville High School moved to the site in 1927. (Courtesy of B. Kenneth Cornett.)

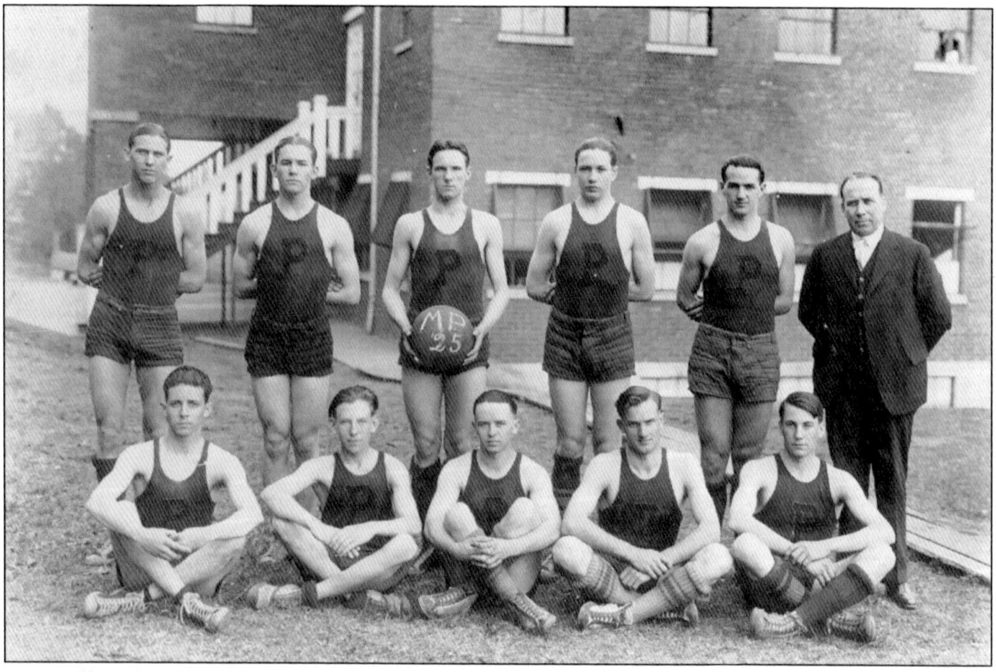

Maryville Polytechnic School's basketball team in 1925 is shown here. The players are, from left to right (first row) unidentified, ? Burns, Cecil McGhee, Walter Peters, and Herman Shields; (second row) Andy Harris, Robert Byerley, Harold Bird, William Cox, Roy Davis, and principal/coach Charles William "Bill Joe" Henry. (Courtesy of Gail Harris.)

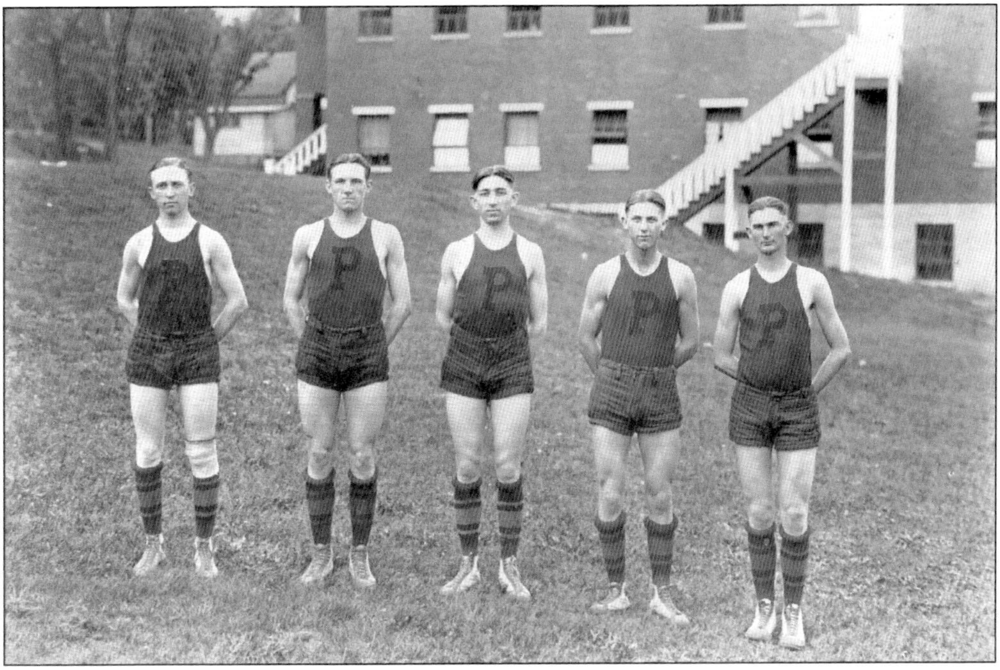

Maryville Polytechnic School's track team photograph was taken in 1924. The team members are, from left to right, Enoch Waters, Harold Bird, John Cox, Andy Harris, and Leonard Davis. (Courtesy of Gail Harris.)

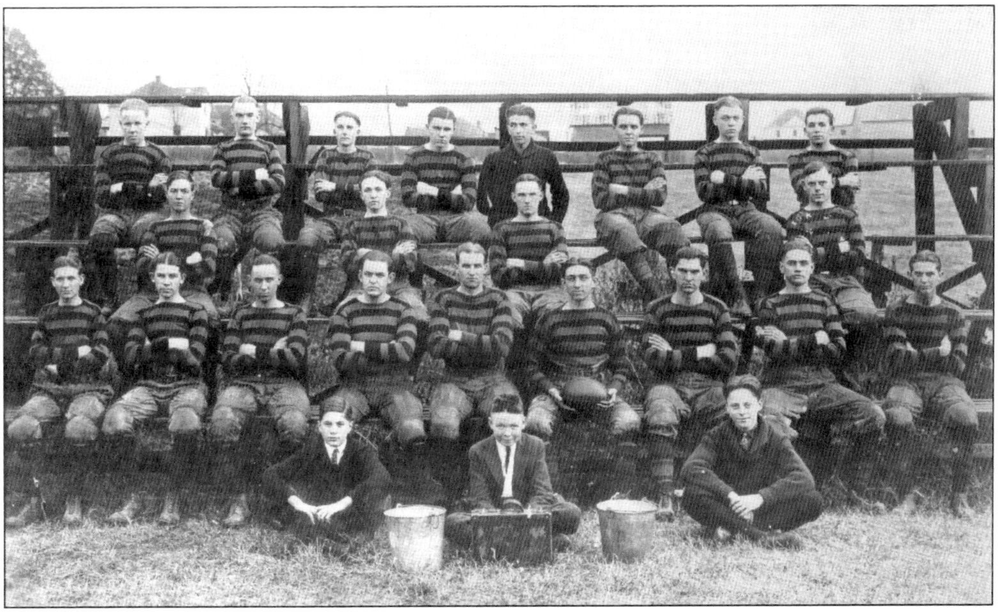

Members of the 1923 football team at Maryville Polytechnic School were, from left to right, (first row) water boys Hugh Hannah, Harry Coile, and unidentified; (second row) Andy Harris, Lester Shields, Clareance Grant, John Cox, Roy ?, James Keen, Fred Bird, Fred Byerley, and Frank Manderson; (third row) Jake Bull, Enoch Waters, Harold Bird, and Charles Alexander; (fourth row) James Hamilton, Roland Grant, Harold Gamble, William Telford, Clyde Jobe, William Crowder, unidentified, and James White. (Courtesy of Gail Harris.)

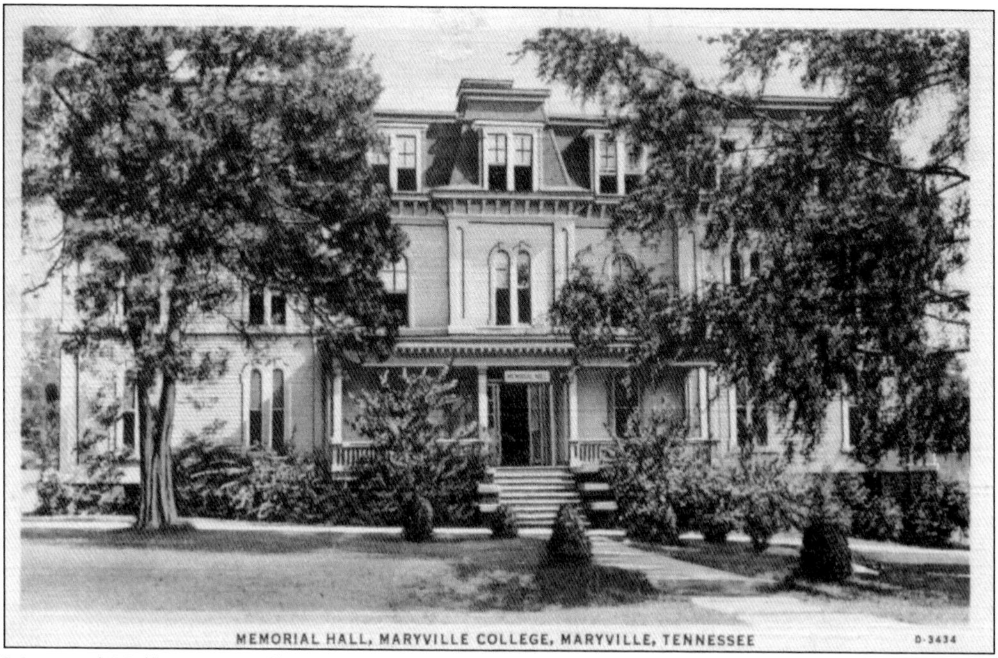

Memorial Hall at Maryville College was completed in 1871. The frame building served as the men's dormitory and boarding hall, where meals were served. Each room was heated by a wood stove, and the male students chopped the wood. The building is no longer in existence, having been torn down in 1975. (Courtesy of B. Kenneth Cornett.)

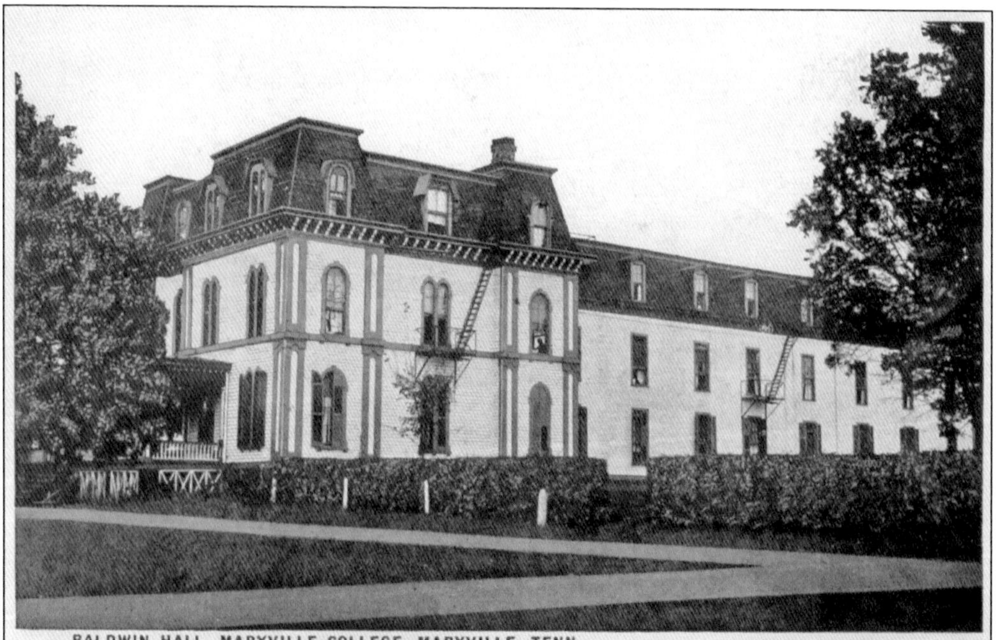

Baldwin Hall at Maryville College was built in 1871. Baldwin, the women's dormitory, was financed by a gift of $25,400 from John C. Baldwin, who was the first large donor to the college. Female students prepared their own meals in several small kitchens located in the basement. This building was removed in 1968 to make room for the Science Center. (Courtesy of B. Kenneth Cornett.)

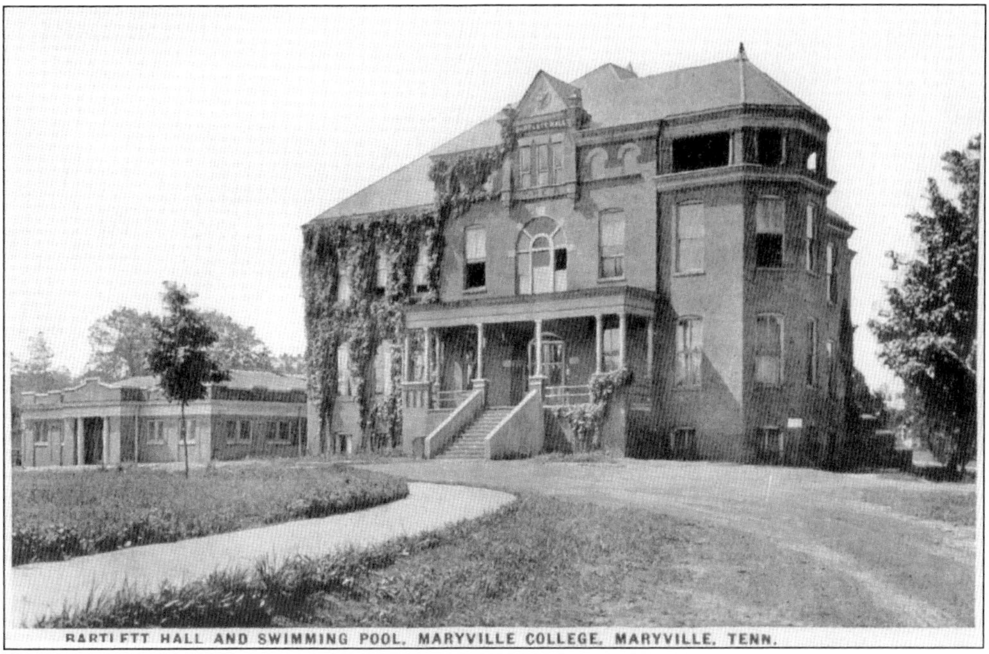

Bartlett Hall and swimming pool on the Maryville College campus are shown around 1940. Philanthropist Nelle McCormick of Chicago, the YMCA, and the students themselves provided the money and labor for Bartlett Hall, which was designed by George F. Barber of Knoxville in 1901. The building still exists, but the swimming pool was removed. (Courtesy of B. Kenneth Cornett.)

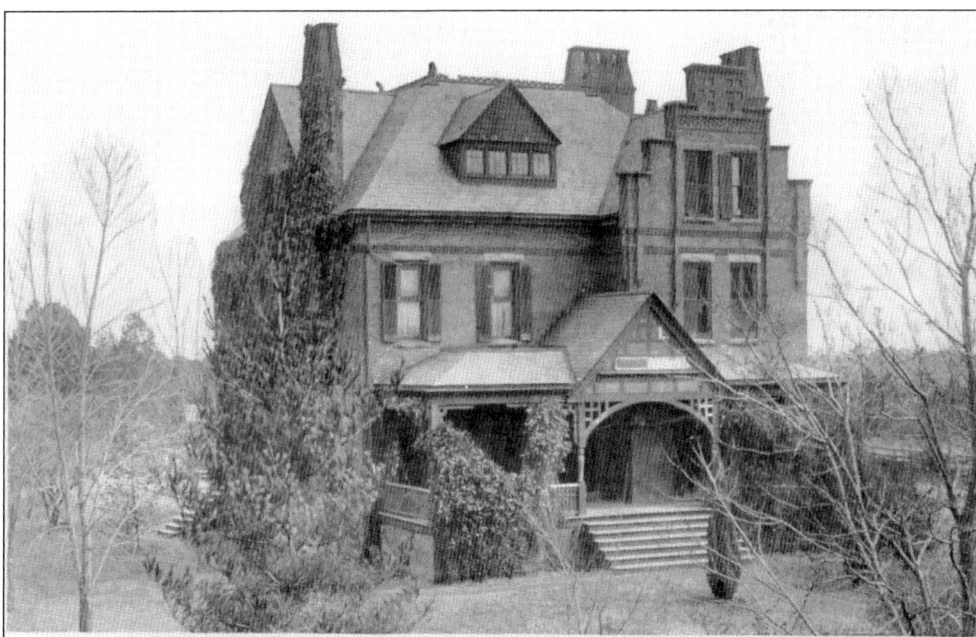

This gracious home served the presidents of Maryville College in the early 20th century. Many of the buildings, along with other historic structures that comprise the Maryville College Historic District, are listed on the National Register of Historic Places. (Courtesy of B. Kenneth Cornett.)

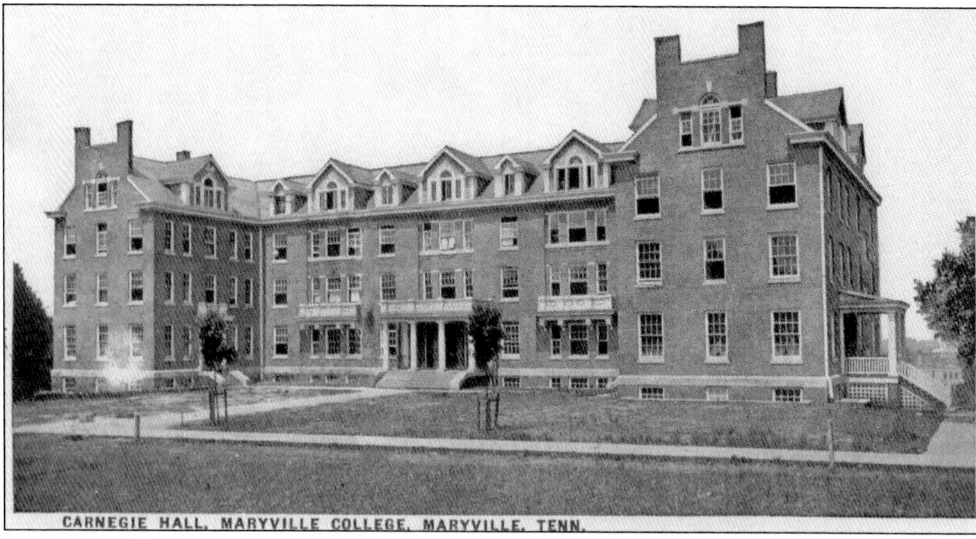

Carnegie Hall is another of the historic buildings on the Maryville College campus. In the 1910s, capitalist Andrew Carnegie provided funds for the five-story Carnegie Hall, which was designed by R. F. Graf and Sons of Knoxville and was completed in 1917. The building is in use today as a men's dormitory. (Courtesy of B. Kenneth Cornett.)

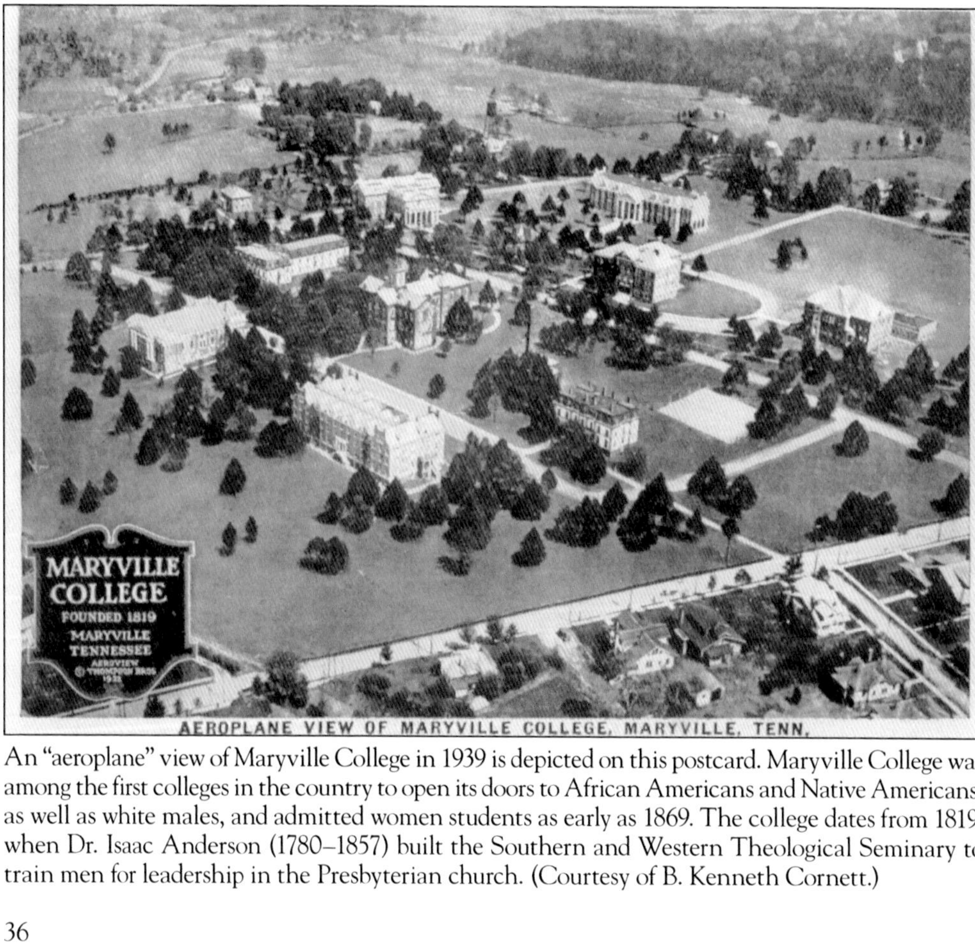

An "aeroplane" view of Maryville College in 1939 is depicted on this postcard. Maryville College was among the first colleges in the country to open its doors to African Americans and Native Americans, as well as white males, and admitted women students as early as 1869. The college dates from 1819, when Dr. Isaac Anderson (1780–1857) built the Southern and Western Theological Seminary to train men for leadership in the Presbyterian church. (Courtesy of B. Kenneth Cornett.)

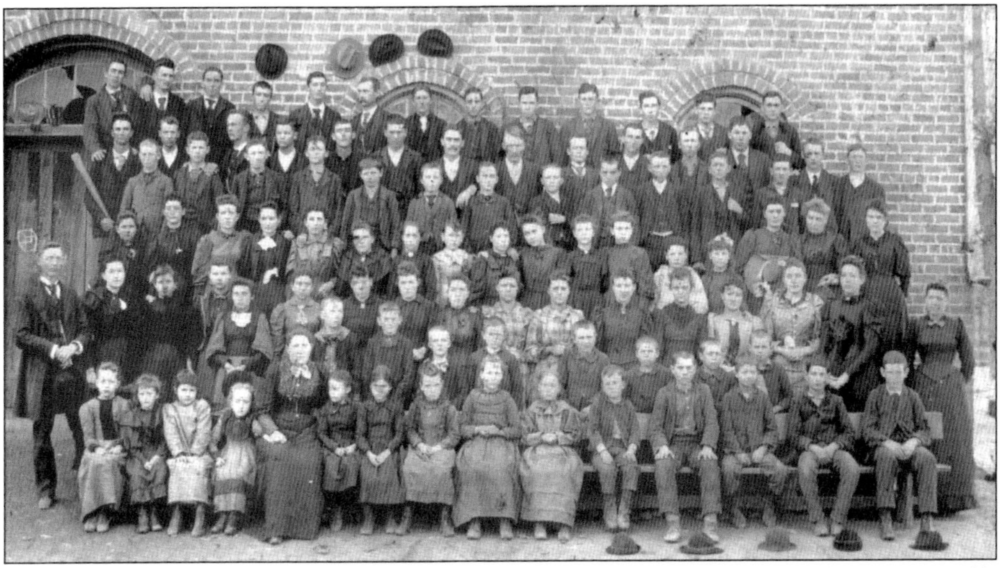

When the Wildwood community outbid Rockford for Porter Academy, which was originally in Maryville, the brick building where these students are gathered was constructed in 1871 at Wildwood. The building was razed in 1918, and some of the brick was used in building Porter High School, Blount County's first public high school. The school, which cost $14,000, contained six classrooms and an auditorium. (Courtesy of Bob DeLozier, D. O. Waters collection.)

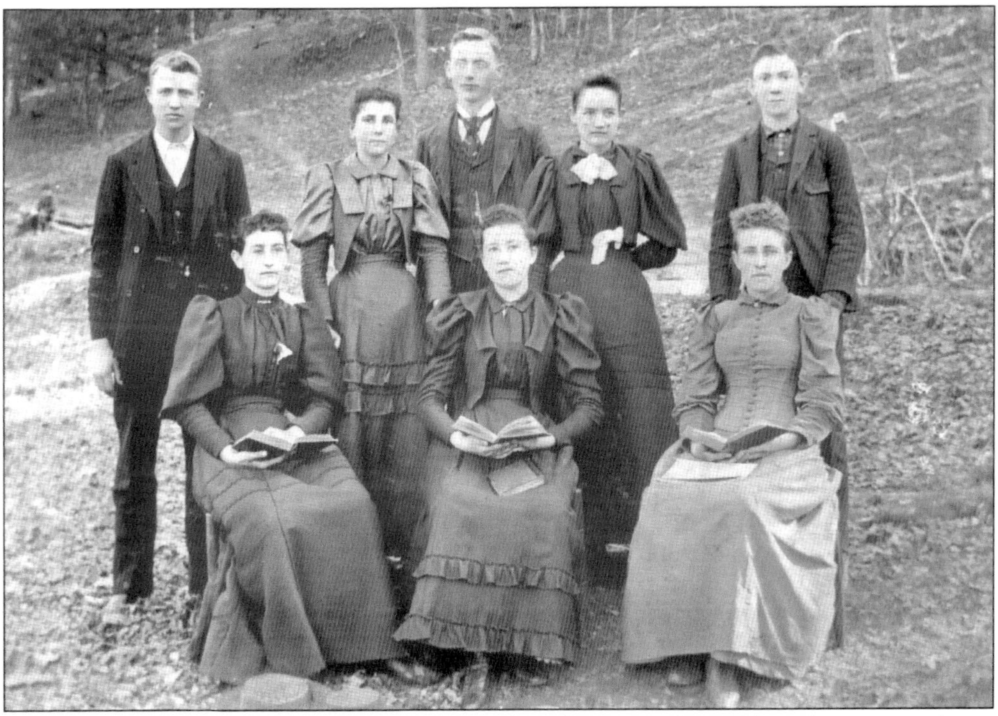

Students at Porter Academy in Bank, Tennessee (now known as the Wildwood community), are, from left to right, (first row) Sophie Goddard, Estelle Hafley, and Frankie Walker; (second row) Tommie Hall, Ina DeLozier, a Prof. Matt Hall, Mae Goddard, and Robert Rose. (Courtesy of Bob DeLozier, D. O. Waters collection.)

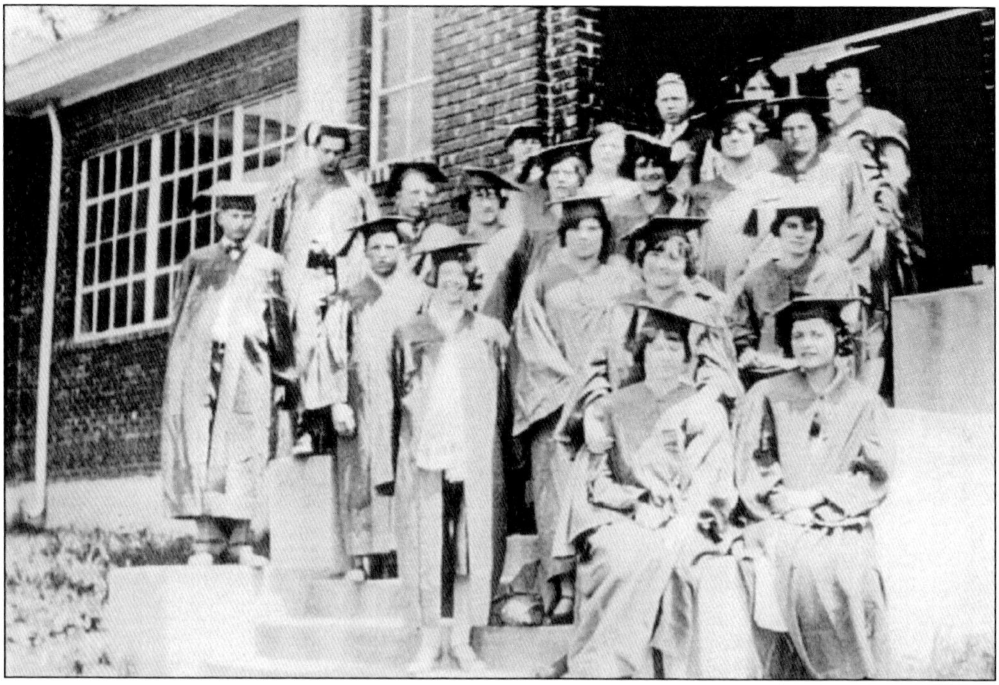

Everett High School opened its doors in 1922 and graduated its last class in 1977, when the new Heritage High School was built. The graduating class of 1926 included Helen Coulter (first row, far right). (Courtesy of Linda Braden Albert, Helen Coulter collection.)

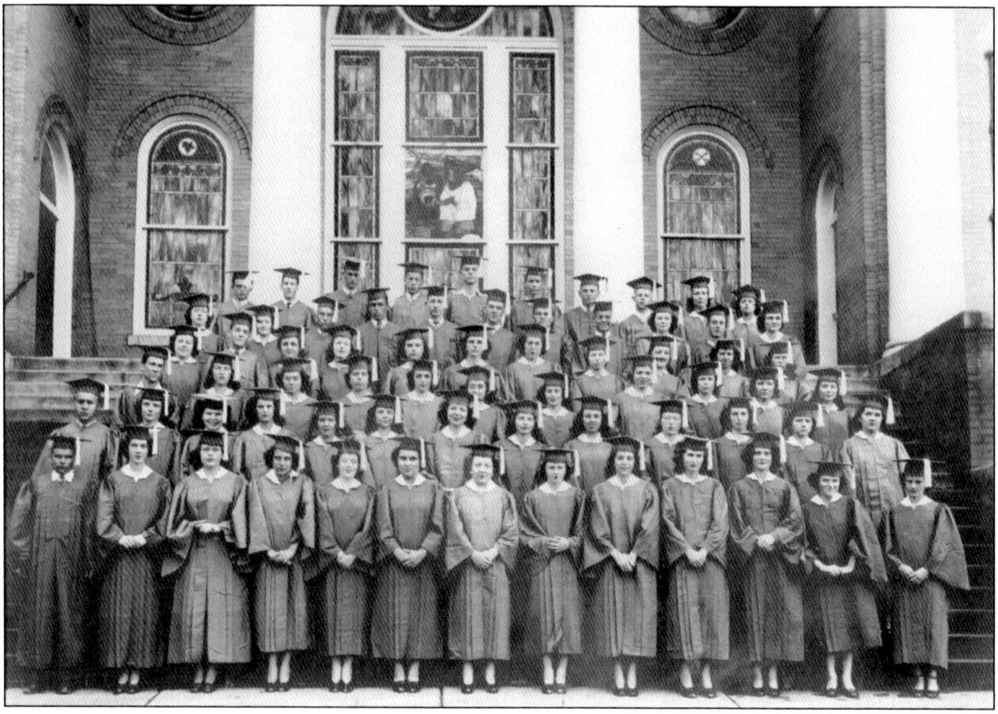

The Everett High School Class of 1944–1945 is pictured here in front of First Baptist Church on Ellis Avenue, Maryville. (Courtesy of Ron and Debbie Teffeteller, Martha Birchfield collection.)

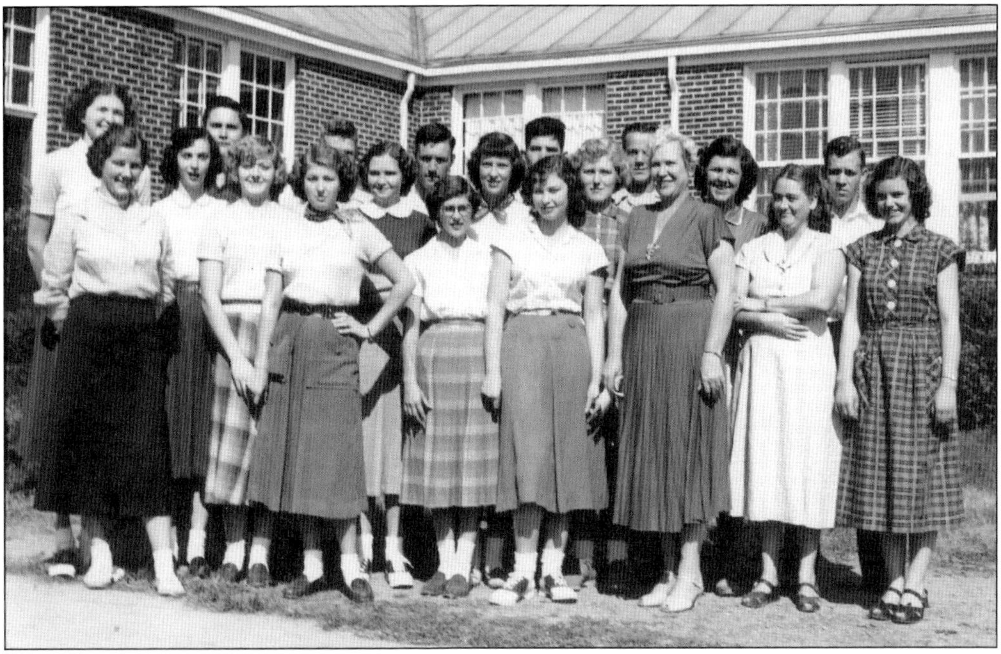

Lanier High School's Beta Club, sponsored by Inez Burns, is shown here in 1954. Burns (first row, third from right), an avid student of history and Blount County historian until her death in 2004, published *History of Blount County, Tennessee: From War Trail to Landing Strip, 1795–1955* in 1957, which was revised in 1988. As a Blount County teacher and librarian for many years, Burns encouraged her students to seek out their own roots. She was successful. Three of these students are actively involved in historical organizations and research: Betty Boone Best, Ralph Lee, and Dorothy Gregory Sutton. (Courtesy of Betty Boone Best.)

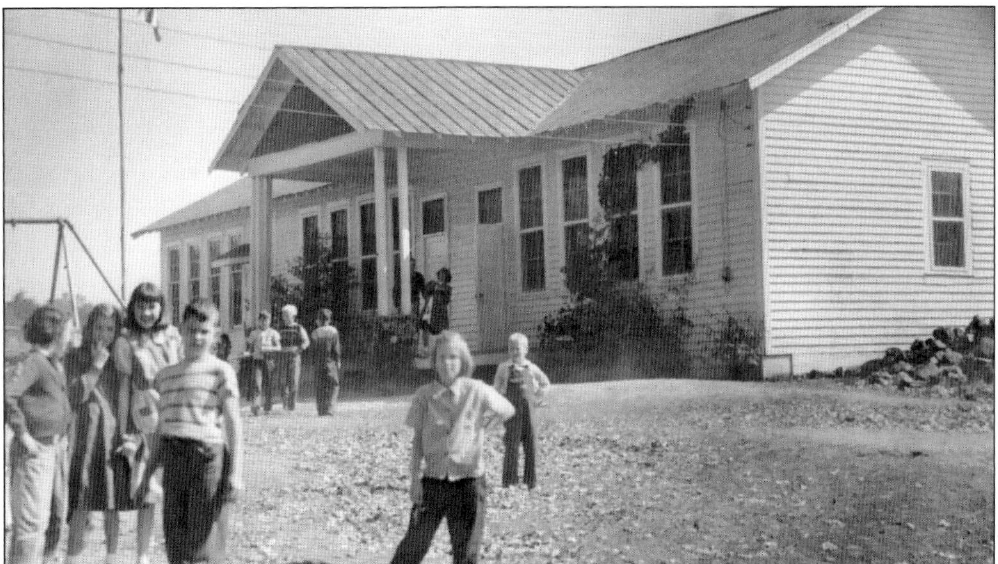

Children are at play in front of the Howard School, which was located in the Lanier community. The school was first called Dunlap, but the name was changed when the school was moved to the Howard property, near Liberty Baptist Church. (Courtesy of Betty Boone Best.)

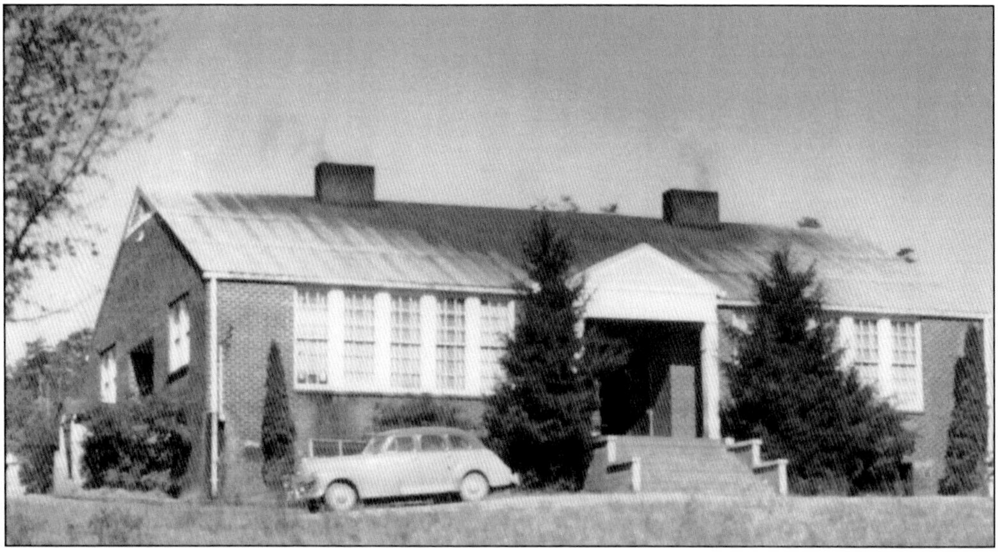

Rush Strong School, named for Knoxville philanthropist Rush Strong, opened in 1921 on Mint Road. Strong left $1,000 to a number of counties with the stipulation that a school be built and named after him, which Blount County did. The school's doors closed in the 1980s, and the building was subsequently modified and turned into apartments. (Courtesy of Betty Boone Best.)

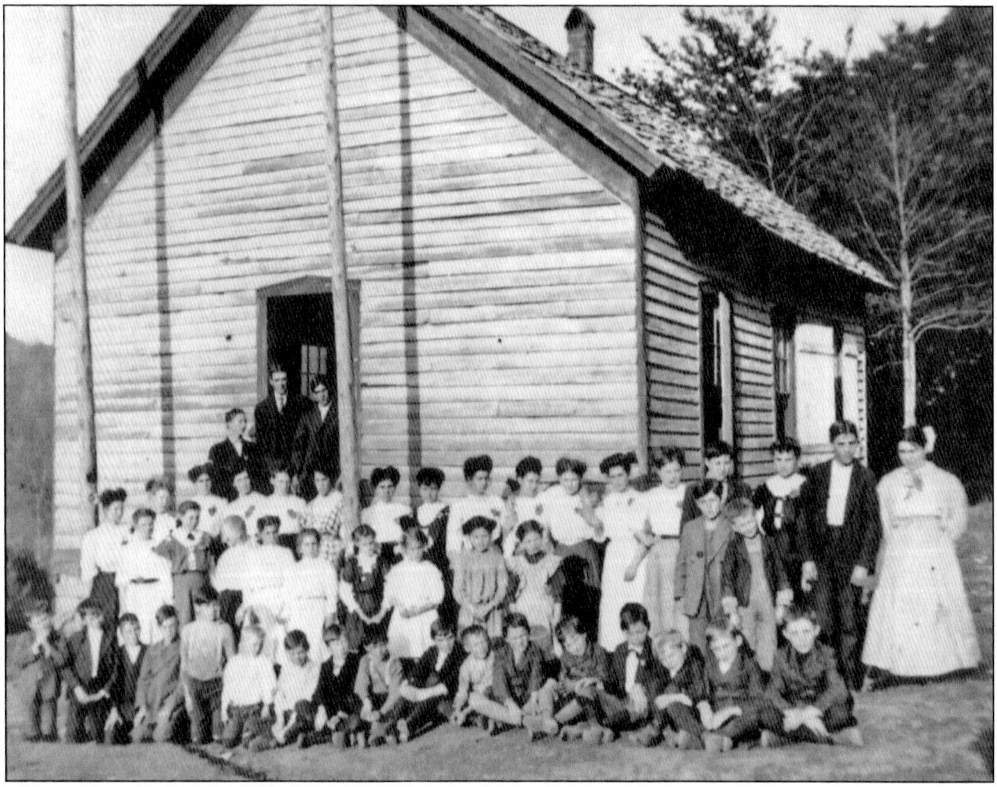

The student body of the Nelson School poses for a photograph in 1907. Students later attended the McCulloch School, which, along with the Bryant School and the Stony Grave School, were consolidated with the Lanier School in 1928. (Courtesy of Betty Boone Best.)

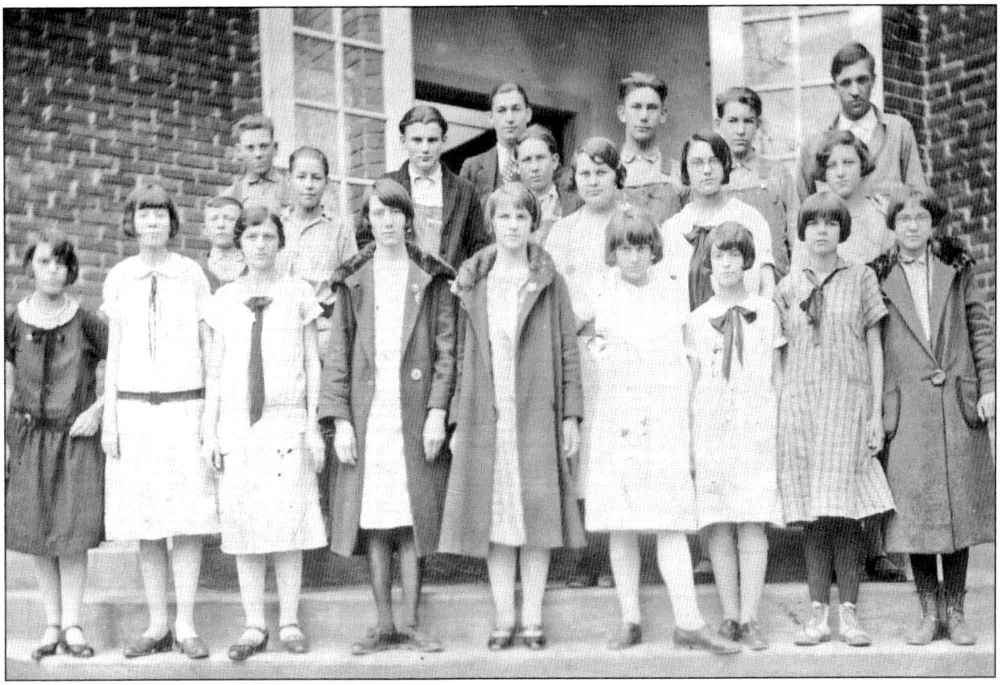

The seventh and eighth grades at the Walland School pose for this 1926 photograph. The teacher, Earl Blazer, is standing at the back in the center. Some of the students were Lois Long, Thelma Thomas, Lela Rudd, Violet Vars Gourmley, Veda Clark, Doyle Martin, and Toots Blazer. (Courtesy of Alleen Powlus.)

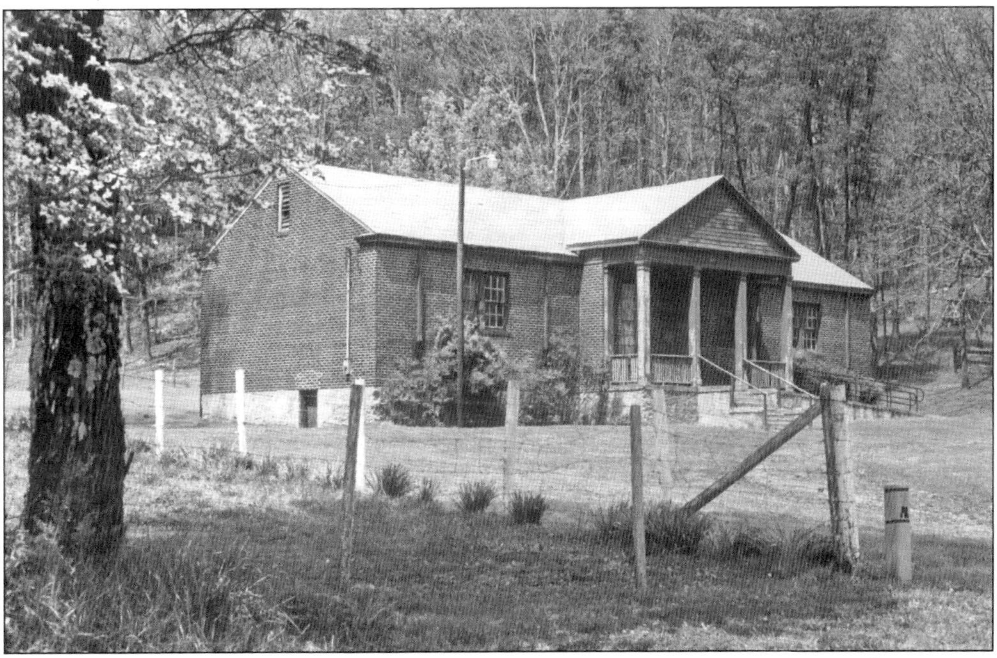

Happy Valley School operated until the 1960s. The brick schoolhouse was built around 1938 in the foothills of Chilhowee Mountain near Abram's Creek and was the third school in Happy Valley. The building now serves as the Happy Valley Community Club. (Courtesy of the *Daily Times*.)

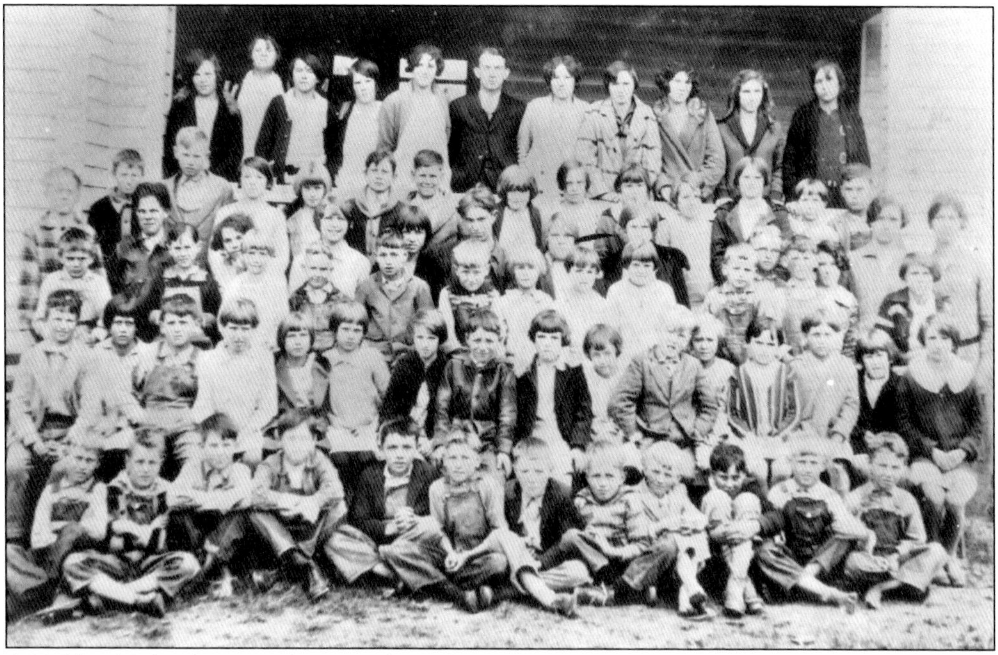

A Hubbard School group takes time for a photograph in the 1930s. Teachers Louise Coulter and Mary Steele are standing in the fourth row at far right. The Hubbard School opened in 1918 with 115 students in grades one through eight. When the school closed in 2000, there were 240 students in kindergarten through third grade. (Courtesy of Margaret Davis Coulter.)

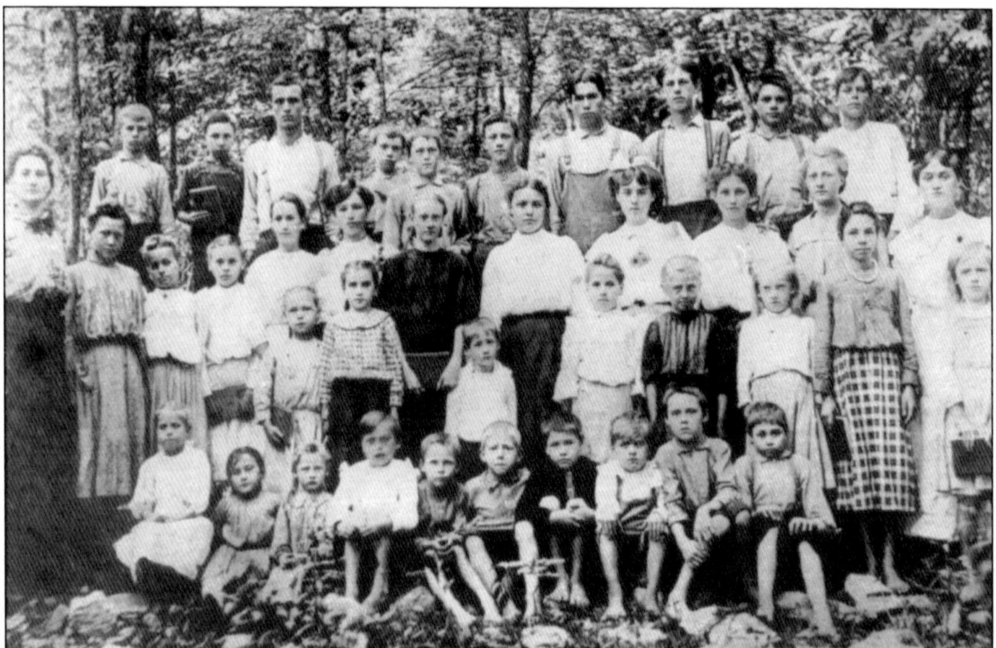

This Howard School group is shown around 1930. A close look shows students with bare feet and boys in overalls. After returning home from school, students completed their chores and did homework by the light of a kerosene lamp. (Courtesy of Betty Boone Best.)

The Townsend School is shown in this aerial photograph from 1964. Townsend High School began in 1929 and continued until 1977, when it was consolidated into Heritage High School. The structure in front of Chilhowee Mountain was built in 1948 to house the elementary school. In 1954, a new gymnasium was added for the high school. The new Townsend Elementary and renovated gymnasium opened in January 1994 and remains a kindergarten through fifth grade school. (Courtesy of the *Daily Times*.)

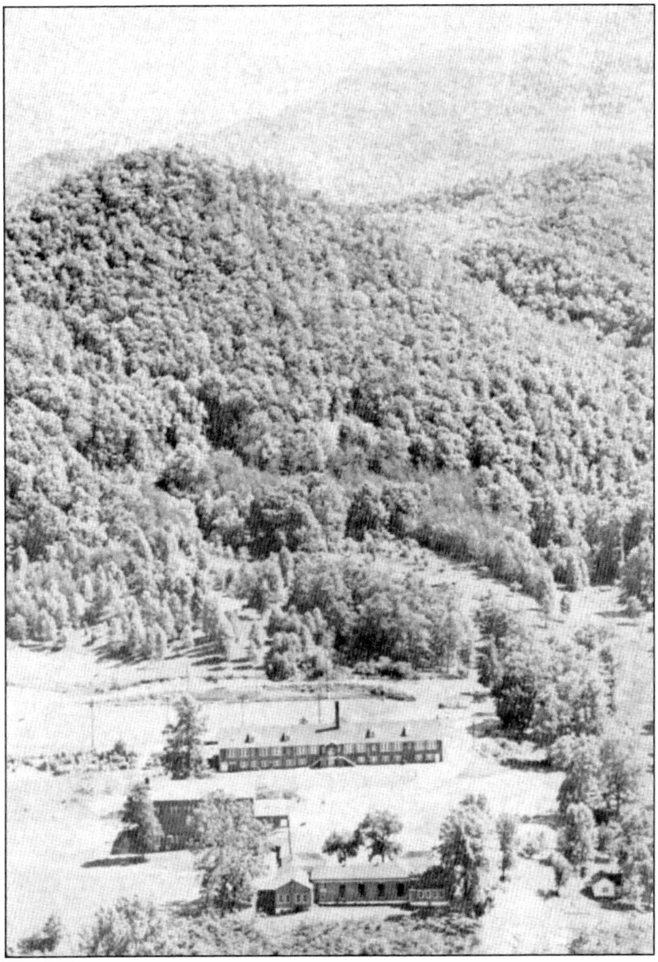

Hubbard School students, shown below about 1938, pause for a class photograph. The school opened in 1918 and closed in 2000. The building now houses the Blount County Community Action Agency and the Blount County Records Management Office. (Courtesy of Margaret Davis Coulter.)

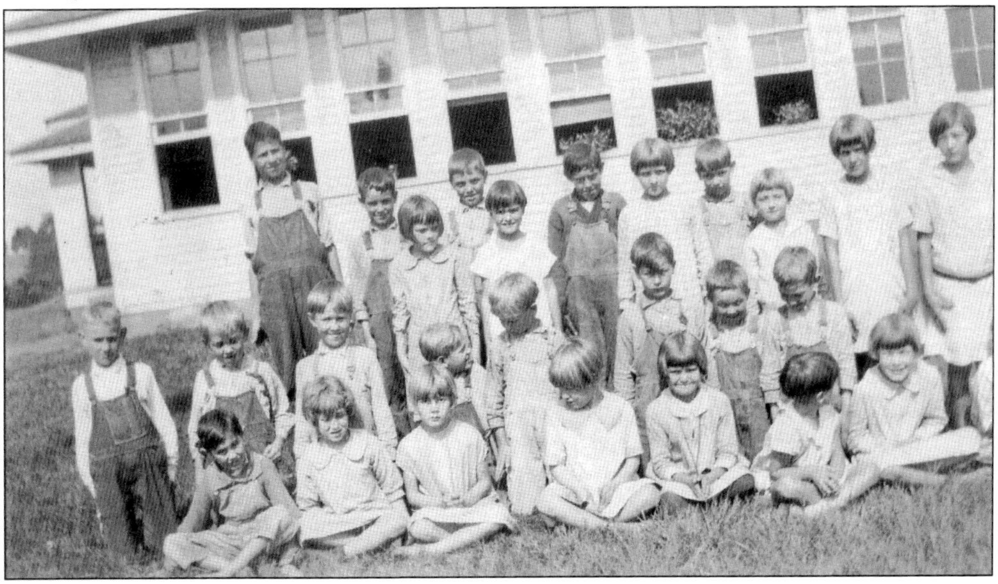

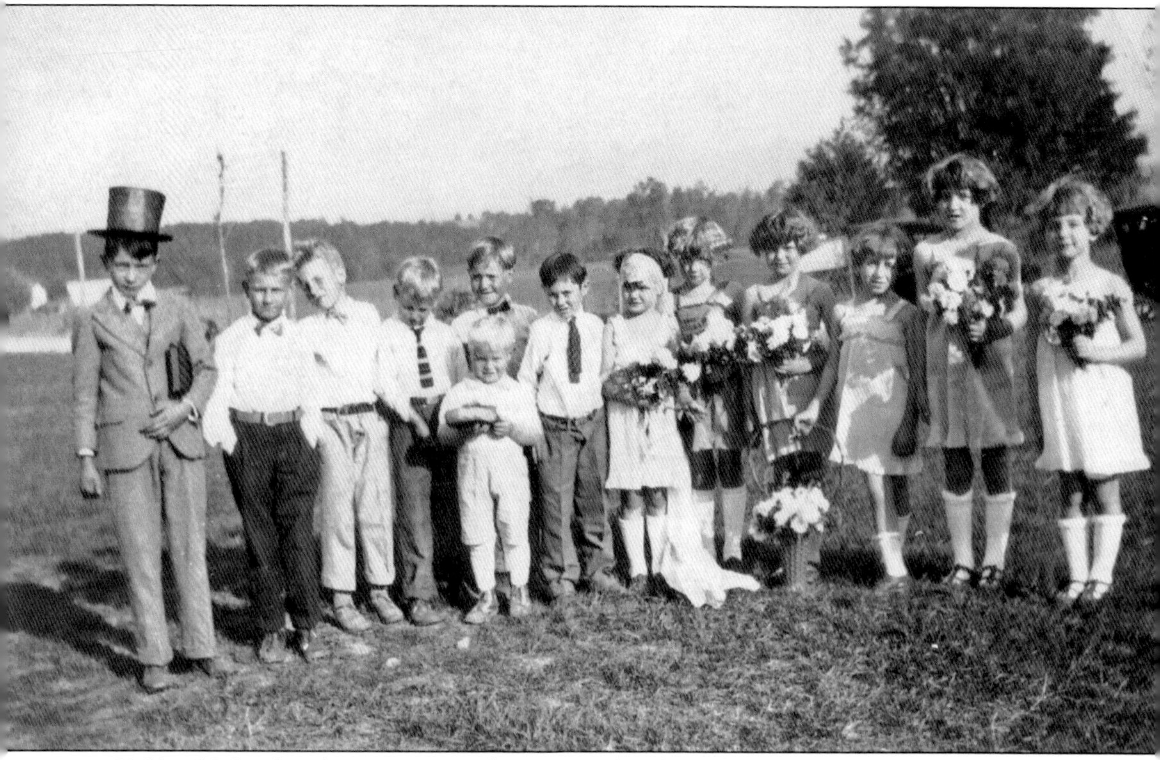

Hubbard School students participated in a Tom Thumb Wedding around 1945. This was a popular event for the students and community in the early 20th century. For a Tom Thumb Wedding, children, including a "bride" and "groom" with all their attendants, have a "wedding." (Courtesy of Margaret Davis Coulter.)

Three

Industry and Business

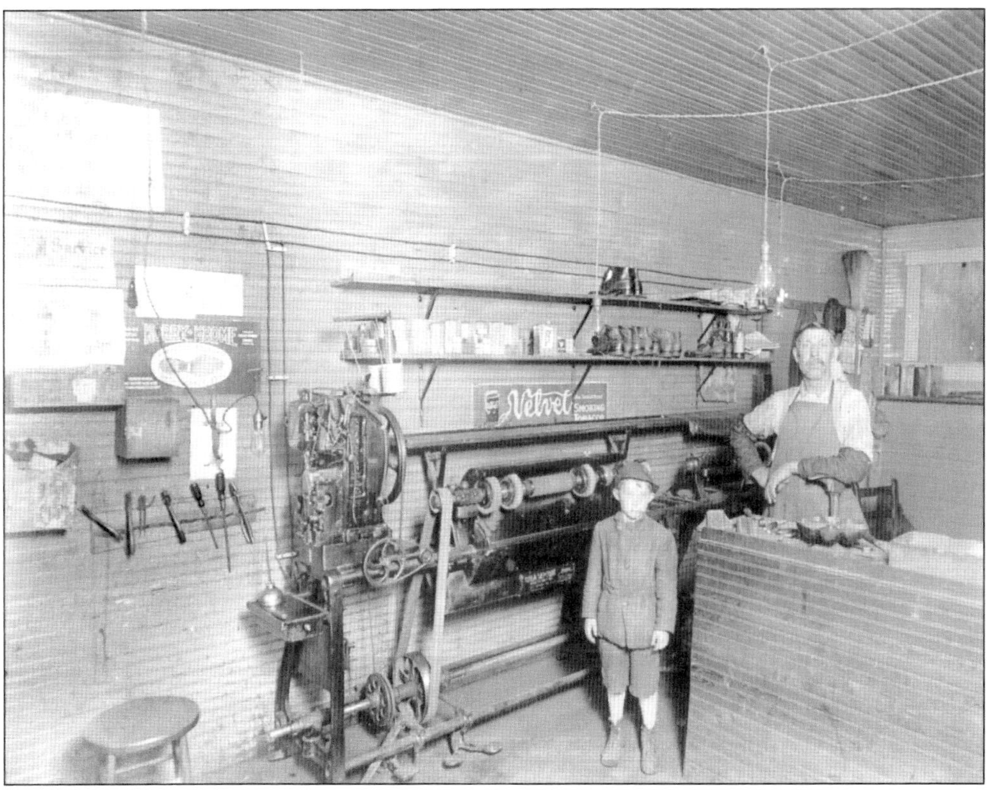

Isaac Johnson (right) and his son, Harold, work in Johnson's shoe shop, which was located at the corner of Washington Street and Sevierville Road in Maryville. The photograph was taken about 1921. (Courtesy of Terry Huffstetler.)

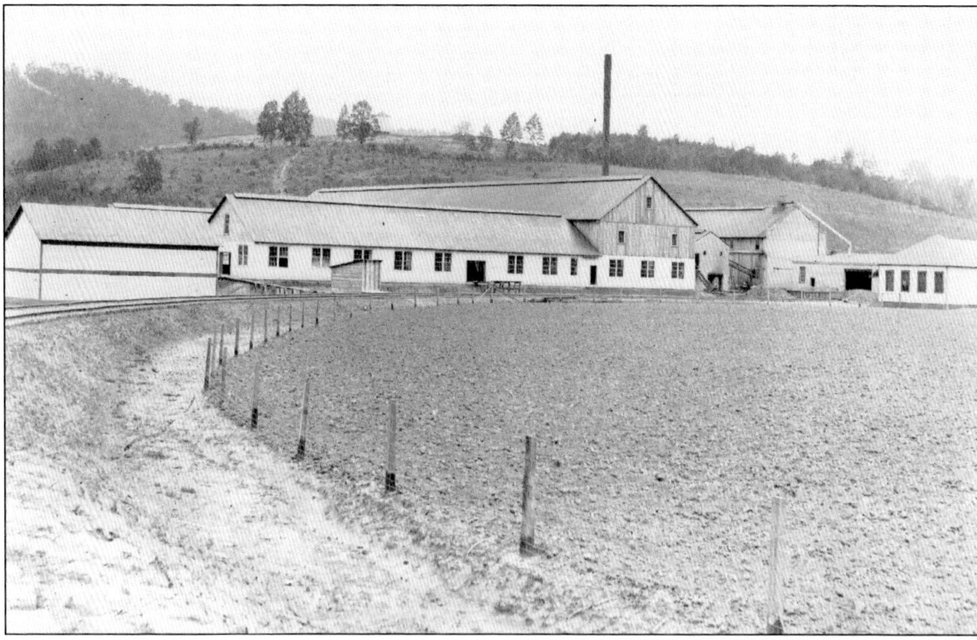

The Schlosser Tannery, also known as the Walland Tannery, was established in 1900 in Miller's Cove. The tannery belonged to the Walton-England Leather Company, giving the name "Walland"—combining "Wal" from Walton and "land" from England—to the community that grew up around the business. The tannery was destroyed by fire in January 1931 and was not rebuilt. (Courtesy of the Blount County Public Library, Adele McKenzie collection.)

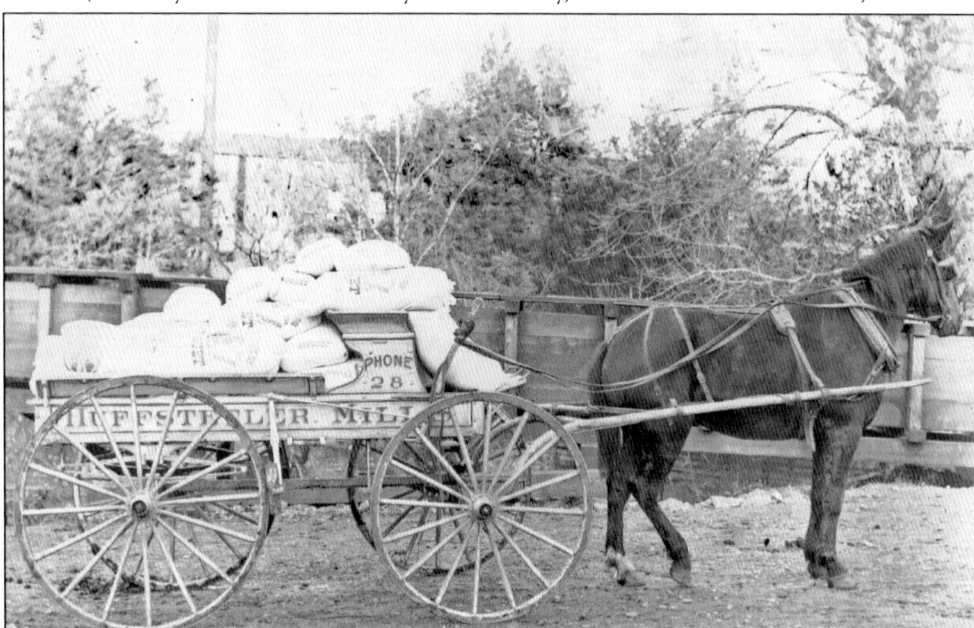

Huffstetler Mill operated in Maryville in the early 20th century. Here a wagon is piled high with flour ready to be delivered to customers. (Courtesy of the Blount County Public Library, Adele McKenzie collection.)

Tollgate House was located beside Parsons Turnpike, a toll road from the mouth of Abrams Creek in Blount County to near Deal's Gap, North Carolina. The turnpike was the main cattle trail and commerce route between this area and Western North Carolina until U.S. Highway 129 was constructed in 1931. George Davis (pictured at right), who ran the tollgate, was responsible for keeping the road in passable condition. (Courtesy of the Blount County Public Library, W. O. Garner's collection.)

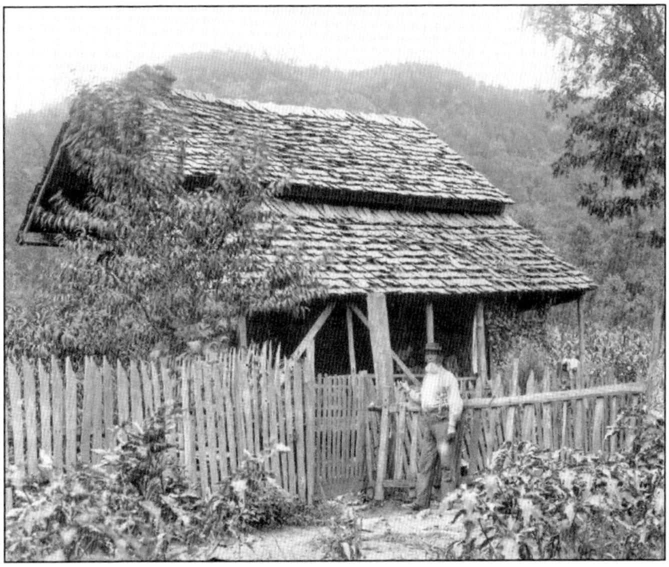

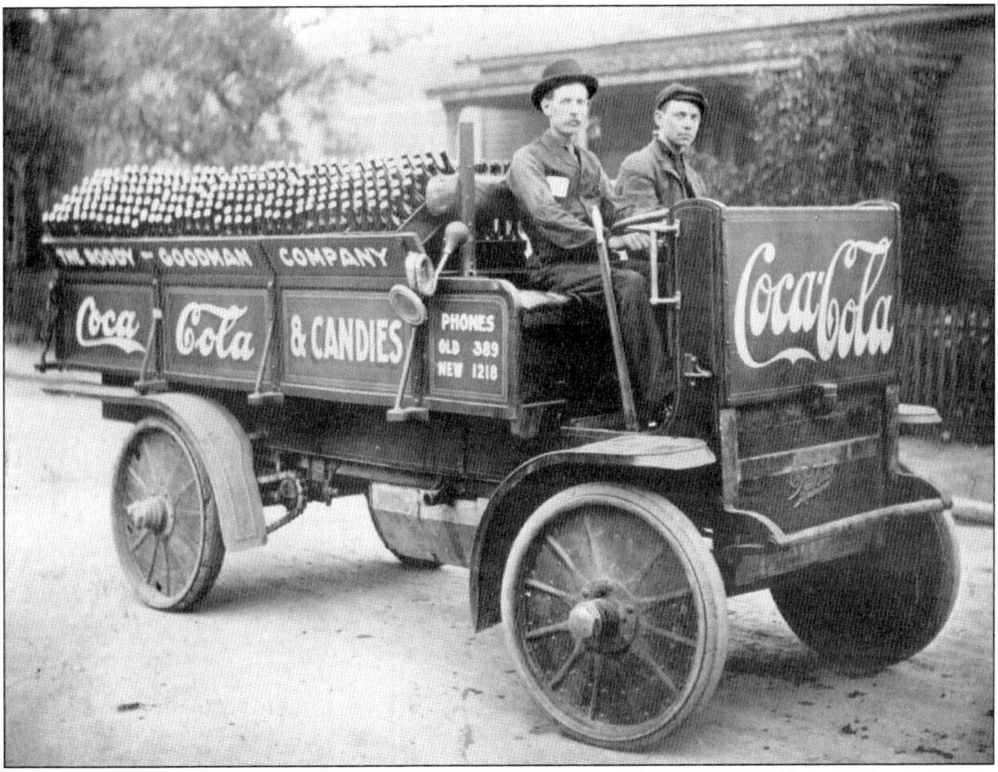

James Patrick Roddy (left) and his partner, William H. Goodman, acquired the rights to bottle and distribute a new product called Coca-Cola in the Knoxville area in 1902. Customers in outlying sections such as Maryville were supplied by truck and rail shipments. In 1920, Roddy Manufacturing was located at the corner of Cusick and Church Streets in Maryville. In 1927, a new company-built plant was located at the corner of College and Harper Streets, and in 1959, a large new facility opened at what is now East Lamar Alexander Parkway. The Blount County Justice Center now occupies the site. (Courtesy of James Pat Roddy III, *75 Years of Refreshment.*)

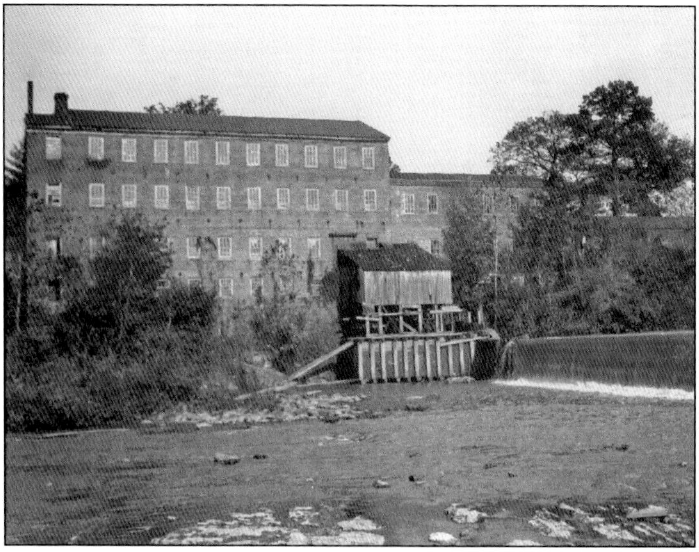

Rockford Manufacturing Company, in continuous operation since 1910, has the distinction of being the oldest manufacturing business in Blount County. It originally began in 1885 with a state charter for the purpose of manufacturing wool, silk, and hemp. The company has been owned and operated in recent years by the Ernest Koella family. (Courtesy of the Blount County Public Library, Adele McKenzie collection.)

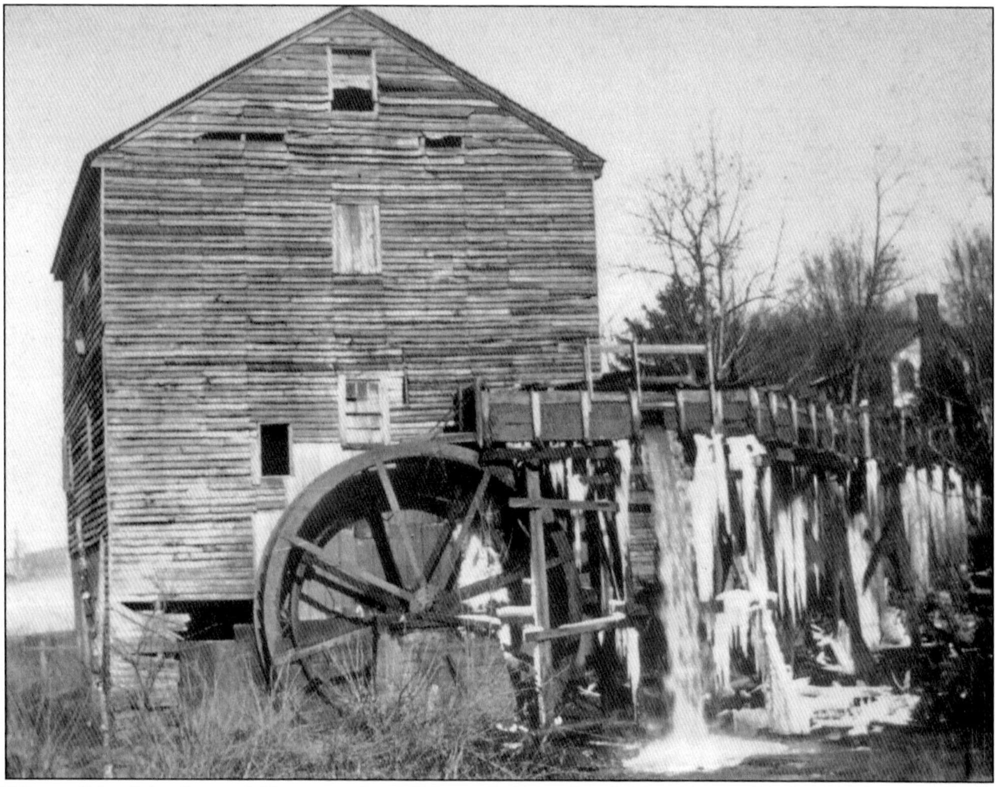

The mill built by Samuel Henry in the 1790s on Baker's Creek was commonly known as Brick Mill because of its construction of brick made by slaves on the site. Henry, a Revolutionary War soldier and cousin of Patrick Henry, received several hundred acres of land on which the mill and his gracious home, built in 1833, were located. The Henry Farm, still owned by Henry's descendants, was named a Tennessee Century Farm in 2009 for being continuously operated as such by the same family. (Courtesy of the Blount County Public Library, Edwin Best collection.)

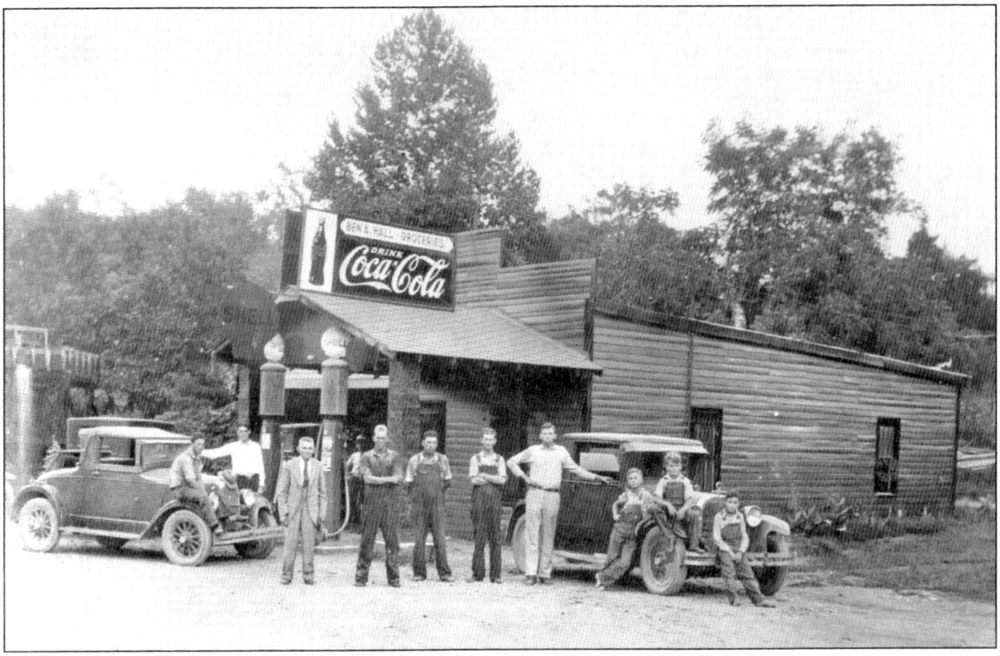

Ben A. Hall Grocery is shown here about 1932. The store was located at Brick Mill, near Greenback. Pictured, from left to right, are unidentified, Ralph Cannon, unidentified, Joe Allen Best, unidentified, Fred Hutton, Ben A. Hall, Jack Seaton, and two unidentified. (Courtesy of the Blount County Public Library, Edwin Best collection.)

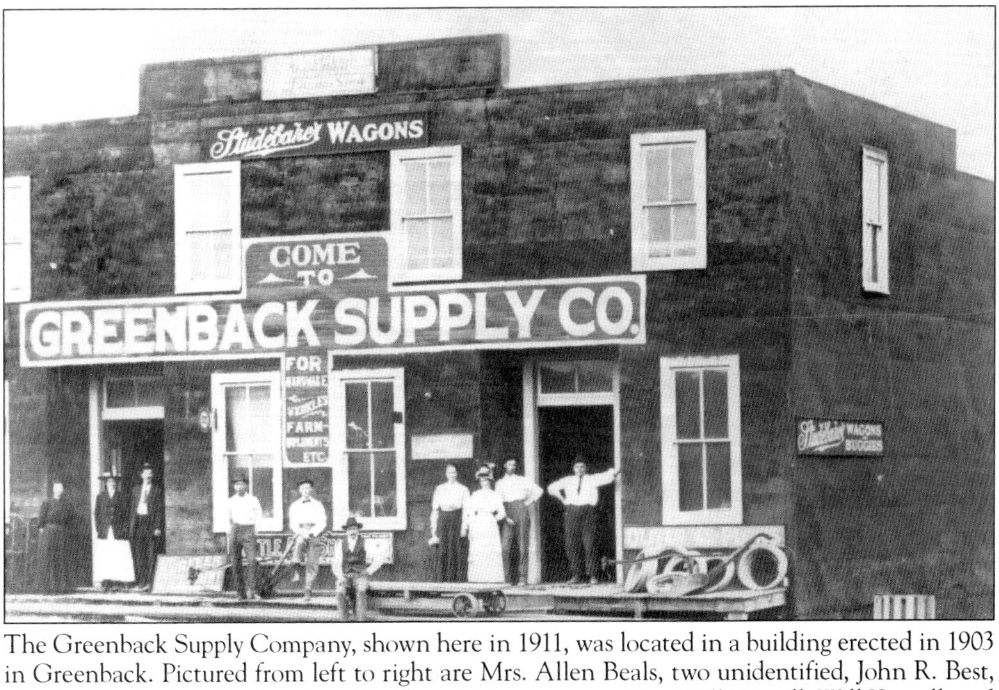

The Greenback Supply Company, shown here in 1911, was located in a building erected in 1903 in Greenback. Pictured from left to right are Mrs. Allen Beals, two unidentified, John R. Best, Charles O. McCall, A. J. Wilson, Mrs. Ira E. Hammontree, Mrs. Will Kittrell, Will Kittrell, and W. H. Jones. The building housed five businesses during its short life, being destroyed by fire in 1917. (Courtesy of the Blount County Public Library, Edwin Best collection.)

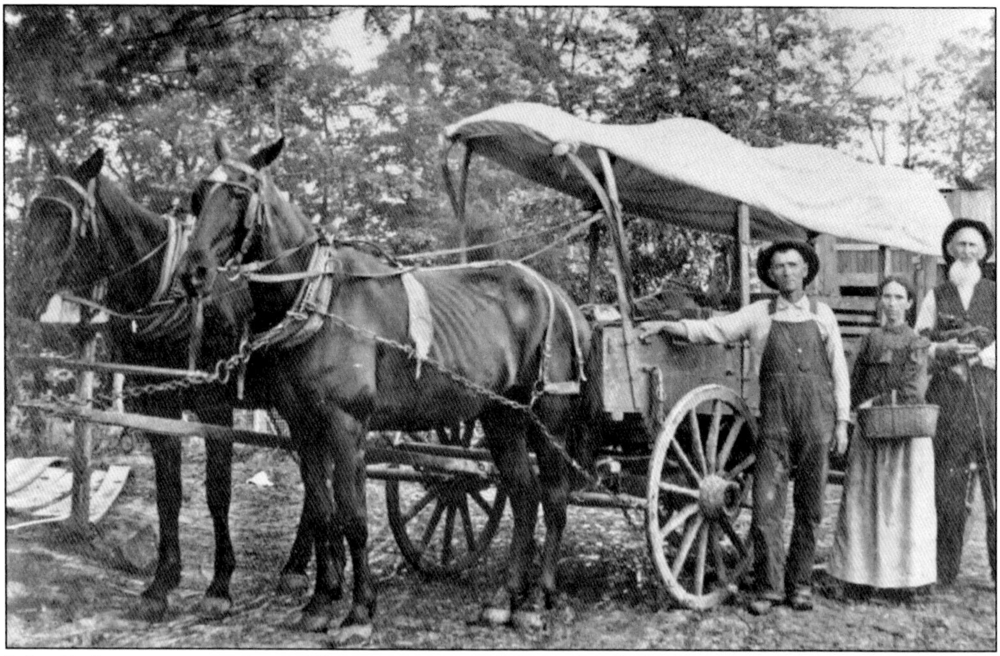

John R. Long operated a peddling route out of Greenback, bartering store goods for country produce. In this *c.* 1920 photograph, Long (left) is shown with Laura (Mrs. Robert) Kerr and John Gilbert. (Courtesy of the Blount County Public Library, Edwin Best collection.)

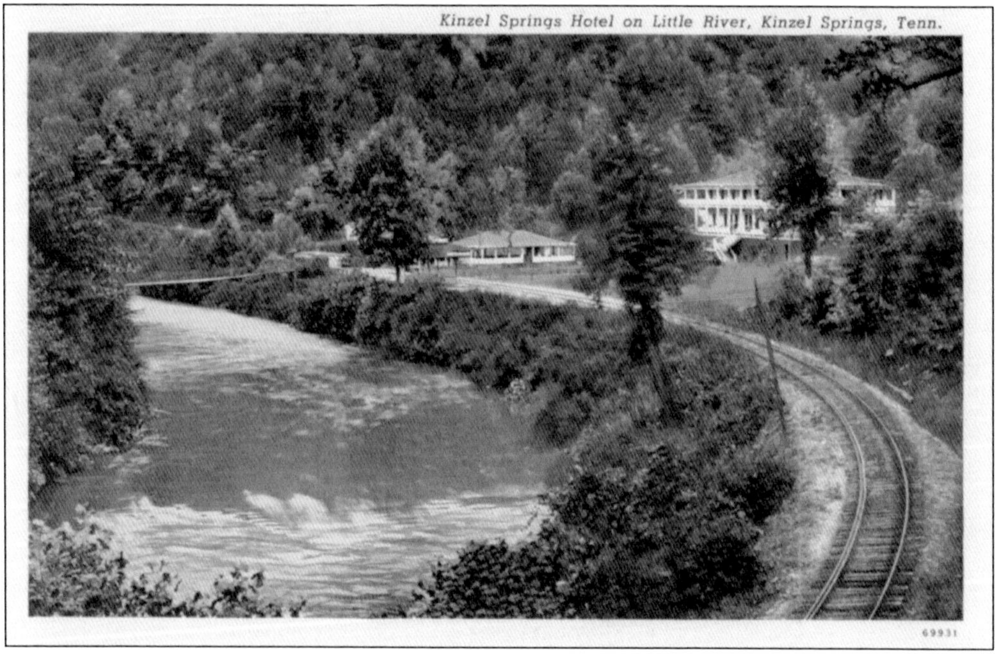

In 1919, Edward John Kinzel and his wife, Catherine, built the 28-room Kinzel Springs Hotel, shown at far right, and 10 cottages beside Little River in Townsend. This postcard shows Little River Railroad and the swinging bridge that crossed the river in front of the hotel. A small depot called Sunshine was near the bridge, which connected the Kinzel Springs Hotel with the Sunshine Hotel on the opposite bank. (Courtesy of B. Kenneth Cornett.)

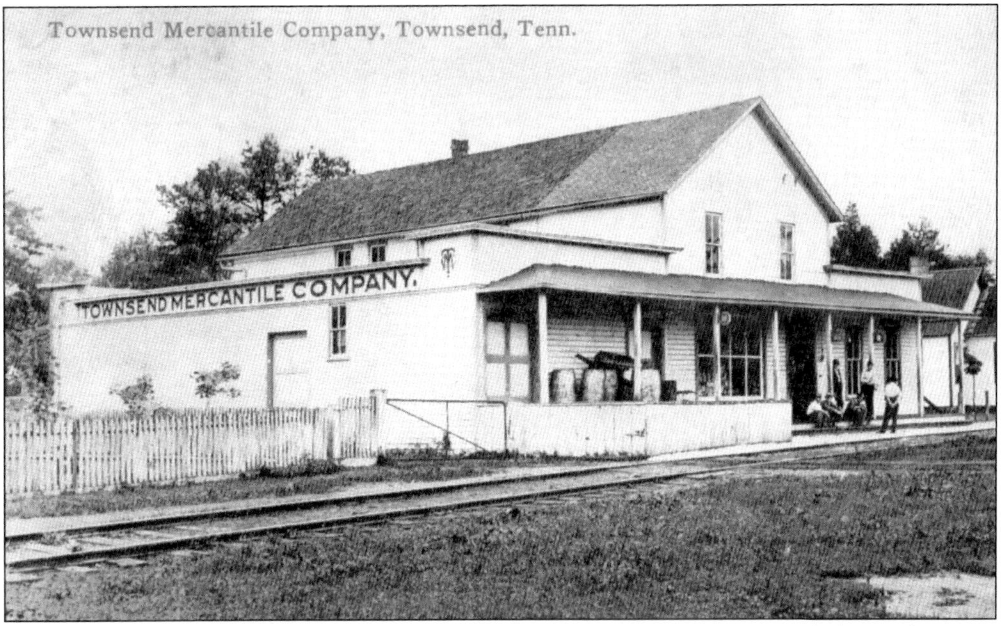

The Townsend Mercantile Company, "the Company Store," was conveniently located next to the lumber mill and pond in Townsend. Workers in the timber industry were paid in company scrip, which could be exchanged for goods at the store. The Townsend Post Office was housed in a small room located at one end of the store. Almost anything families needed could be found there. (Courtesy of B. Kenneth Cornett.)

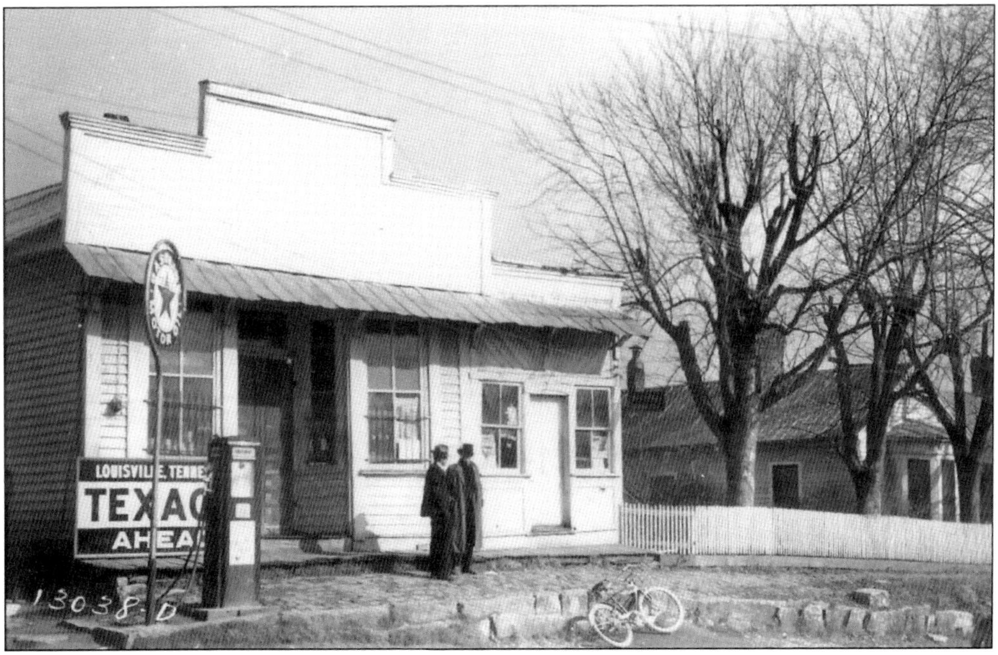

In 1886, brothers L. R. "Doc" and John Harper built a general merchandise store in Louisville. A smaller wooden structure was built adjacent to the store and housed the post office. Doc Harper sold his share of the store to his brother in order to serve as postmaster. The wooden store building with its false front still stands near the entrance to Louisville Point Park. (Courtesy of Kathleen McCammon.)

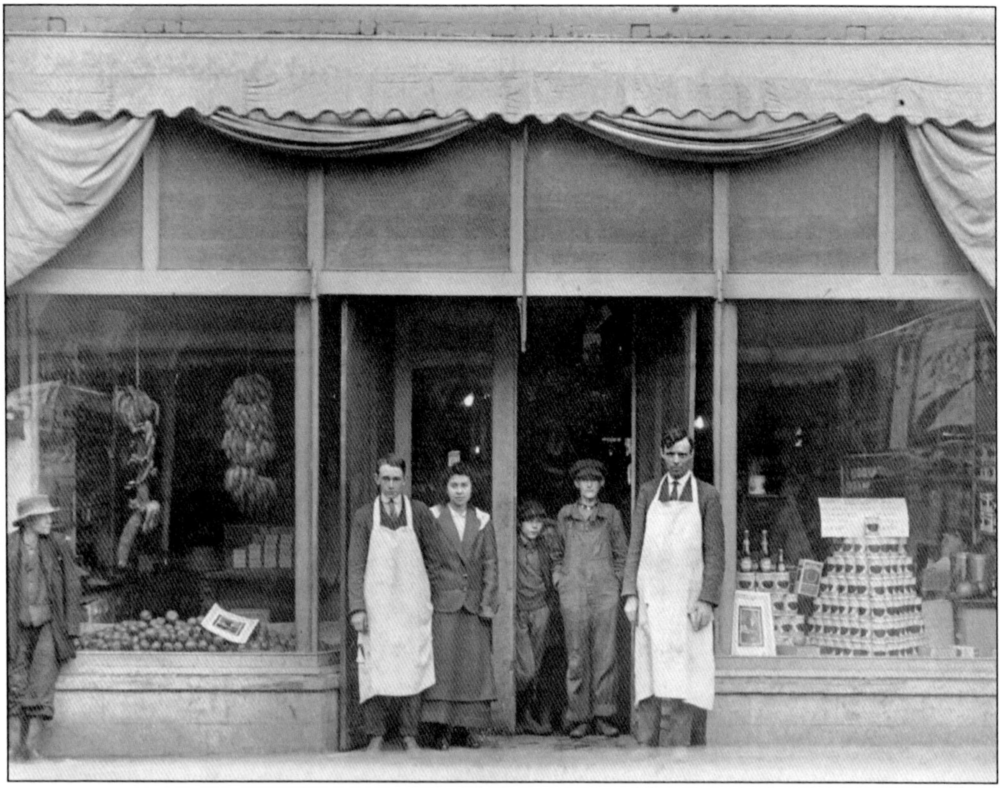

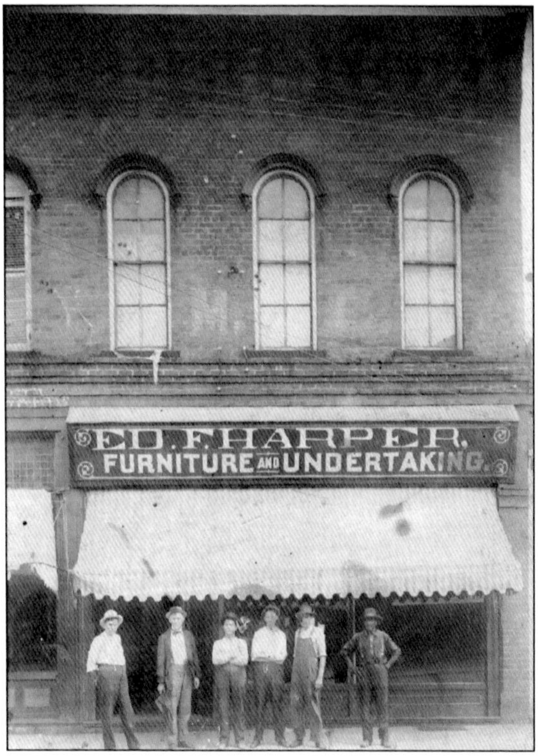

The McCammon Grocery Store in Maryville was owned by C. P. McCammon and Otto McCammon. A letterhead from the store promised "Quality Groceries," including fresh vegetables and fruits. Note the bunches of bananas hanging in the display window. The telephone number was "No. 329." (Courtesy of Kathleen McCammon.)

Ed F. Harper Furniture and Undertaking on Main Street (Broadway), Maryville, was the forerunner of the modern funeral home known as McCammon-Ammons-Click. Ed F. Harper operated an undertaking business establishment along with a furniture business at what is now National School Products on Broadway Avenue. Roy Ammons, one of McCammon-Ammons-Click Funeral Home's founders, is pictured fourth from left. (Courtesy of Tom Click, McCammon-Ammons-Click Funeral Home.)

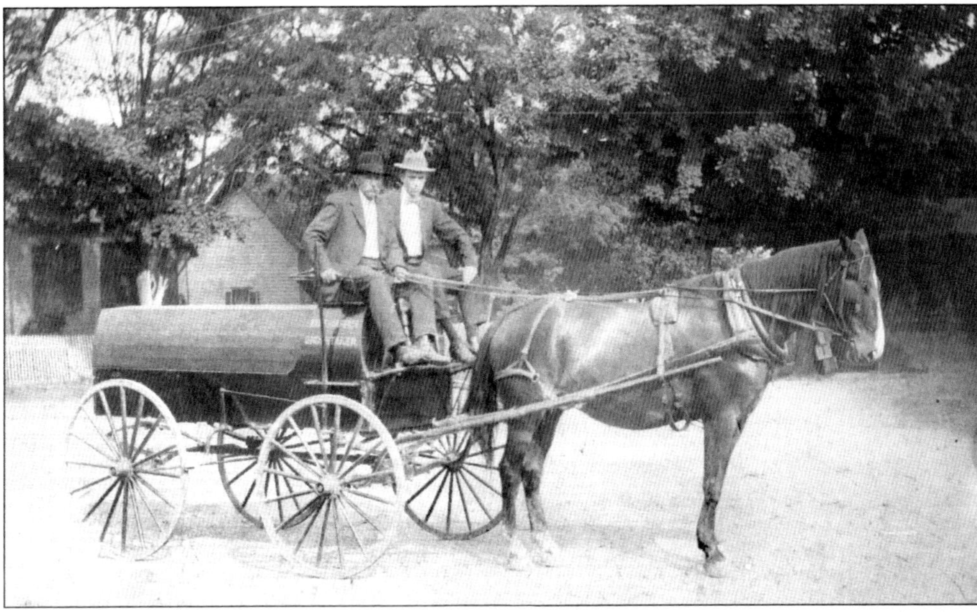

A black-draped, horse-drawn hearse, shown here in the 1920s, was part of Ed F. Harper's undertaking business. Driver Blackbarn Ross is pictured with Roy Ammons at Broadway Avenue and College Street. Coffins of that day were smaller and made locally of wood. (Courtesy of Tom Click, McCammon-Ammons-Click Funeral Home.)

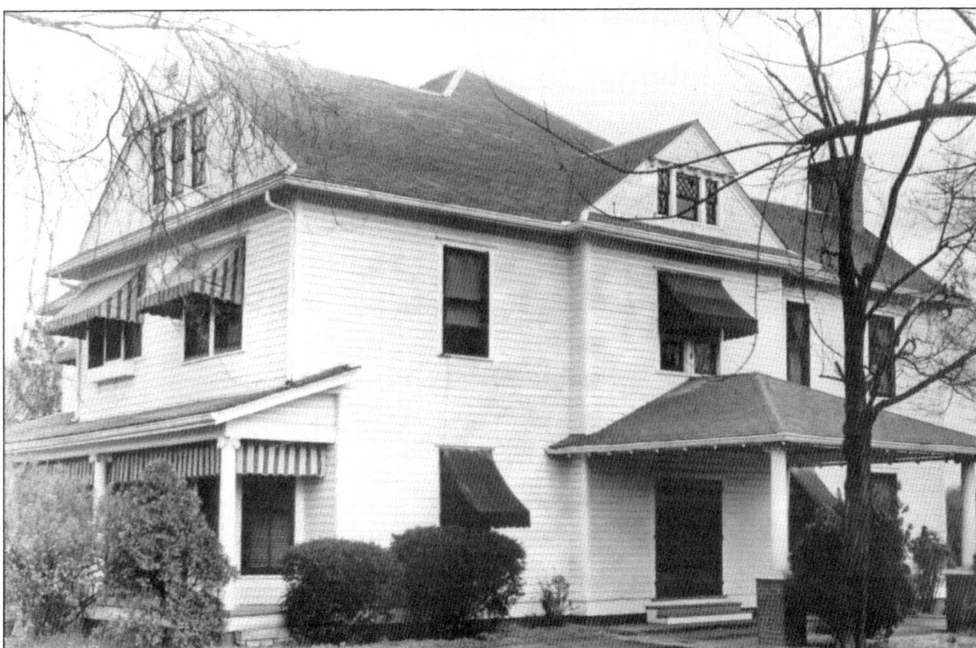

McCammon-Ammons Funeral Home, located on Broadway Avenue, Maryville, is shown here in 1940. In 1927, Roy Ammons and Sam McCammon established Blount County's first business devoted exclusively to undertaking. Both of the founders had been in the funeral business with furniture stores, which also provided undertaking services. Tom Click joined the firm in 1954. (Courtesy of Tom Click, McCammon-Ammons-Click Funeral Home.)

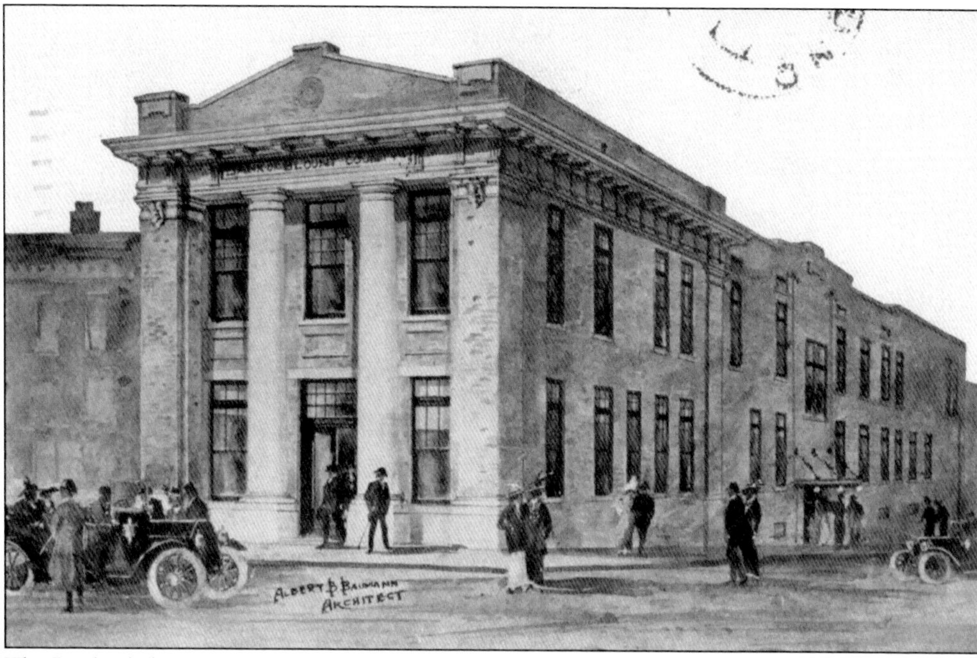

The Bank of Blount County operated in downtown Maryville in the early 20th century. (Courtesy of B. Kenneth Cornett.)

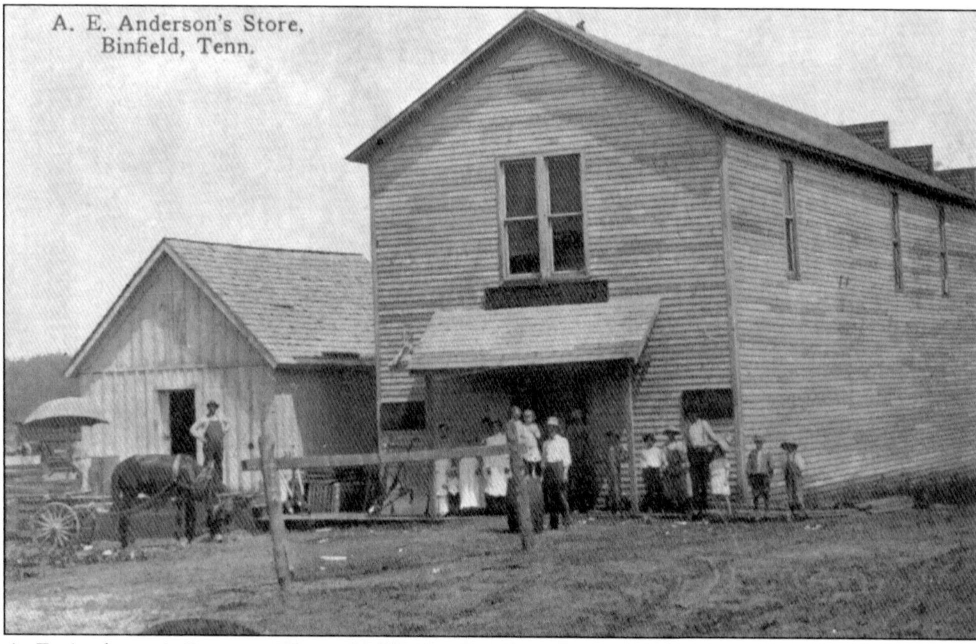

A. E. Anderson's Store on Clover Hill Ridge Road in the Binfield community is pictured in this pre-1920 postcard. The store was originally built by Wright Logan in 1904. The store was also the Binfield Post Office from 1915 to 1934. "Binfield" got its name from the fact that Logan had "bins" and owned a "field" nearby. (Courtesy of B. Kenneth Cornett.)

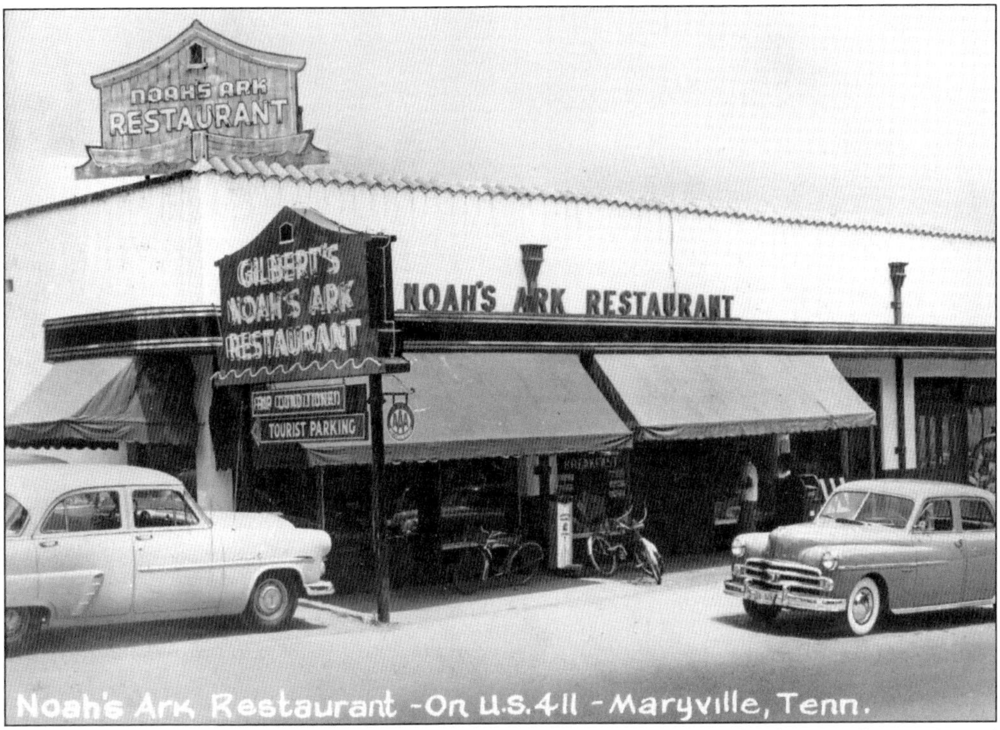

Noah's Ark was a popular destination for Blount County teenagers and others in the 1940s and 1950s. Located on West Broadway, Maryville, just below the Dwarf Drive-In, the restaurant was owned and operated by the Gilbert family. (Courtesy of B. Kenneth Cornett.)

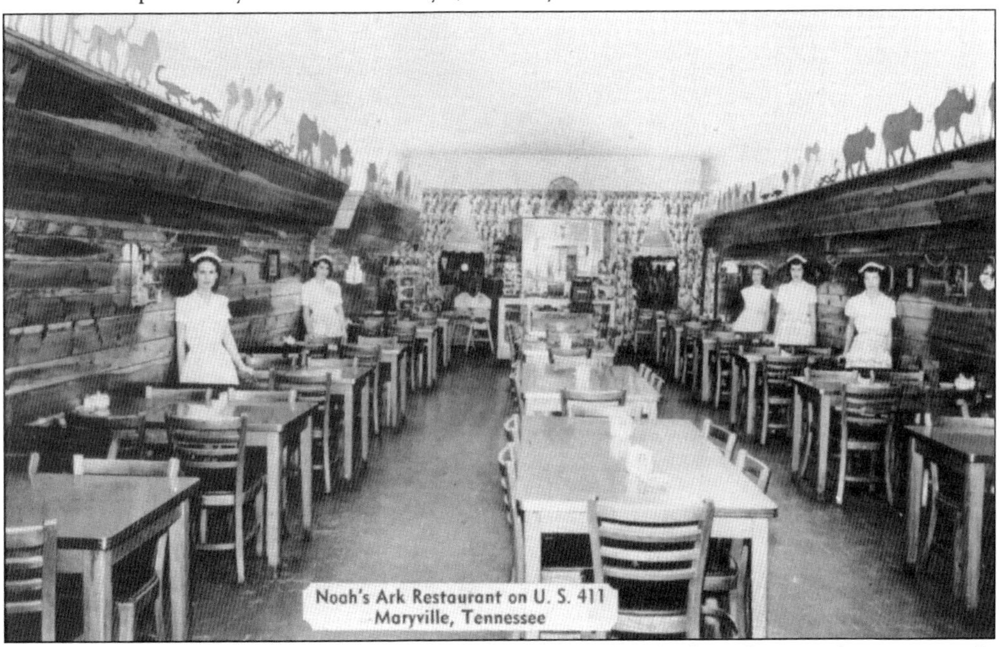

Waitresses stand ready to help customers at Noah's Ark, which is decorated appropriately with a progression of animals marching two by two along the walls. (Courtesy of B. Kenneth Cornett.)

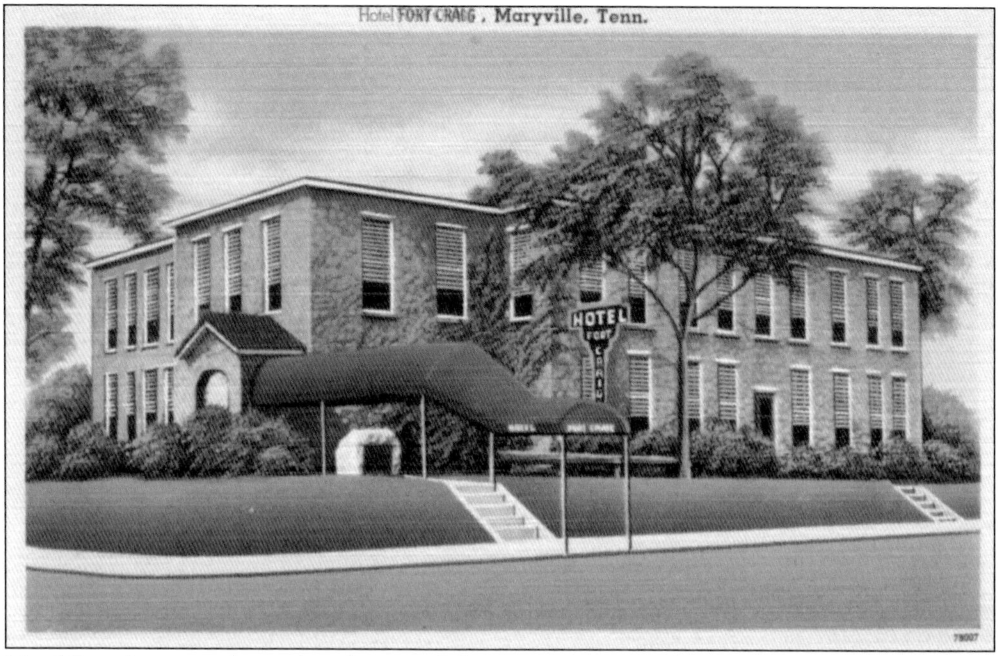

Hotel Fort Craig was located at the site of the Sam George residence on Washington and East Main (Broadway) Streets in Maryville, near the original Fort Craig (now the Blount County Chamber of Commerce). The property was purchased by Dr. J. E. Carson in 1928 and was operated as a hospital until 1944. In 1948, it was remodeled as Hotel Fort Craig, a tourist hotel. (Courtesy of B. Kenneth Cornett.)

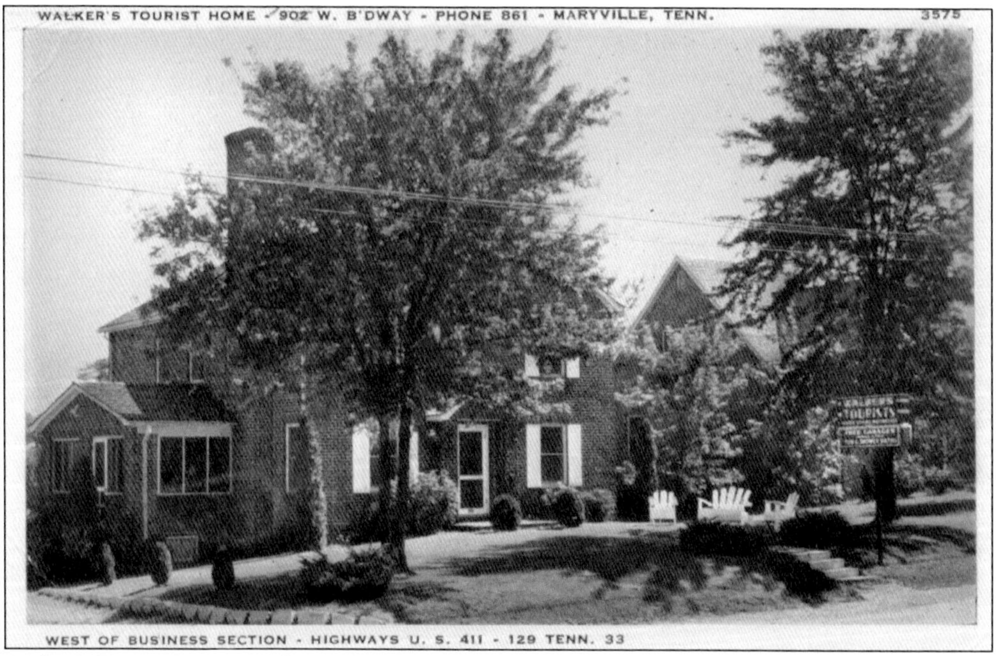

Walker's Tourist Home was located on West Broadway Avenue in Maryville near Kay's Ice Cream, which is now Sweet Celebrations. It was popular with parents coming to Maryville to visit their children who were attending Maryville College. (Courtesy of B. Kenneth Cornett.)

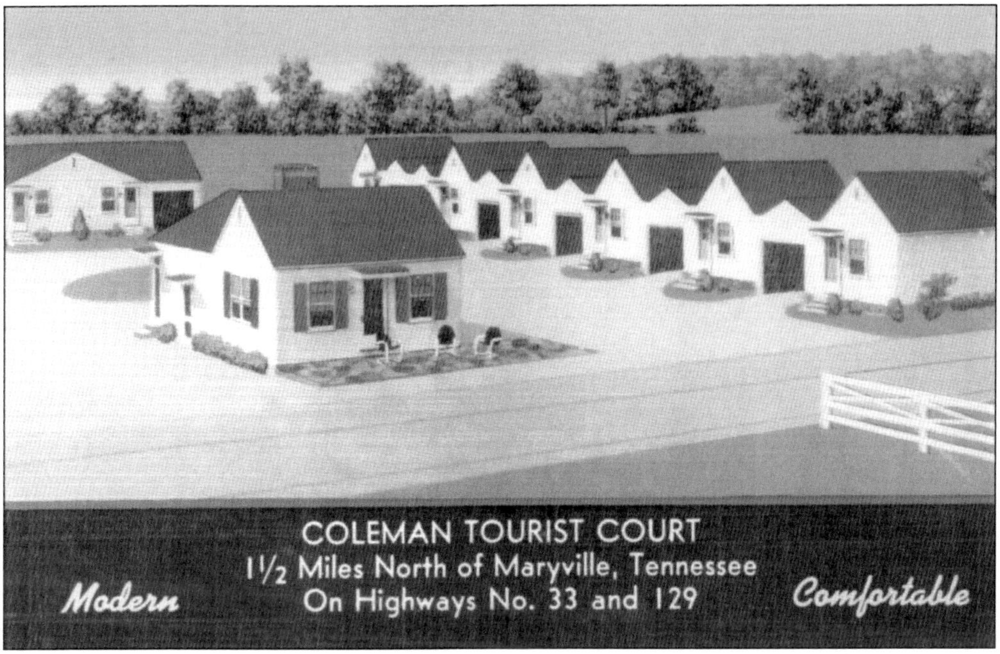

Coleman Tourist Court was another of the many small family-owned places of lodging for tourists in Blount County. It was located north of Maryville on Highways 33 and 129, now Old Knoxville Highway and Alcoa Highway. (Courtesy of B. Kenneth Cornett.)

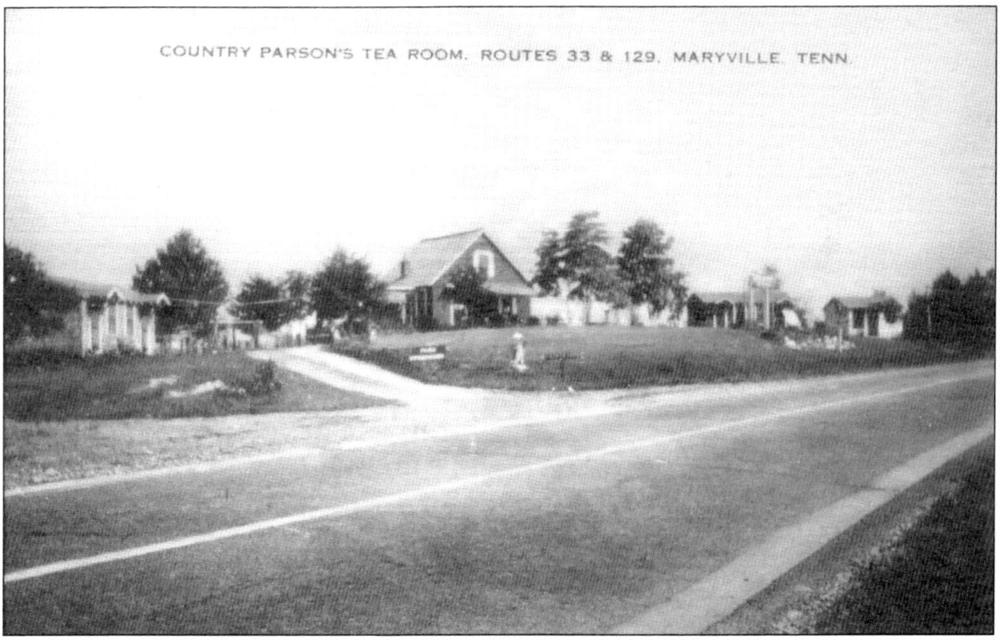

Country Parsons Tea Room and rental cabins were operated by "Pop" Goodman on Old Knoxville Highway near Rockford. It was often referred to as "the Lighthouse" because of Reverend Goodman's religious activities. He often handed out religious tracts and held meetings/services at the facility. (Courtesy of B. Kenneth Cornett.)

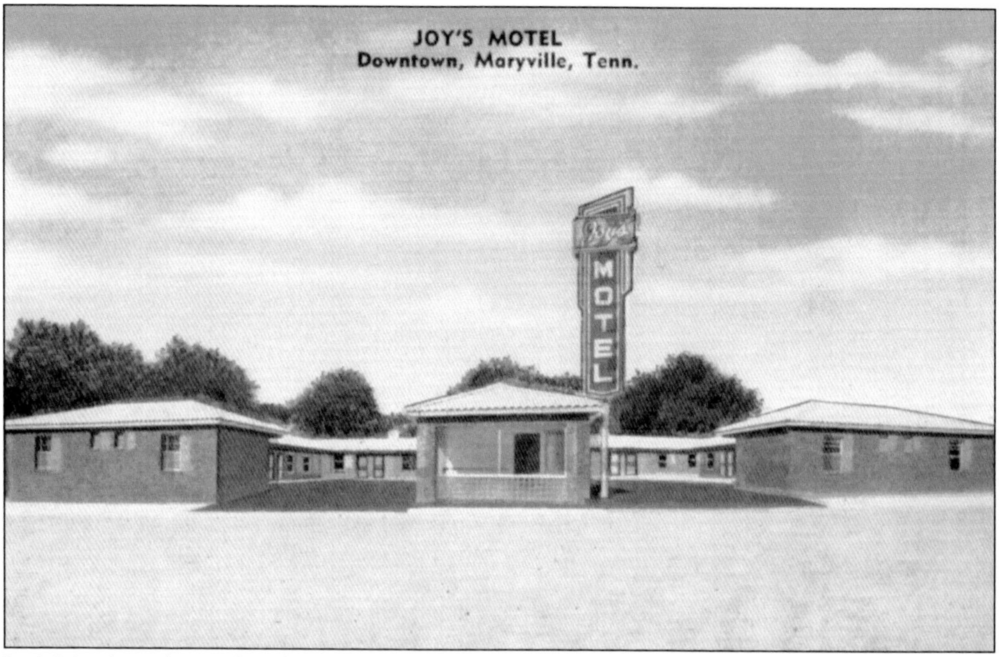

Joy's Motel was located at the corner of Main (Broadway) and Washington Streets in Maryville. Completed in the summer of 1953, the motel—which was in walking distance to the business district, restaurants, and theaters—had 25 units with features including air-conditioning, radiant heat, fireproofing, wall-to-wall carpeting, and tiled baths. The telephone number was 5180. Joy's Motel was named for owner Buzz Vineyard's daughter, Joy. (Courtesy of B. Kenneth Cornett.)

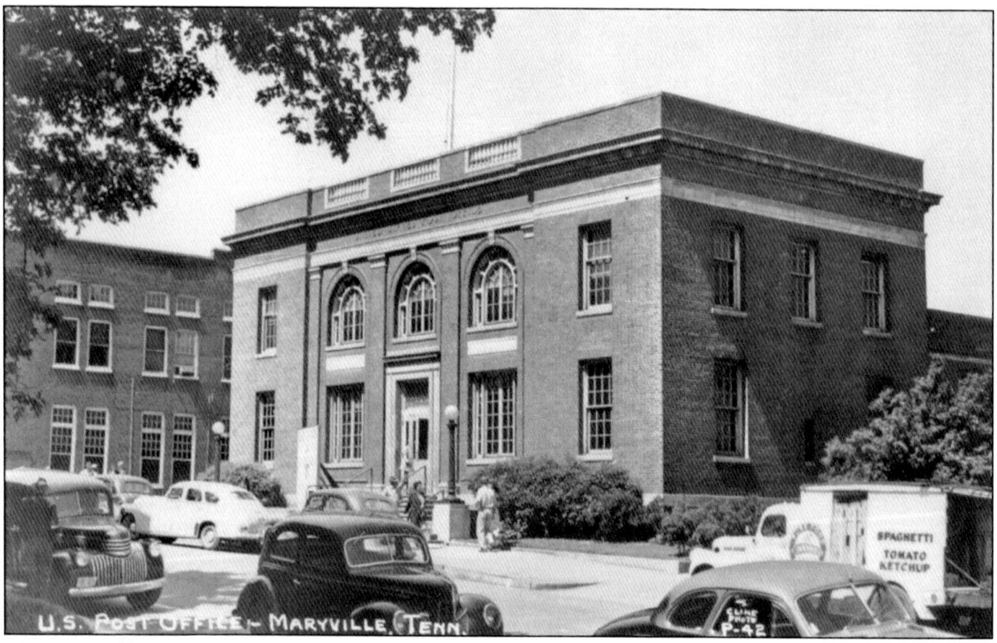

The post office in Maryville was established on October 6, 1800. The facility shown here in the 1940s is located on Broadway Avenue in downtown Maryville. It operated until the 1980s and now houses several offices. (Courtesy of B. Kenneth Cornett.)

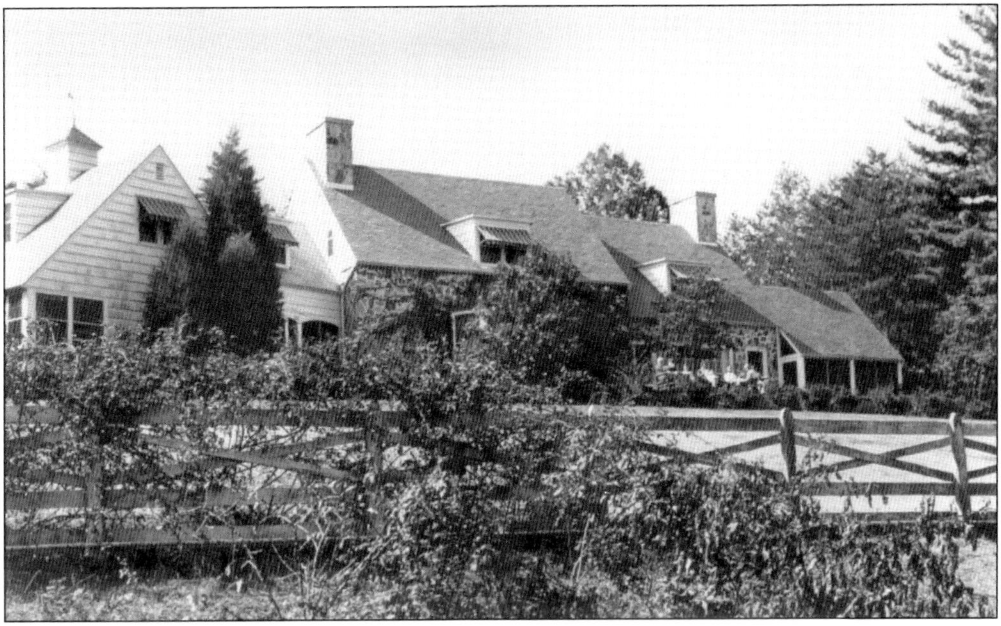

Blackberry Farm Inn, located in the southeastern portion of Blount County, is surrounded by the Chilhowee Mountains. David and Florida Lasier vacationed in the Smokies and decided to purchase 300 acres of land in West Miller's Cove. They originally planned to build a retirement and summer home. Instead, the plans changed, and they opened an inn in 1939. Blackberry Farm is owned today by the Beall family and has been recognized by publications such as *Southern Living* for its gracious accommodations. (Both, courtesy of B. Kenneth Cornett.)

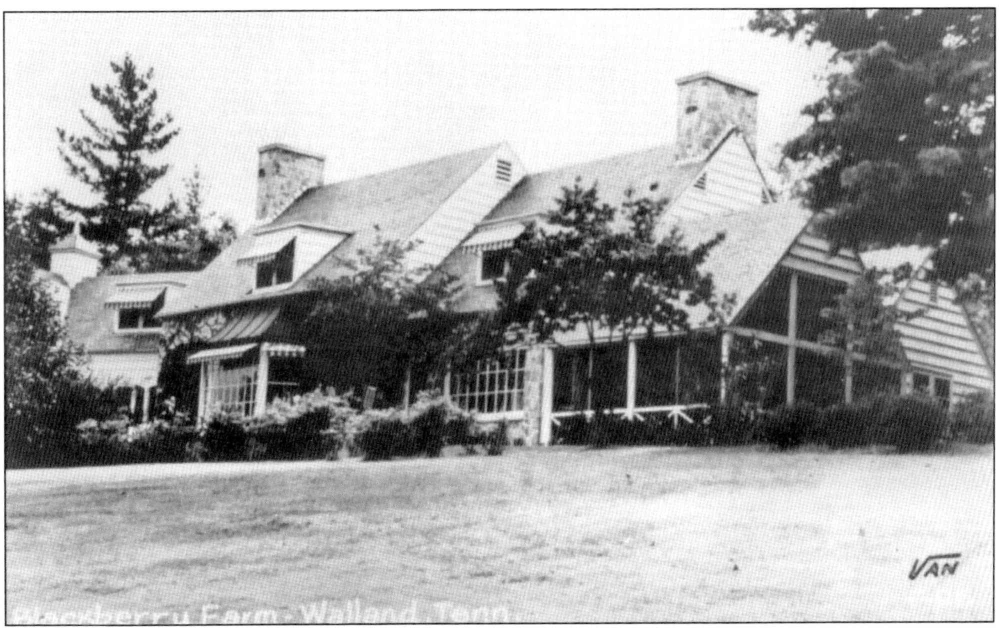

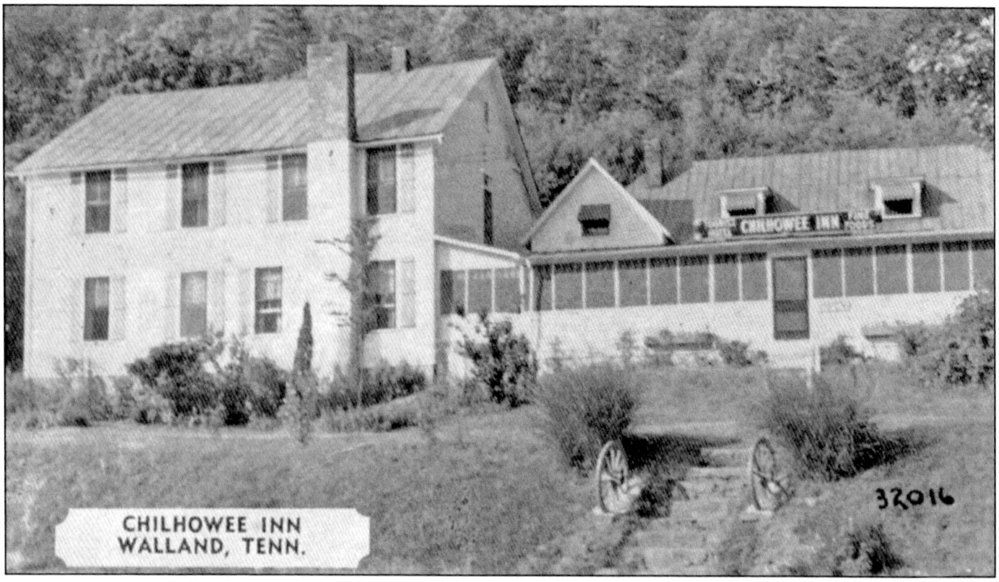

In 1903, a five-room cottage was built on Little River in Walland to accommodate out-of-town officials of the Schlosser Leather Company. The following year, a 10-room inn, Chilhowee Inn, was built, incorporating the house to accommodate guests and provide lodging for teachers. The inn became famous for its fine food and was a popular weekend resort. It is now under private ownership, again offering hospitality to guests. (Courtesy of B. Kenneth Cornett.)

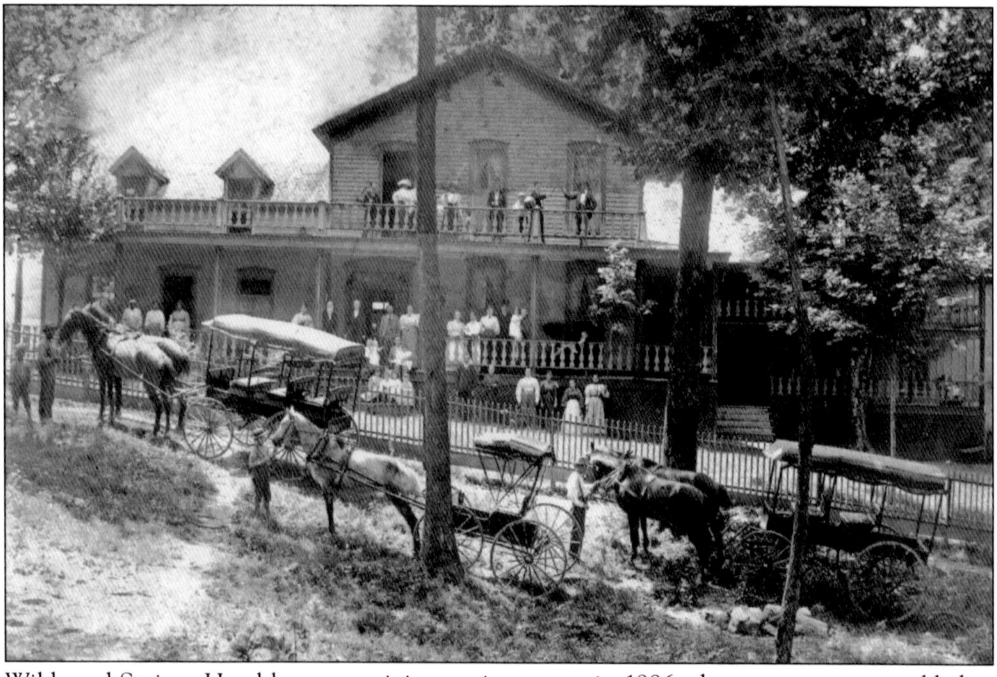

Wildwood Springs Hotel began receiving paying guests in 1886 when an annex was added to the original log and frame home of Rev. Claudius B. Lord and family. In 1902, sixty guests were recorded. The last season Wildwood Springs was open as a resort was 1925. Holding the horses for the surreys are (left) Marion Frazier and Ben Carter, (center) Ed Bond, and (right) John Bond. (Courtesy of Bob DeLozier.)

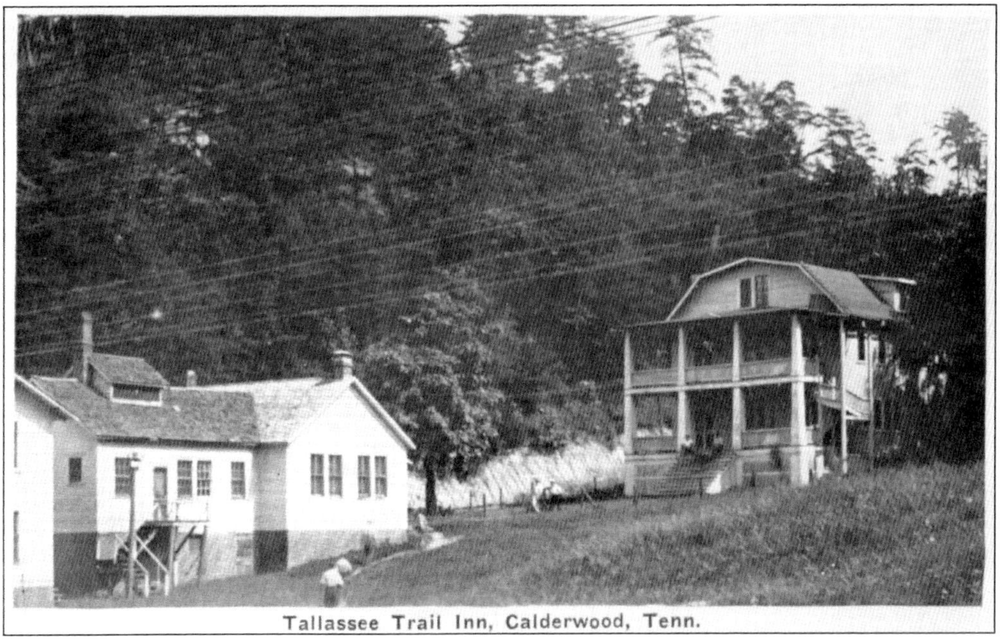

Tallassee Trail Inn was located at the town of Calderwood. Many workers of the Aluminum Company of America's dam projects either stayed in the hotel and/or brought their families to stay there. (Courtesy of B. Kenneth Cornett.)

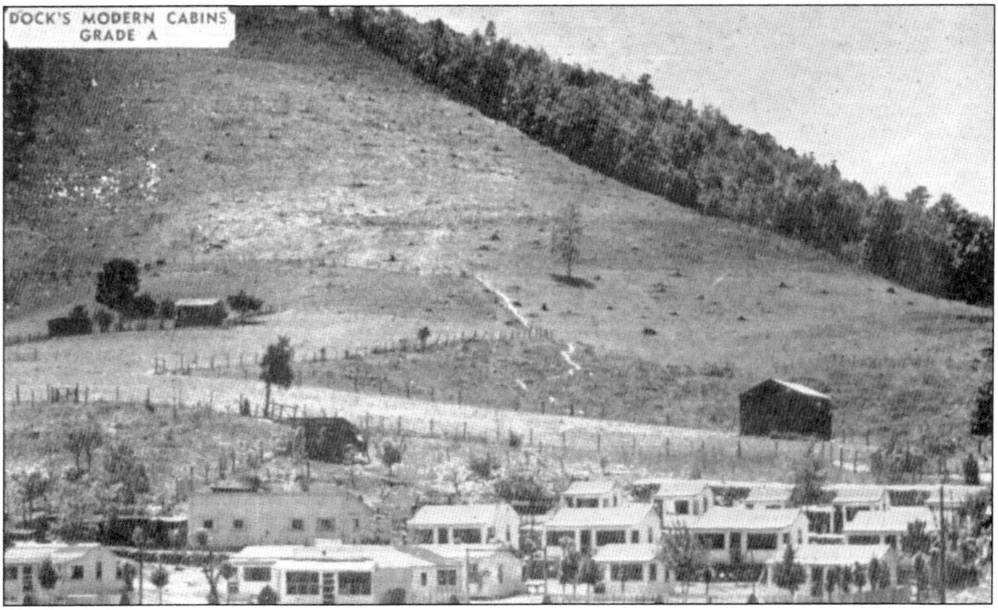

Dock's Modern Cabins welcomed tourists to the Great Smoky Mountains National Park during the Great Depression years in the 1930s. This popular Townsend facility, with its original sign, continues to provide lodging for today's tourists. (Courtesy of B. Kenneth Cornett.)

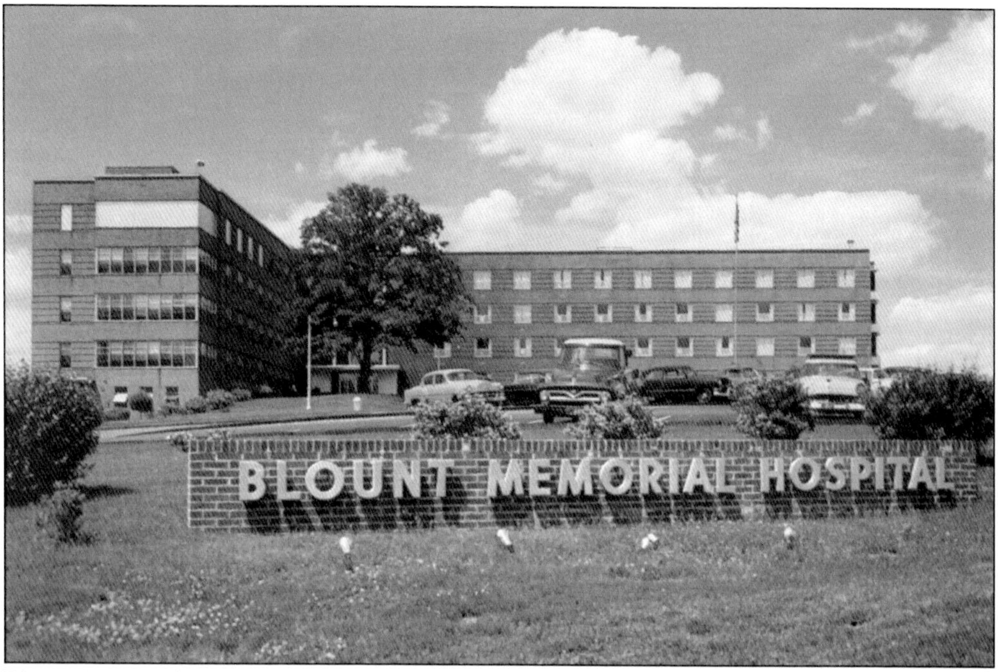

Blount Memorial Hospital is shown here in the 1950s. The hospital, which opened in 1947, has grown substantially since its early days and is now one of Blount County's largest employers. (Courtesy of B. Kenneth Cornett.)

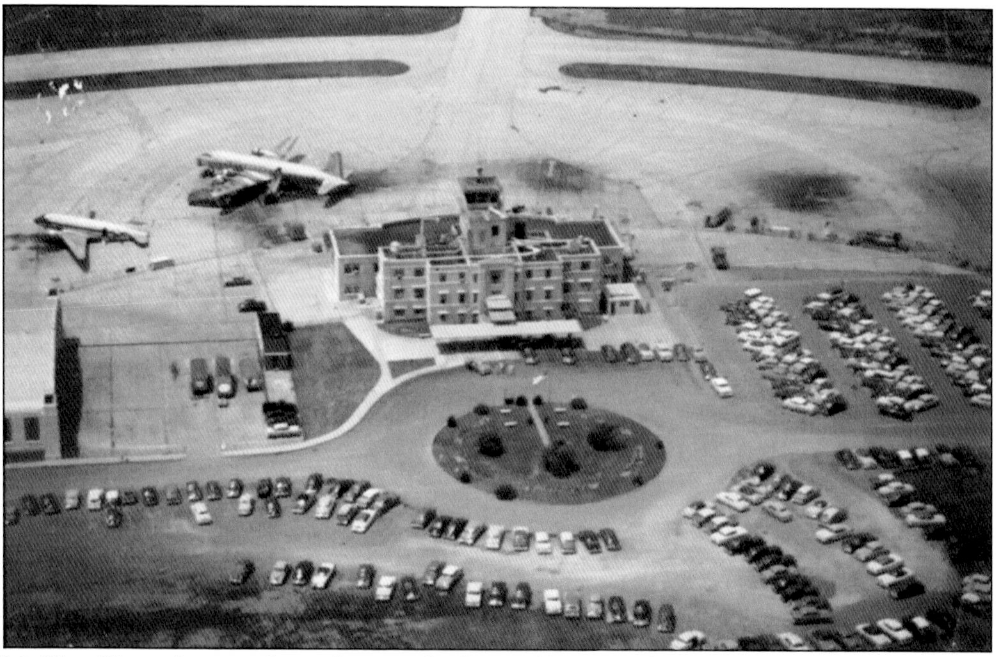

McGhee Tyson Airport, shown here in the late 1950s, opened in 1934. At first, there were no buildings, but in 1936, work on the passenger terminal began. It was named for Charles McGhee Tyson, a Knox County pilot killed over the North Sea in 1918. Although located in Blount County, the airport serves Metropolitan Knoxville. (Courtesy of B. Kenneth Cornett.)

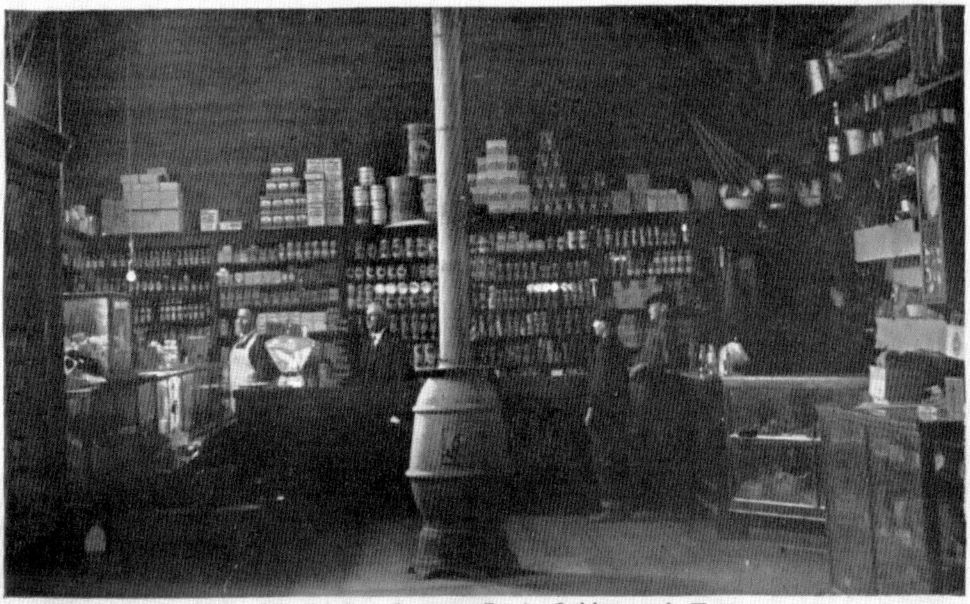

Alcoa Supply Co., Grocery Dept., Calderwood, Tenn.

The Alcoa Supply Company was located in the Calderwood community, originally known as Alcoa. It supplied provisions for the men who were constructing dams to provide hydroelectric power for the Aluminum Company plants and for the men's families. All staple items necessary for a family were available at this store. (Courtesy of B. Kenneth Cornett.)

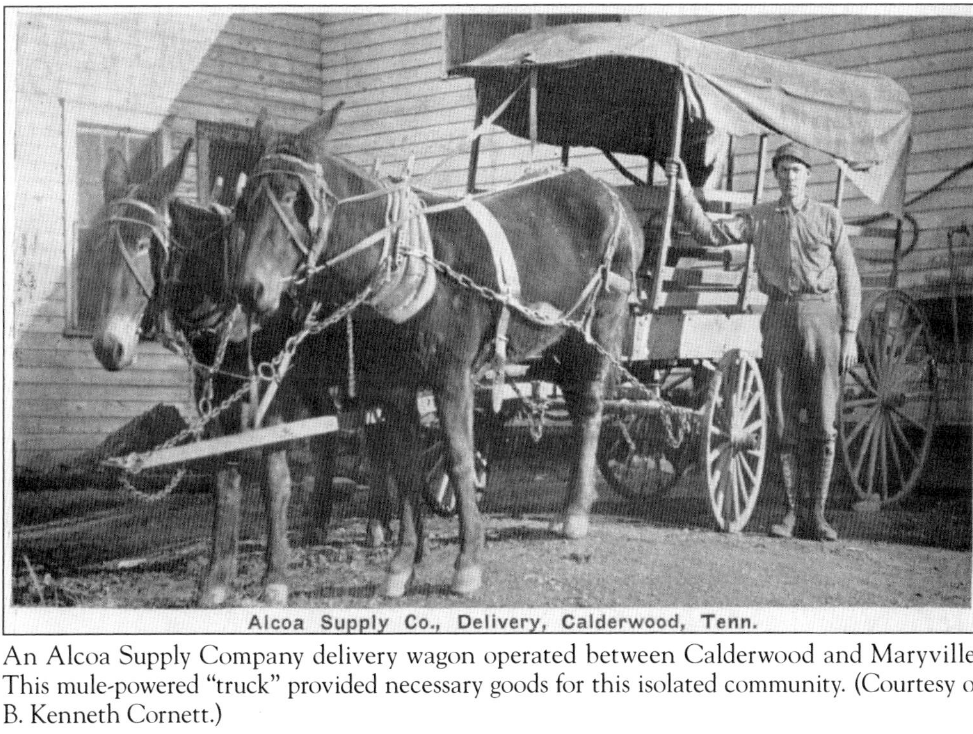

Alcoa Supply Co., Delivery, Calderwood, Tenn.

An Alcoa Supply Company delivery wagon operated between Calderwood and Maryville. This mule-powered "truck" provided necessary goods for this isolated community. (Courtesy of B. Kenneth Cornett.)

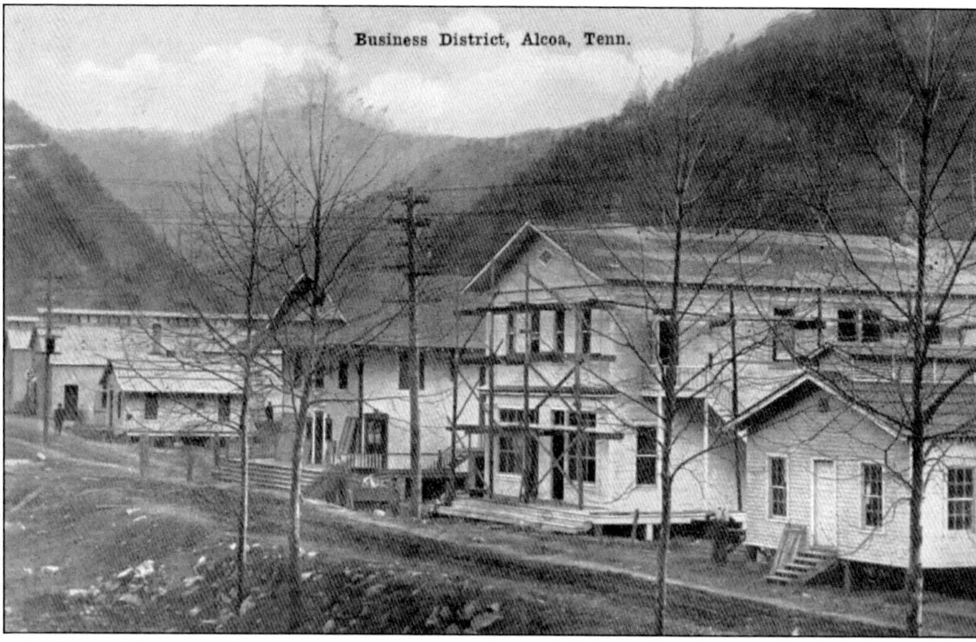

The "Alcoa" business district shows the town of Calderwood, which was originally called Alcoa when the Aluminum Company of America (Alcoa, Inc.) built Calderwood Dam on the Little Tennessee River. The name was changed to Calderwood in honor of one of Alcoa, Inc.'s officials, and the town of Alcoa was chartered in 1919 at what had been called North Maryville. (Courtesy of B. Kenneth Cornett.)

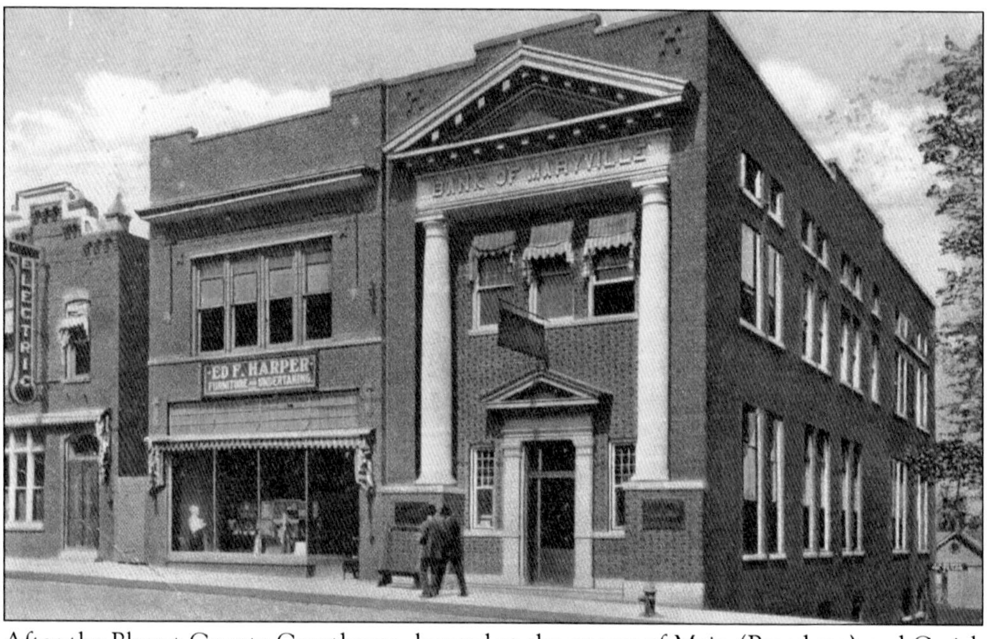

After the Blount County Courthouse, located at the corner of Main (Broadway) and Cusick Streets, burned in the early 1900s, it was relocated to Court Street, where it still stands. The Bank of Maryville, chartered in 1885, was built at the old courthouse site. It still continues its operation in Maryville. (Courtesy of B. Kenneth Cornett.)

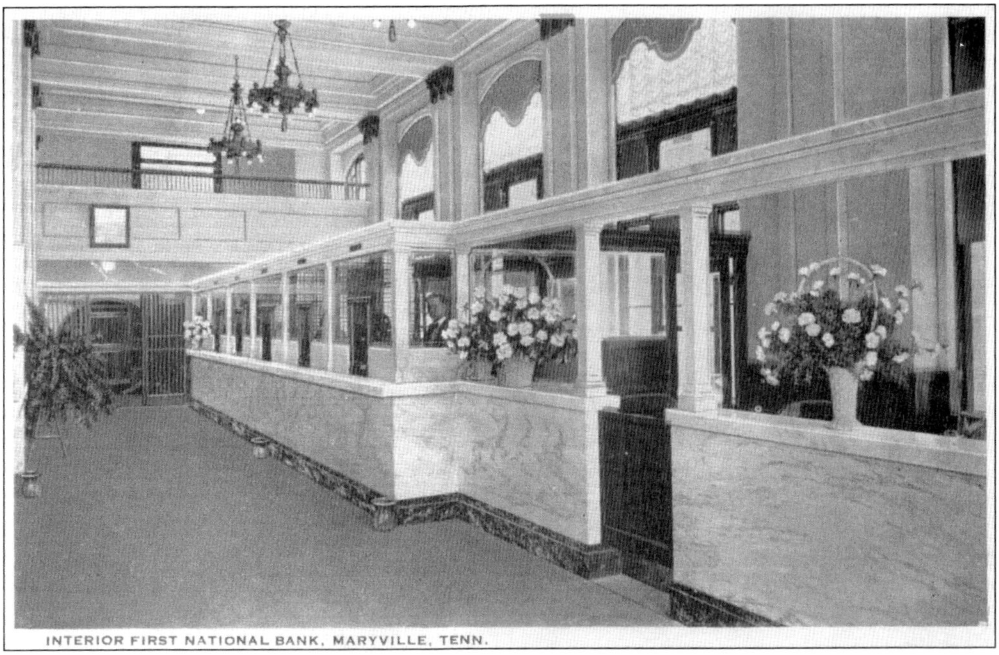

The teller cages at Blount National Bank are shown here about 1940. The bank was located in a five-story brick building in downtown Maryville. (Courtesy of B. Kenneth Cornett.)

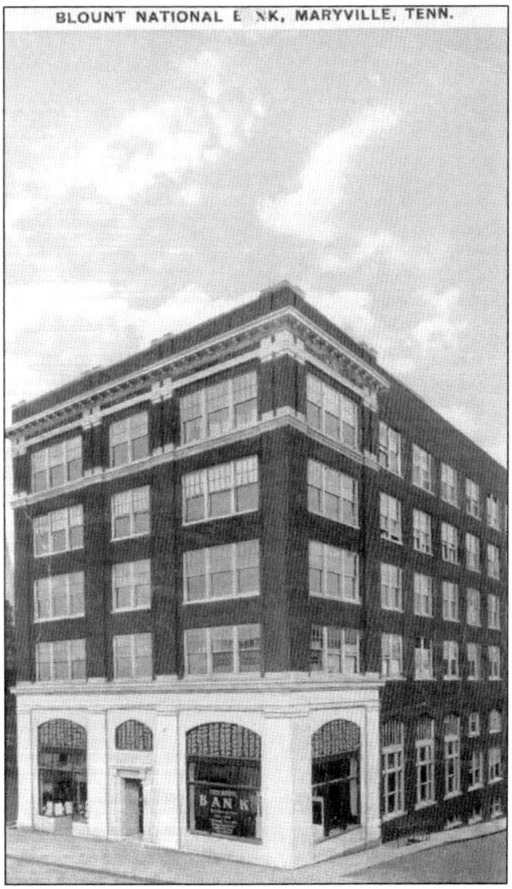

This building, shown here about 1940 on Main Street (Broadway) in Maryville, was built in 1921 as the First National Bank. First National closed in 1932, and then Blount National Bank was organized at the same location in 1934. The building is now known as Preservation Plaza. (Courtesy of B. Kenneth Cornett.)

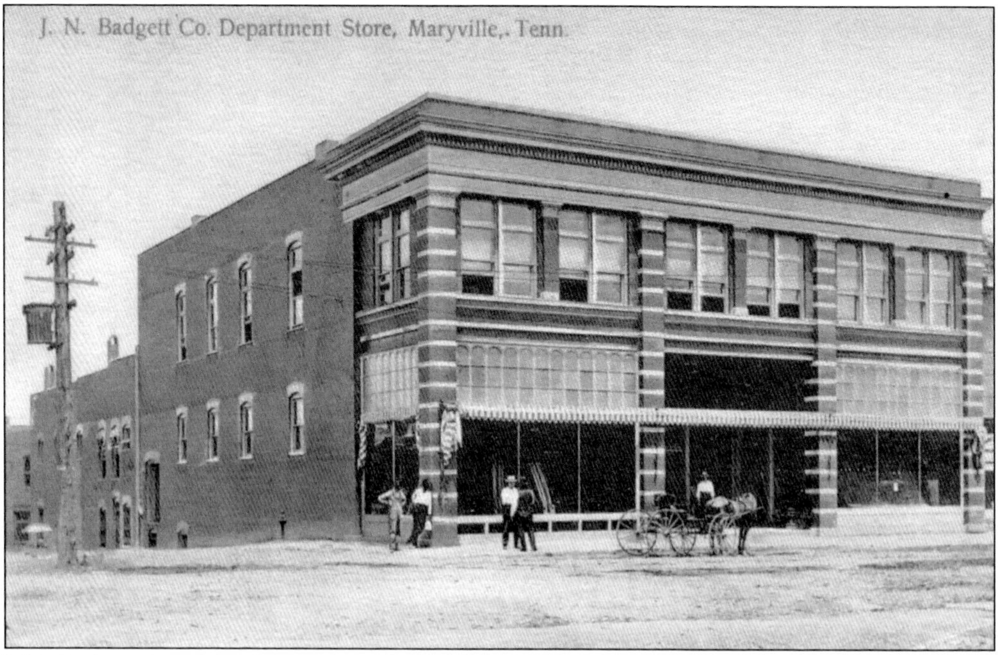

J. N. Badgett Company Department Store, shown here around 1910, operated on the corner of Main (Broadway) and Cusick Streets. This was later the location of Proffitt's Department Store. National School Supply now occupies the building. (Courtesy of B. Kenneth Cornett.)

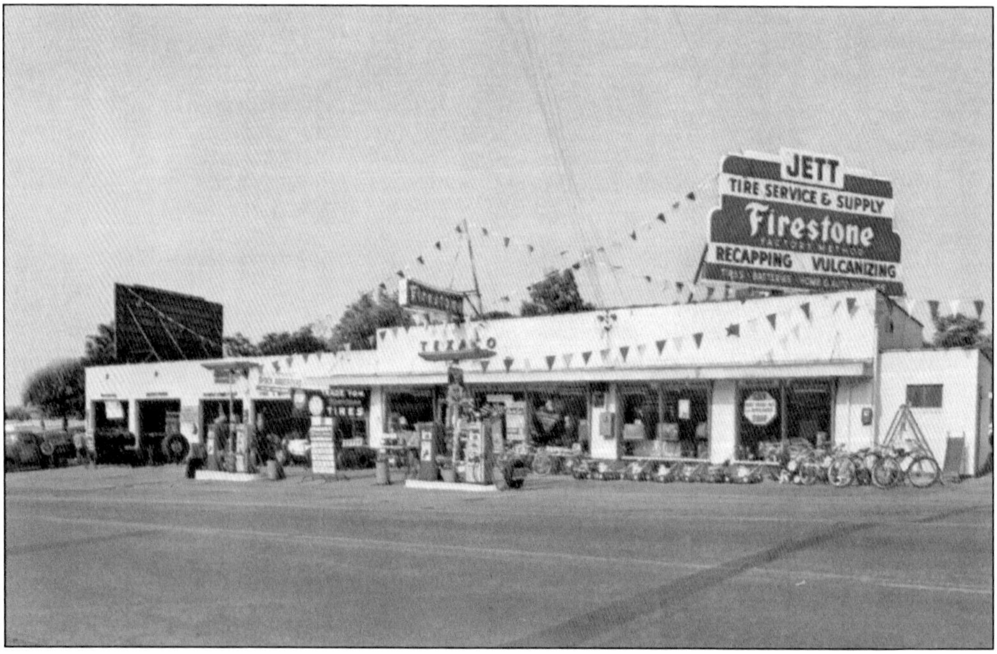

Jett Service and Supply, located at Five Point in Maryville, has offered car care to Blount County residents for many years. Shown here around 1970, the business was a landmark at the east end of Maryville and, according to the postcard from which this image was taken, was "headquarters for quality merchandise for car, home, and farm." (Courtesy of B. Kenneth Cornett.)

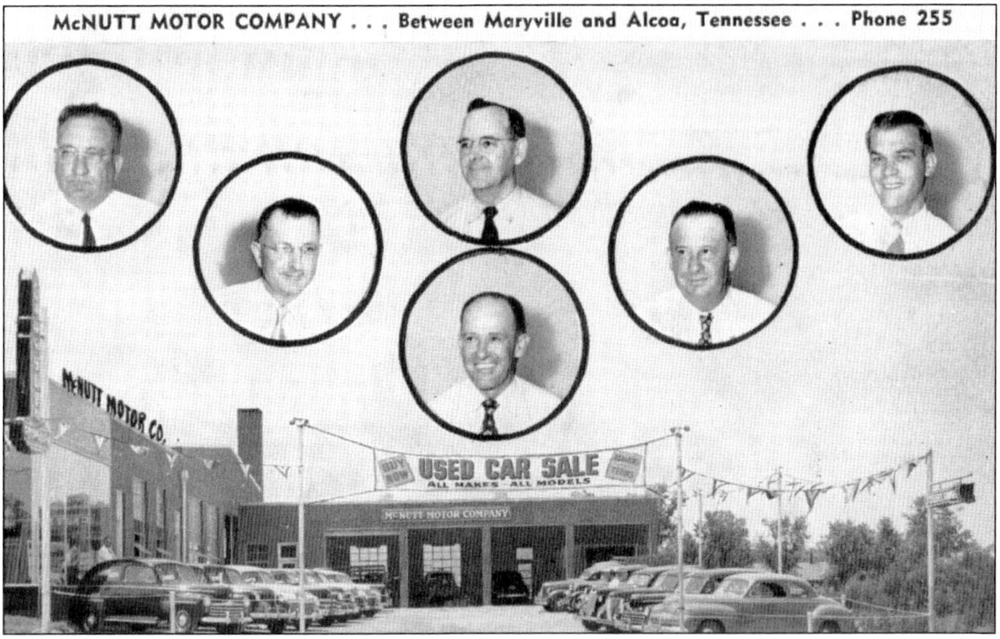

McNutt Motor Company, located on Church Avenue in Maryville in 1948, moved to West Hunt Road in Alcoa in 1951. McNutt Motor Company was the dealer for Chrysler, Plymouth, and Dodge cars and trucks. The owner, Hugh McNutt, is shown at bottom center, and employees, from left to right, are Pop Prather, Ott Jenkins, W. L. Goddard, Hubert Ford, and Jack Reynolds. (Courtesy of B. Kenneth Cornett.)

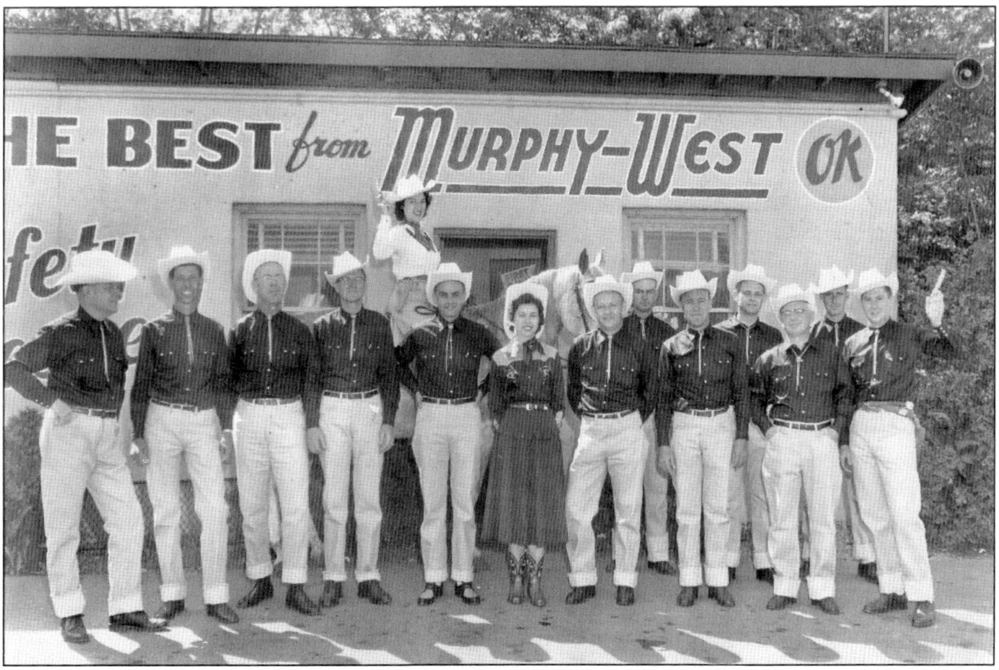

Employees at Murphy-West Motors, including Milburn Waters (far right), who later served as Blount County clerk, pose for this advertisement. (Courtesy of Ron and Debbie Teffeteller, Martha Birchfield collection.)

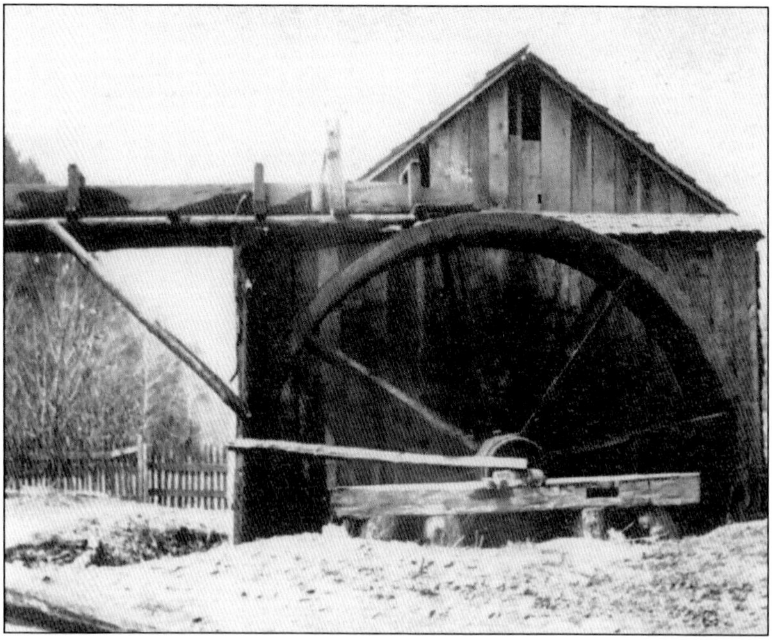

This is the only known photograph of the mill built by Warner Martin on Nails Creek in 1788–1789. Records show that Martin's Mill was one of this area's earliest public mills for grinding grain into fine flour. Martin and his son, John, owned all of Tarklin Valley, more the 1,400 acres. (Courtesy of Bob DeLozier.)

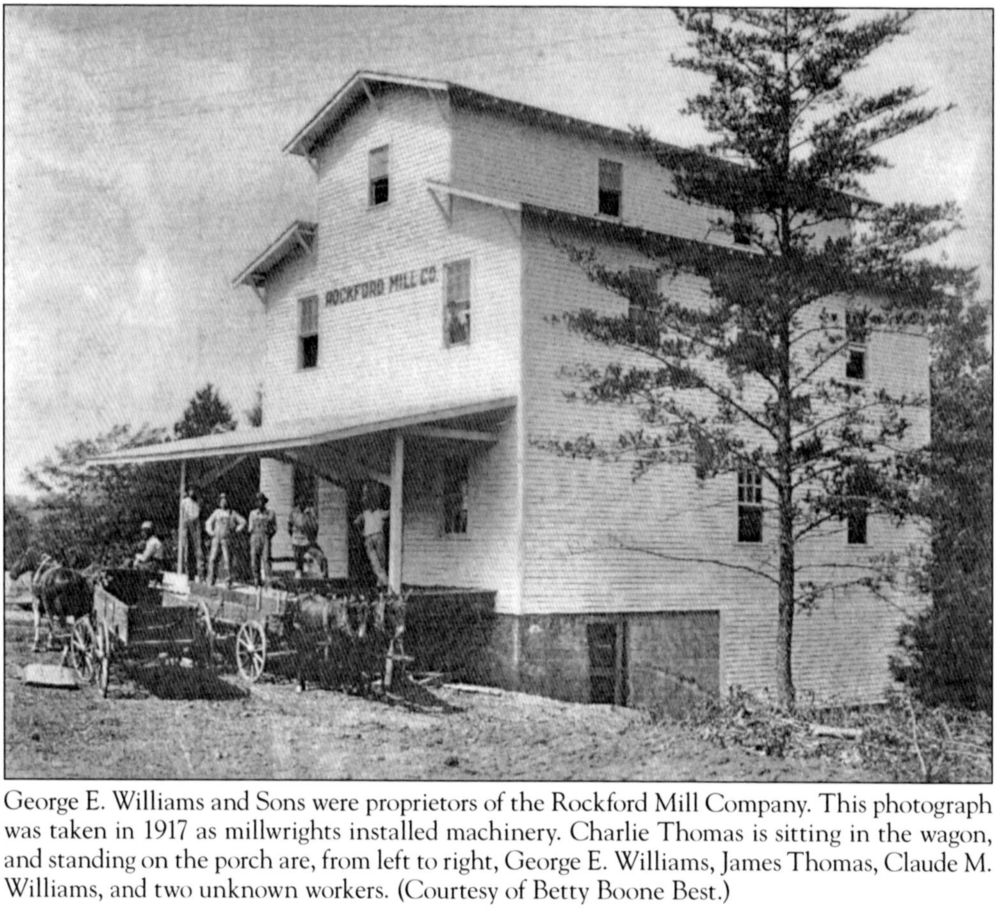

George E. Williams and Sons were proprietors of the Rockford Mill Company. This photograph was taken in 1917 as millwrights installed machinery. Charlie Thomas is sitting in the wagon, and standing on the porch are, from left to right, George E. Williams, James Thomas, Claude M. Williams, and two unknown workers. (Courtesy of Betty Boone Best.)

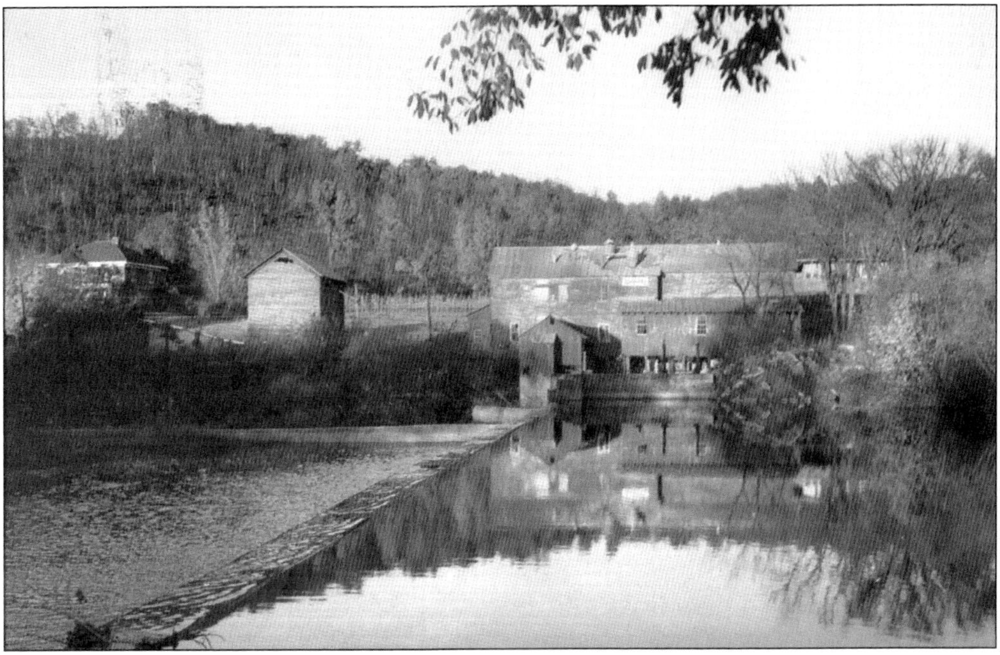

Located in the Little River Gorge, Peery's Mill used water power to grind corn into meal and wheat into flour. The original permit to build a mill at the site was obtained by Samuel Henry in 1842. The mill was destroyed by arson on August 30, 1986. (Courtesy of B. Kenneth Cornett; photograph by Dean Stone.)

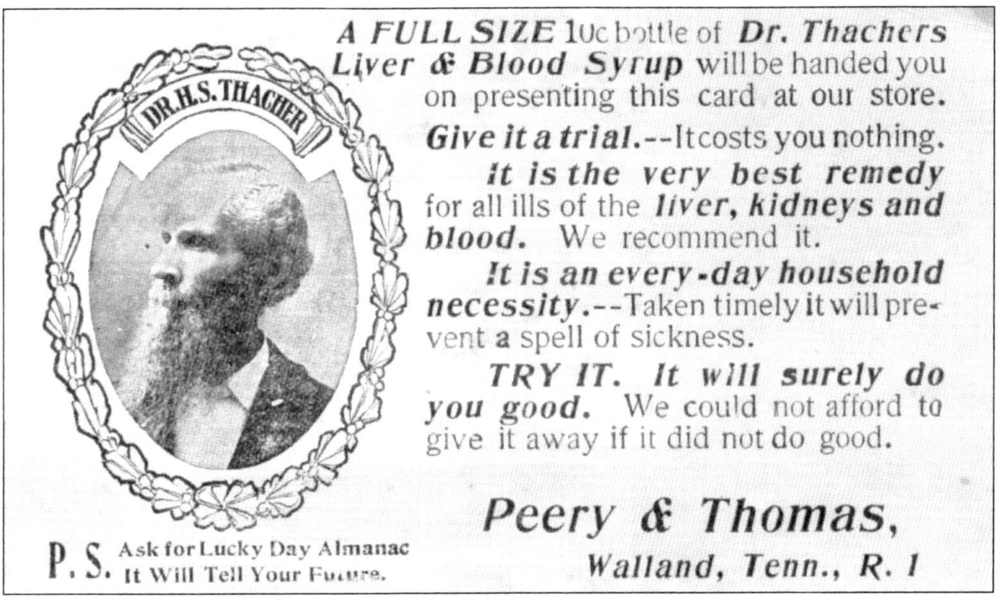

The Peery and Thomas Store was located near Peery's Mill in Walland and carried a variety of items, such as Dr. Thatcher's liver and blood syrup, which was supposed to "cure any ills of the liver, kidneys and blood." The postcard dates from about 1920. (Courtesy of B. Kenneth Cornett.)

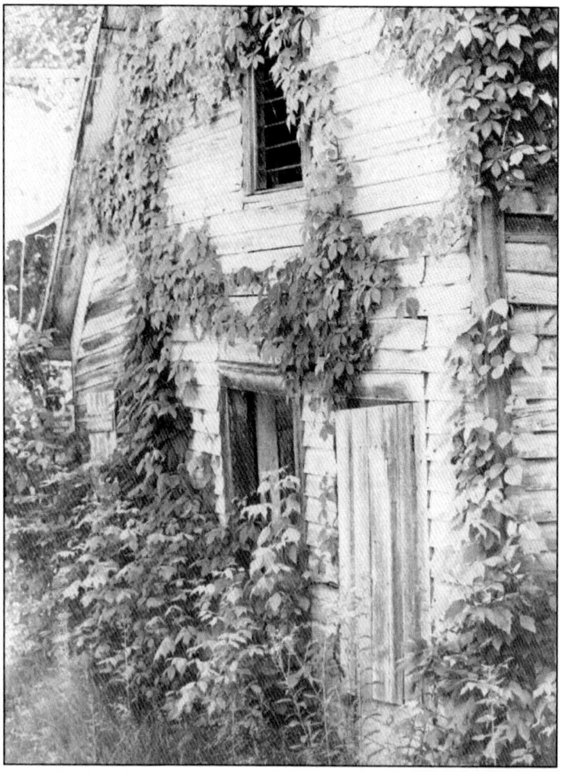

Ova Belt Lindsay was the well-known operator of the rural grocery store and post office in the Wellsville community. The post office, shown in the photograph at left and again below, right, behind the Esso sign, was destroyed by fire. The store, located near the intersection of Six Mile Road and Calderwood Highway (U.S. 129), offered everything needed by local farmers. The store was originally started by Lindsay's father. (Both, courtesy of the *Daily Times*.)

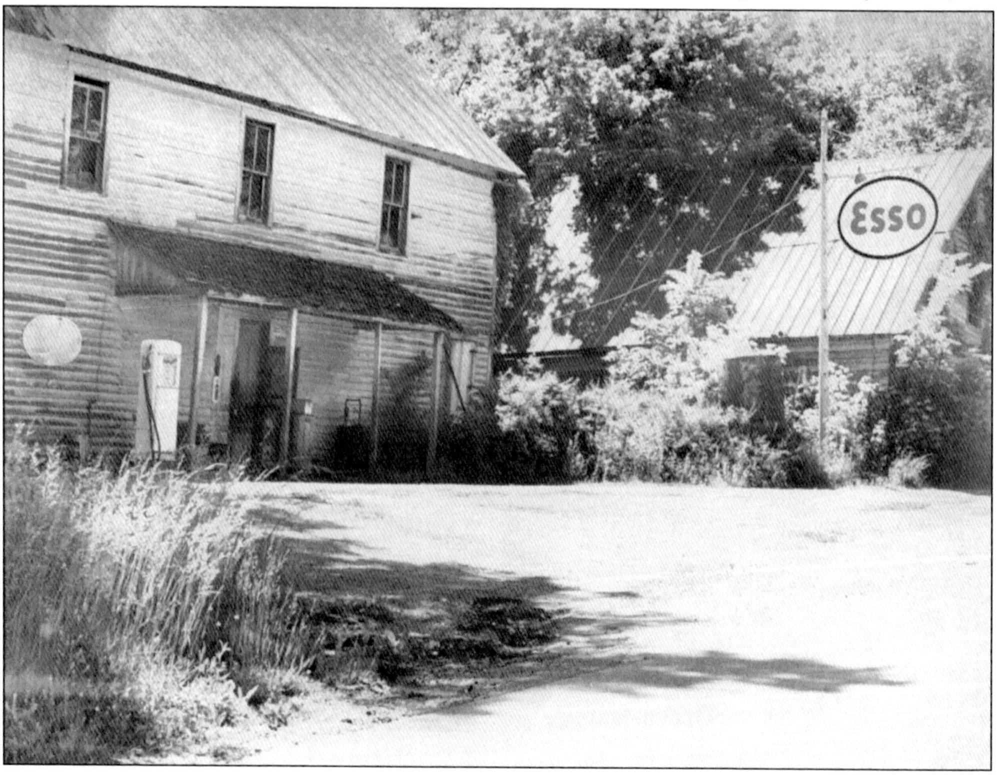

This 1962 photograph shows workmen at the Aluminum Company of America's Alcoa plant. Alcoa, Inc., is still one of Blount County's major employers. (Courtesy of the *Daily Times.*)

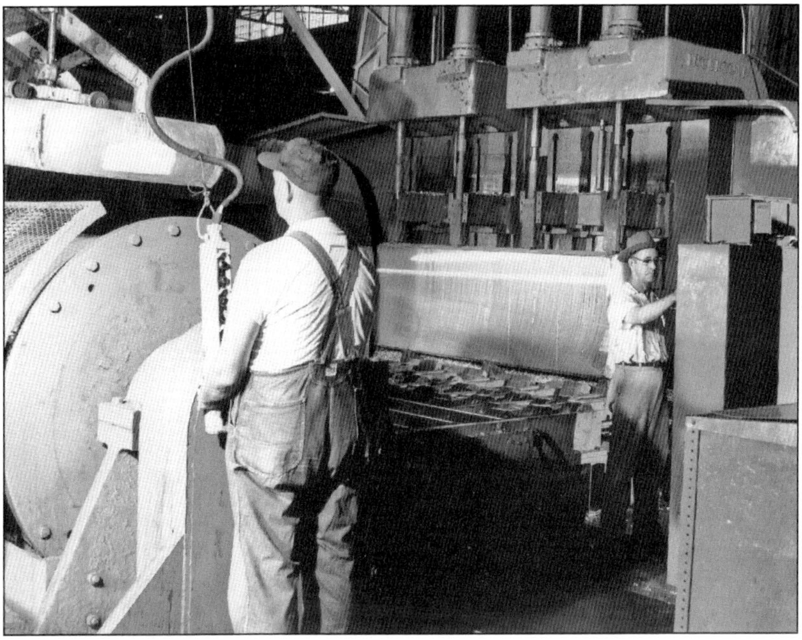

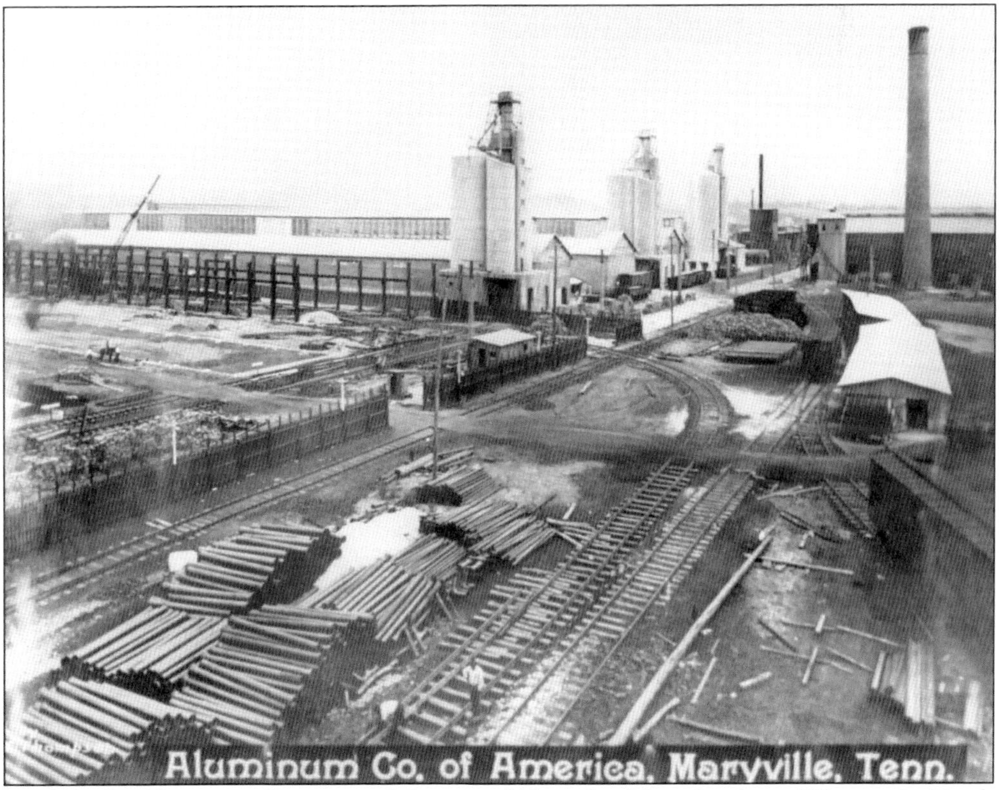

In 1913, the Aluminum Company of America (Alcoa, Inc.) bought about 700 acres in North Maryville and, the following year, began building the first of its plants in Blount County. The city of Alcoa grew up around the plants, and the city charter became effective on July 1, 1919. (Courtesy of the *Daily Times.*)

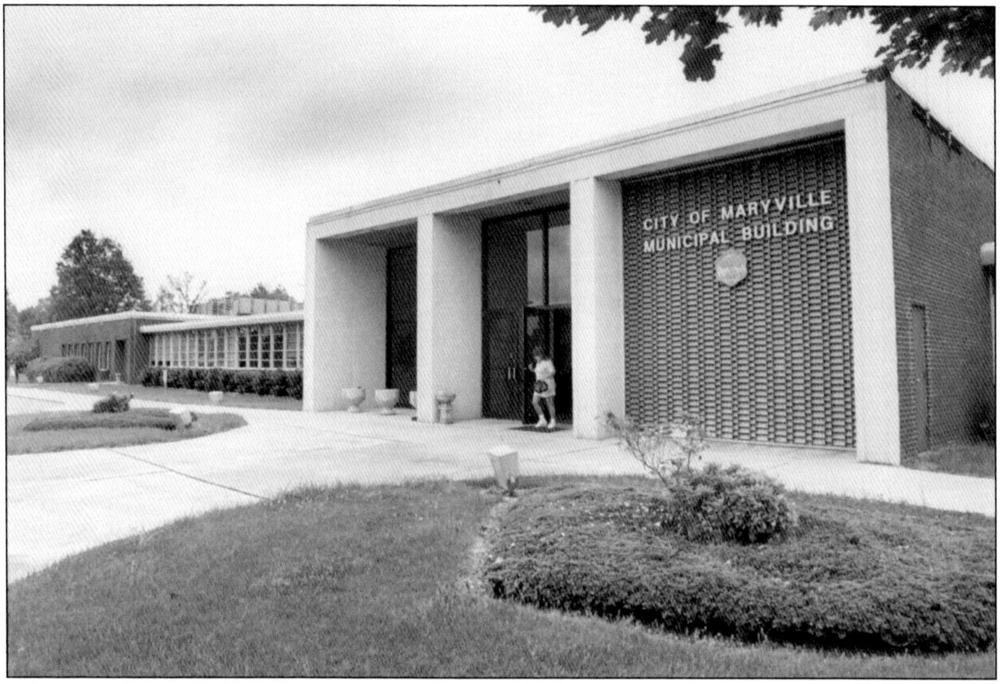

The Maryville Municipal Building, shown here in 1995, was constructed in 1956 and remained in use until it was razed to make way for the current facility, which was finished in 2005. (Courtesy of the *Daily Times.*)

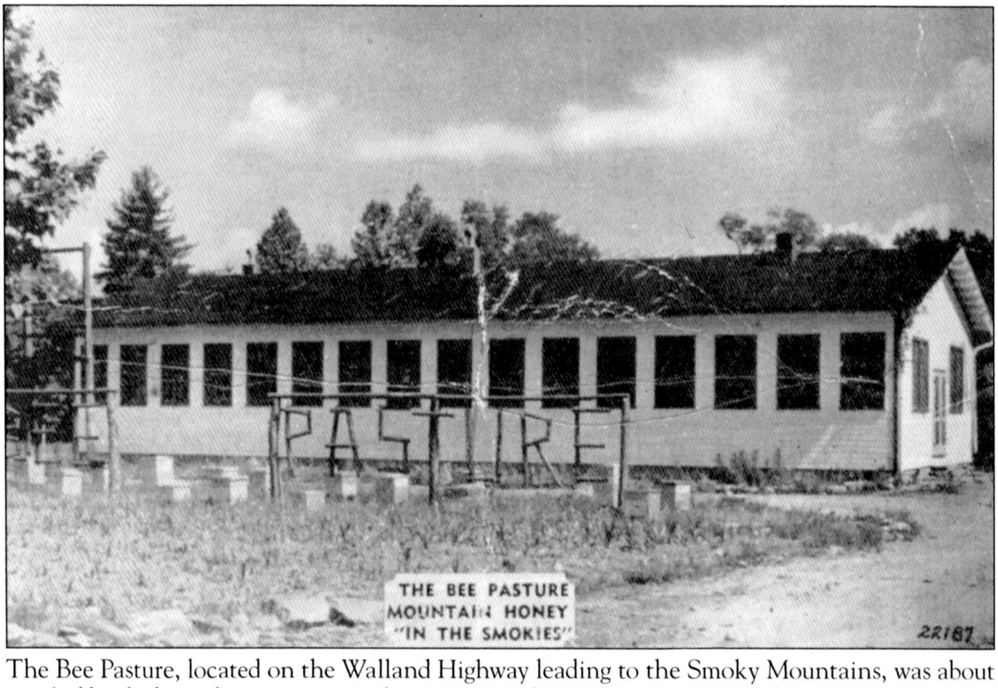

The Bee Pasture, located on the Walland Highway leading to the Smoky Mountains, was about one-half mile from the entrance to the Great Smoky Mountains National Park. The store sold mountain honey, waffles with honey, and country ham and chicken dinners to tourists on their way to the Smokies. This postcard is from around 1935. (Courtesy of B. Kenneth Cornett.)

Four

AGRICULTURE

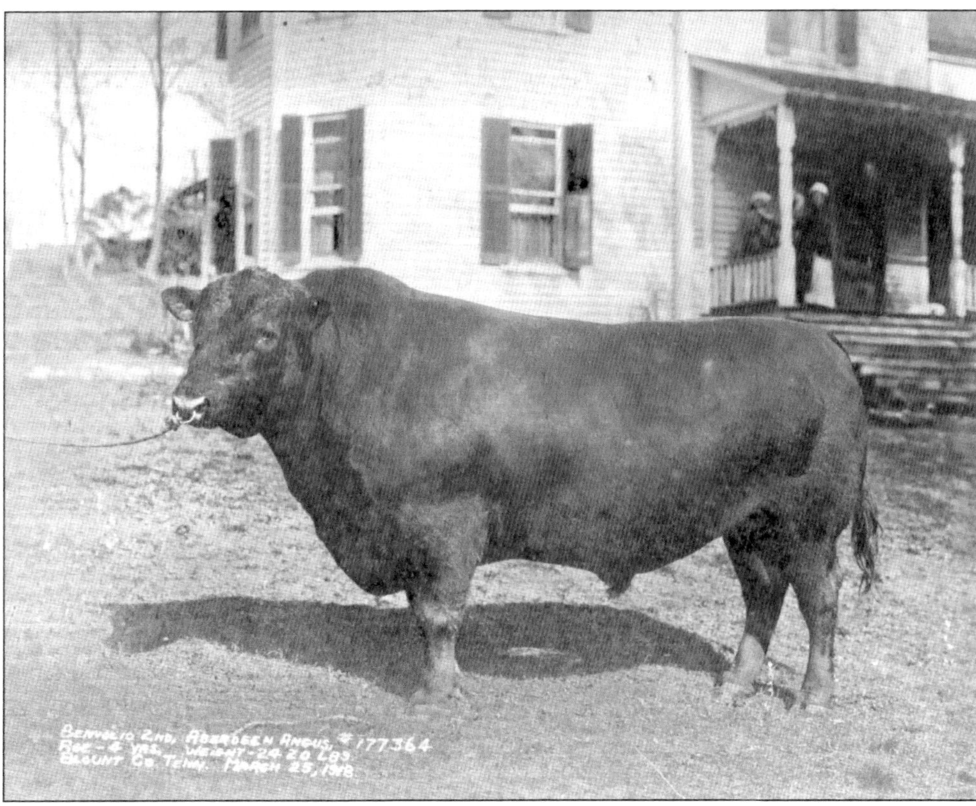

Brookwave Farm proudly displays Blount County's prize bull, weighing 2,420 pounds, in 1918. The farmhouse in the background was built by J. R. Harris in 1850. The farm was later operated as a dairy farm by Harris's daughter and son-in-law, Troy and McNutt Clark. (Courtesy of Gail Harris.)

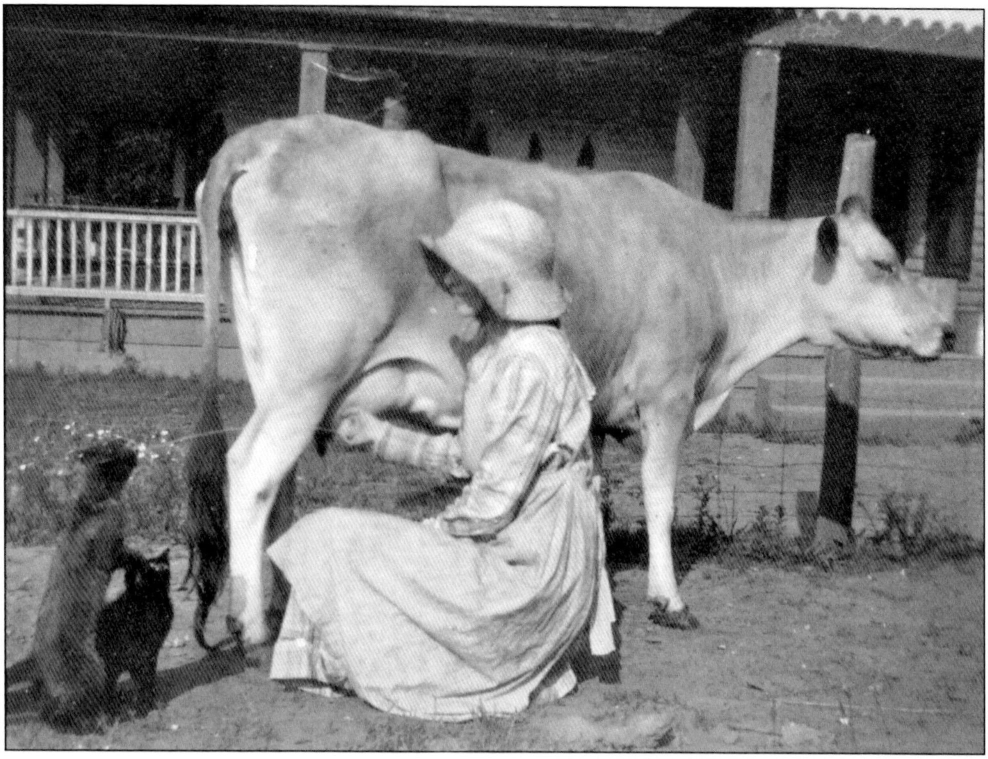

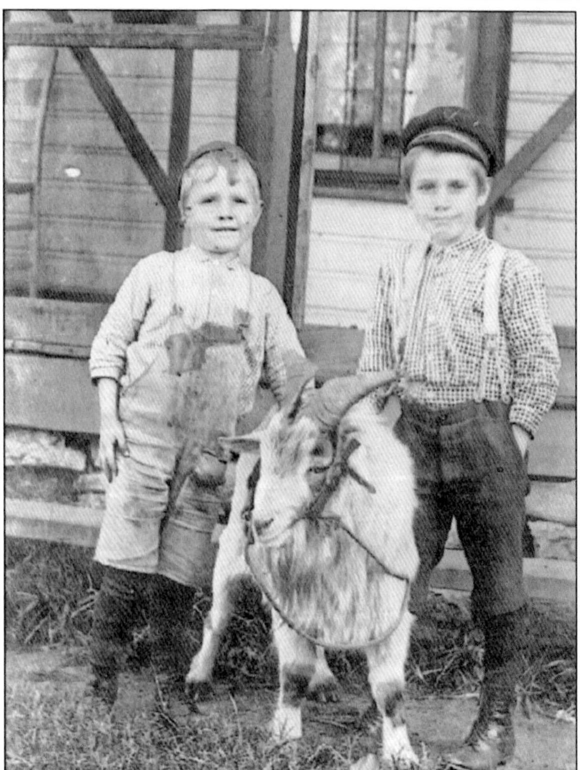

Milking the cow was a daily chore, and sometimes the cats received a treat while the milking was going on. Most rural families owned a Jersey cow, which provided milk for the family plus an opportunity to sell cream to Sugar Creek Creamery in Knoxville. Sugar Creek had a route and purchased cream throughout Blount County. (Courtesy of Kathleen McCammon.)

Joe and Laura Myers always kept a herd of goats on their farm at Townsend. Here brothers Leonard (left) and Lee Myers stand with one of their "pets." (Courtesy of Marilyn Myers Byrd.)

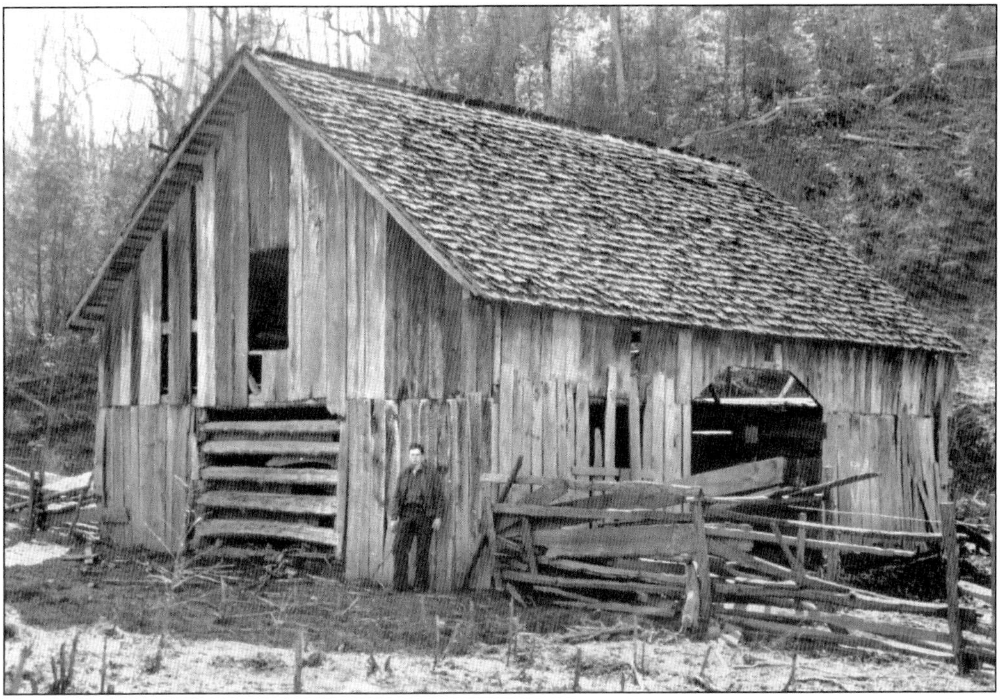

John McCaulley stands in front of the barn at his home on Chestnut Flats Road in Cades Cove in 1937. Tourists to the popular destination within the Great Smoky Mountains National Park often do not realize this was a community of people who lived, worked, raised families, and died right here in the shadow of the Smokies. (Courtesy of B. Kenneth Cornett.)

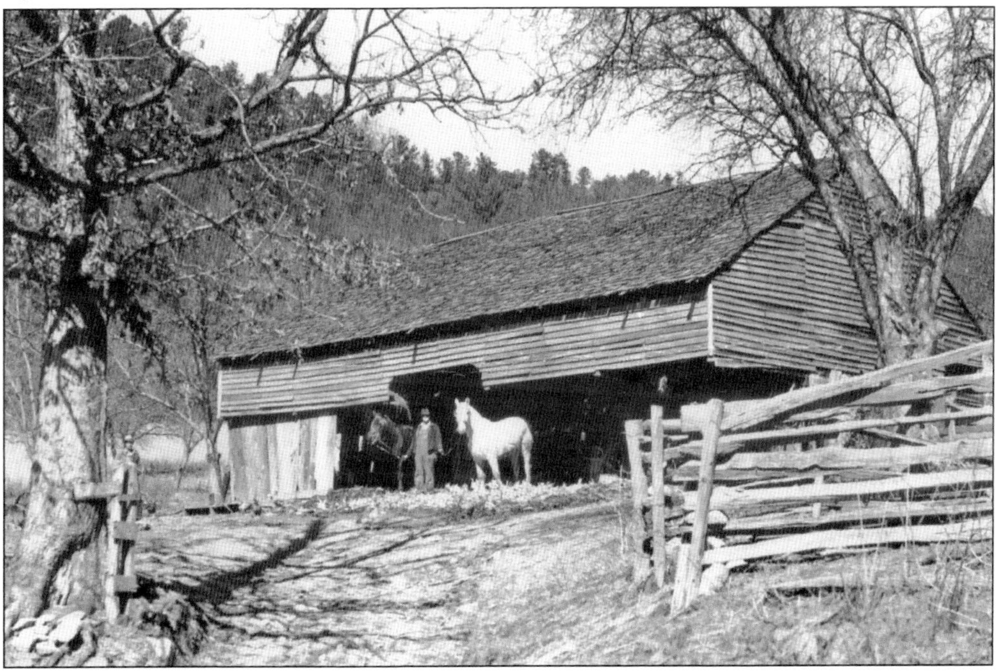

Sherman Myers, of Cades Cove, is captured in this 1937 photograph as he goes about his work at the barn. His home was on North Cove Road. (Courtesy of B. Kenneth Cornett.)

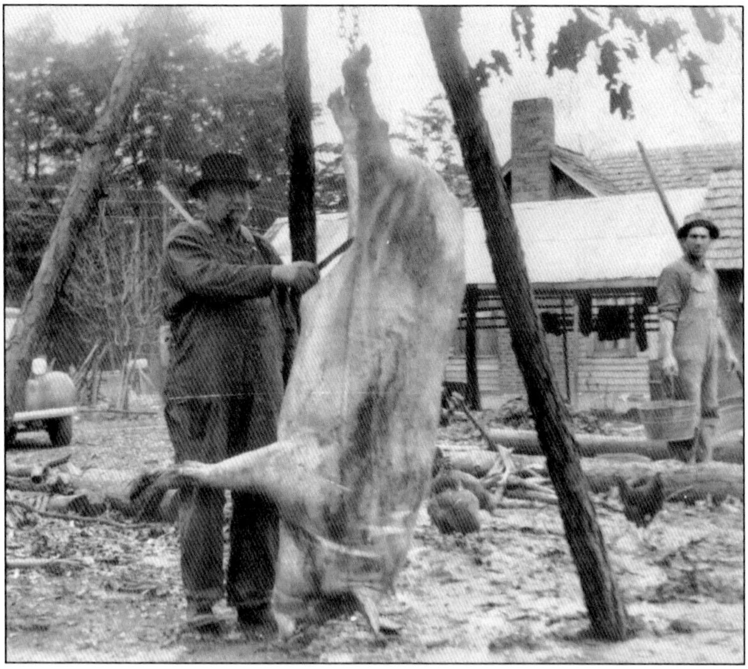

Hog-killing time on the farm took place as soon as the weather was cold enough. In this 1943 photograph, Will Huffstetler stands next to a huge hog, which would provide meat for the family for some time. At right is his brother, Fred Huffstetler. Carpenters Elementary and Middle Schools are located on the Huffstetler farm today. (Courtesy of Terry Huffstetler.)

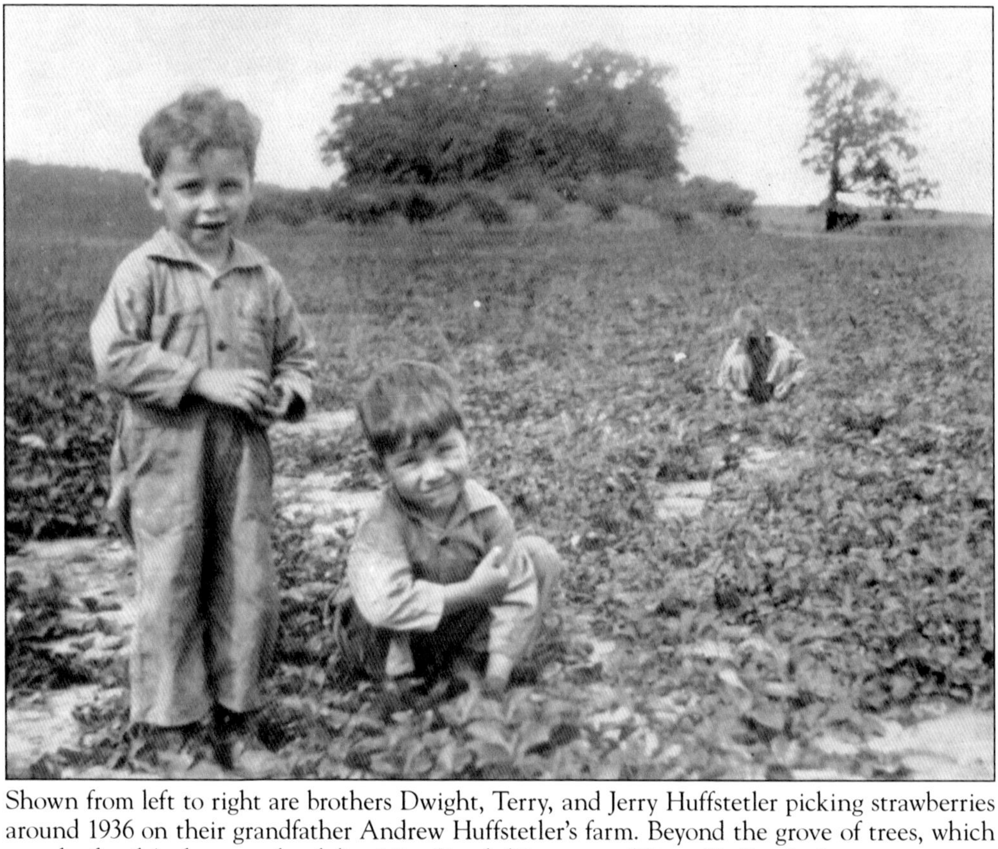

Shown from left to right are brothers Dwight, Terry, and Jerry Huffstetler picking strawberries around 1936 on their grandfather Andrew Huffstetler's farm. Beyond the grove of trees, which was the family's cherry orchard, lies Mint Road. (Courtesy of Terry Huffstetler.)

Plants were raised for their beauty as well as their function. Nancy Teffeteller shows off her prized elephant ears in this photograph. (Courtesy of Ron and Debbie Teffeteller, Martha Birchfield collection.)

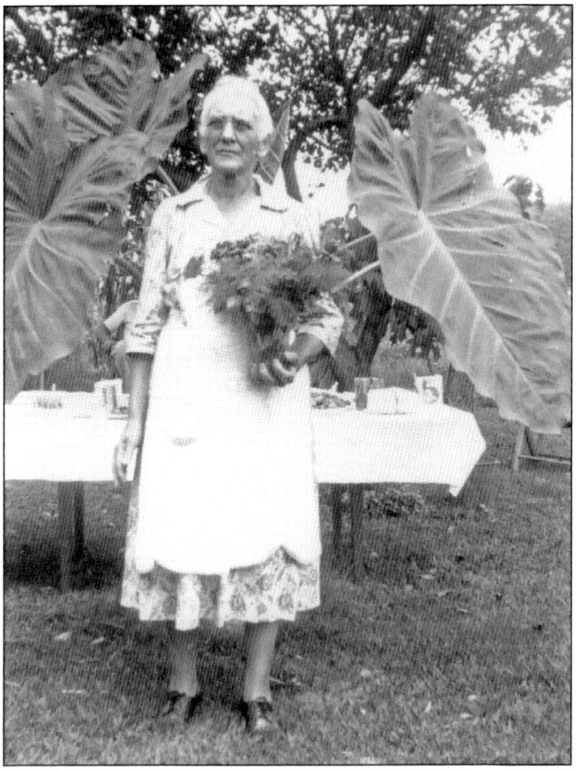

Pictured from left to right are Martin Simerly, Cora Lee Teffeteller Pollard, and John Pollard, posing for a photograph in 1948 as the chickens flock around them. Simerly is holding the container with chicken feed. (Courtesy of Ron and Debbie Teffeteller, Martha Birchfield collection.)

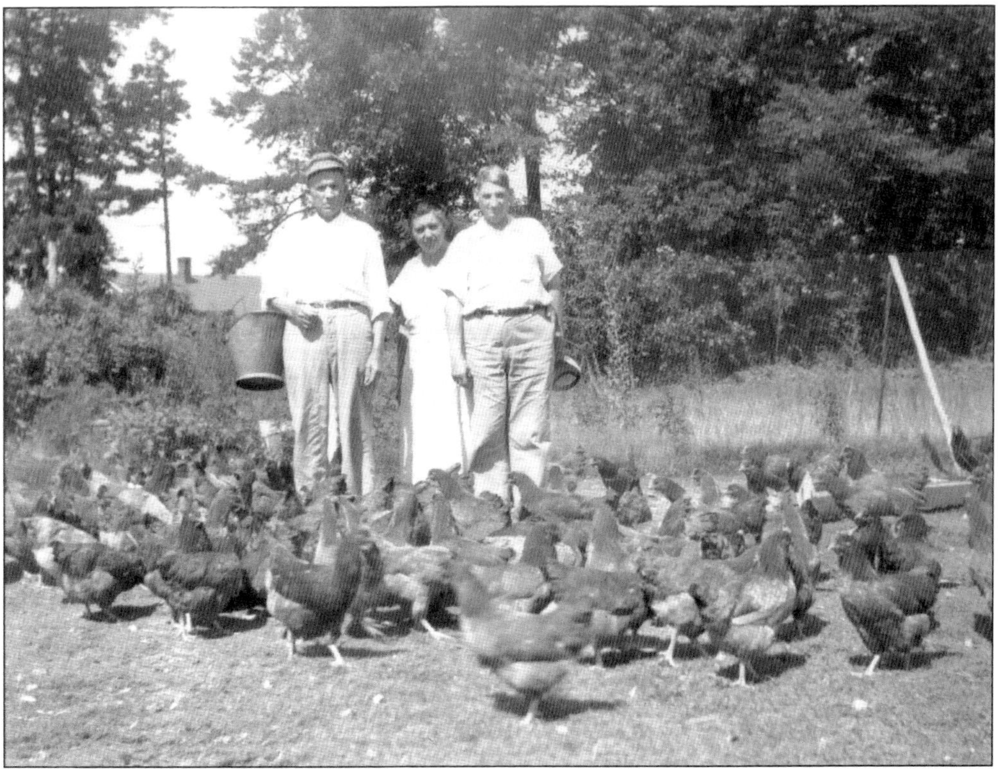

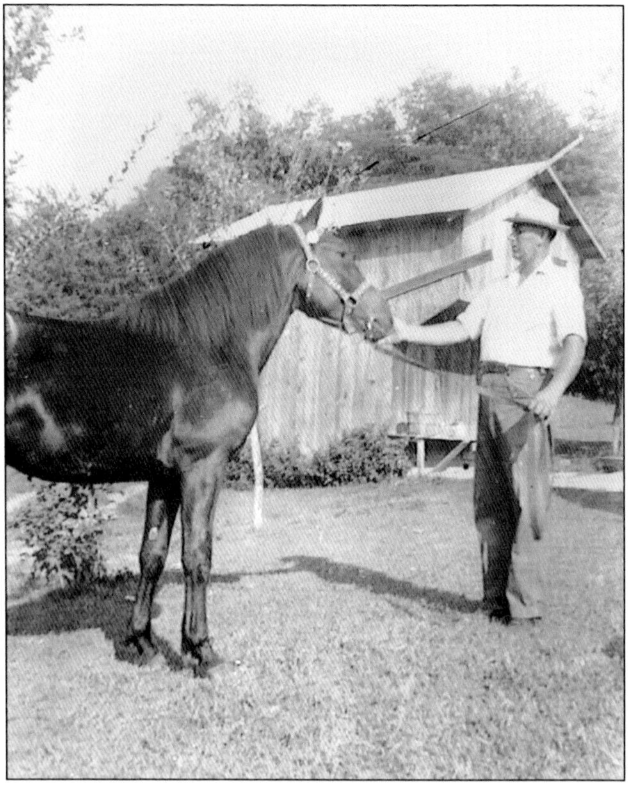

Ira Abbott (1903–1970) lived in the Law's Chapel community of Blount County, where he farmed and raised a family with his wife, Elizabeth Davis Abbott. Abbott, shown with one of his favorite horses, was head of the maintenance department for the Blount County schools for many years. His son, Harold Davis Abbott, later held that same position. (Courtesy of Harold D. and Mary Abbott.)

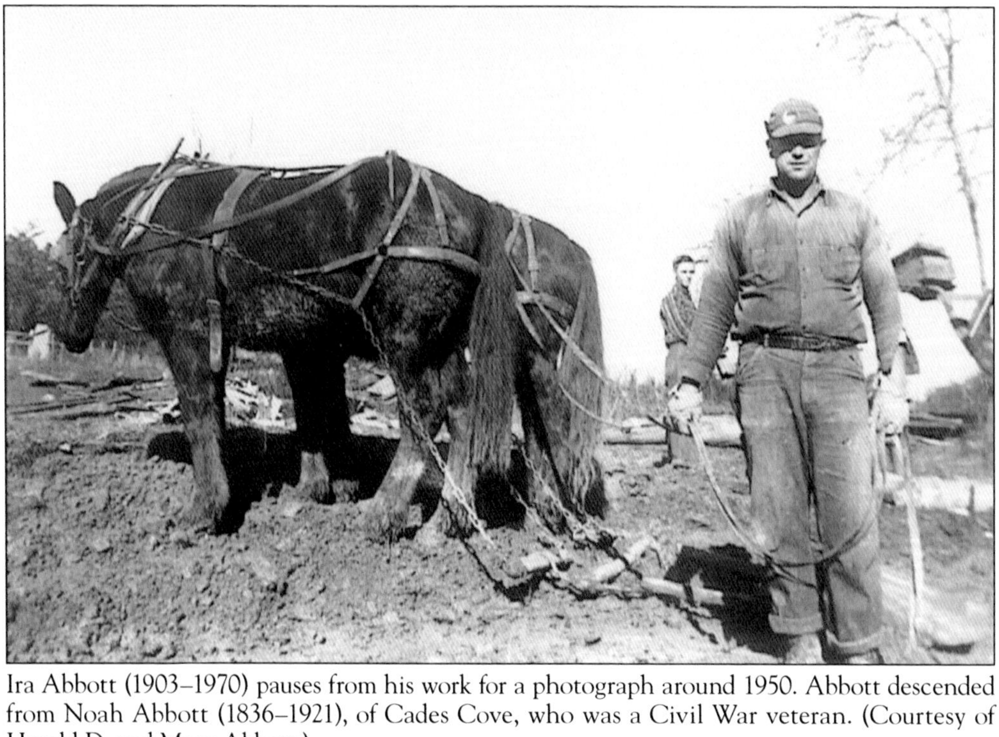

Ira Abbott (1903–1970) pauses from his work for a photograph around 1950. Abbott descended from Noah Abbott (1836–1921), of Cades Cove, who was a Civil War veteran. (Courtesy of Harold D. and Mary Abbott.)

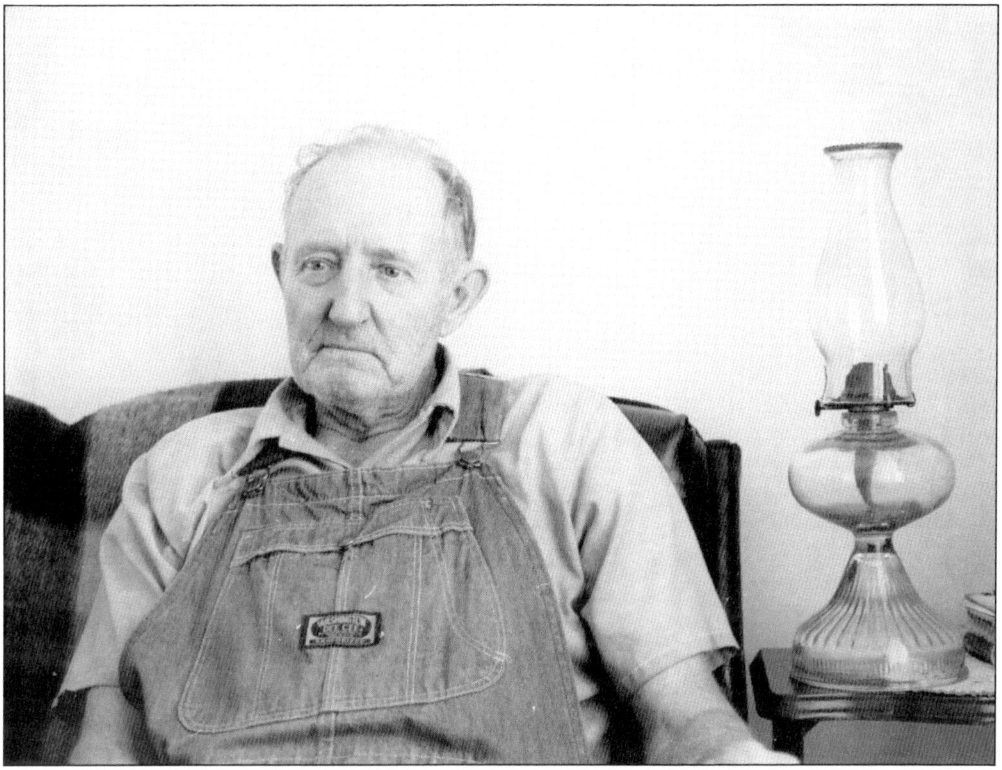

Kermit Caughron, shown above at his Cades Cove home around 1988, and his wife, Lois Shuler Caughron, were the last permanent residents of Cades Cove. They were allowed to farm the land and kept cattle and bees. They sold the honey to tourists, who often stopped by to get a glimpse of life from a bygone era. After Kermit's death in 1999, Lois moved to Maryville, and the Cades Cove property reverted to the National Park Service. The Caughron home and most of the outbuildings were dismantled in 2002. (Courtesy of the *Daily Times*.)

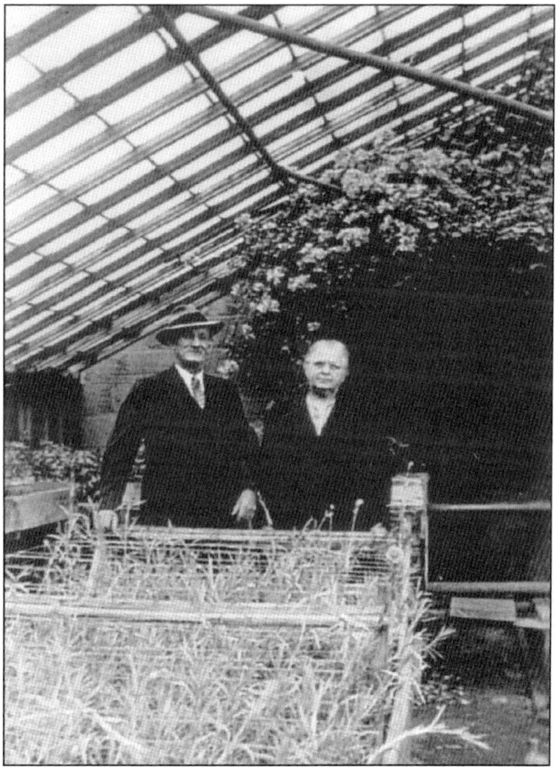

Charles R. Coulter and his wife, Nancy Millsaps Coulter, pause for a photograph in 1947 in one of the greenhouses at Coulter Florists on Sevierville Road. A bougainvillea plant is shown climbing the ceiling above them. (Courtesy of Linda Braden Albert, Helen Coulter collection.)

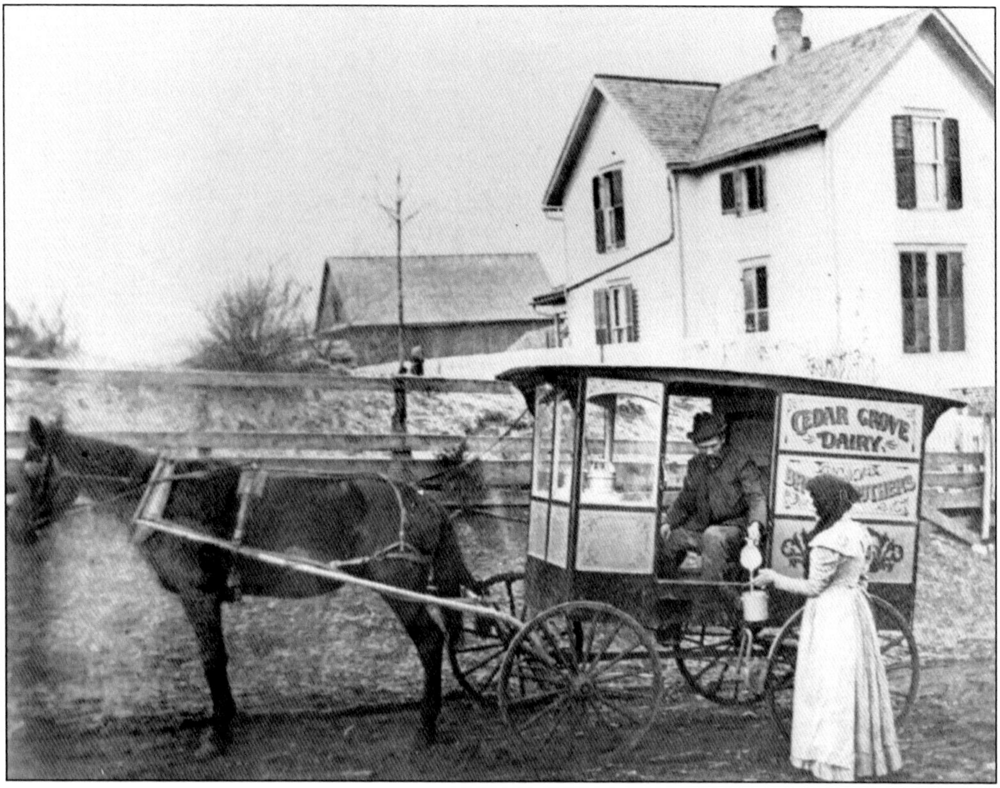

John F. Brown pours milk for Emily Webb at the corner of Washington and Lamar Streets in Maryville. Cedar Grove Dairy offered Maryville's first home delivery milk service beginning in 1901, with the customers supplying their own containers. The 160-acre Brown Brothers farm and dairy was acquired by Maryville College in 1934 and continued to operate as a dairy farm. (Courtesy of the Blount County Public Library, Adele McKenzie collection.)

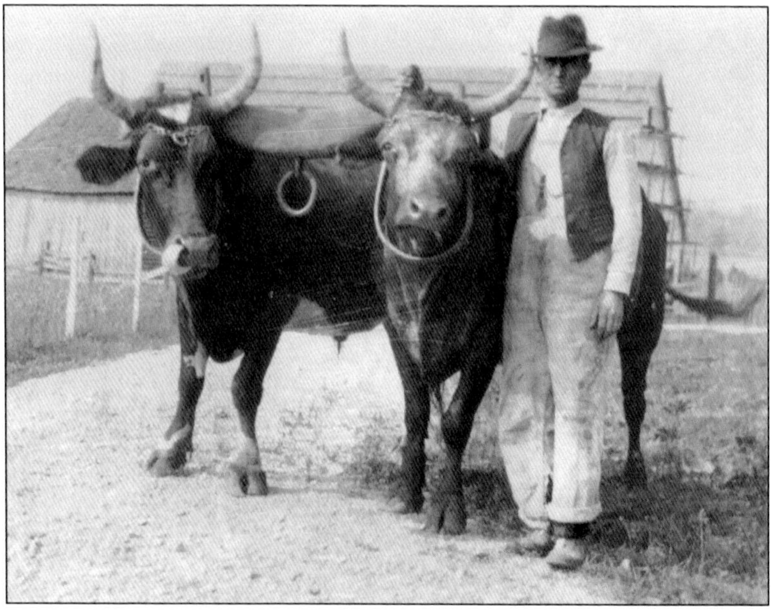

H. F. "Bert" Anderson stands with his team of oxen that was used to build the large barn at Limestone Dairy and Farm in Rockford. The Anderson family and their descendants owned and operated the Limestone Farm beginning in 1873. (Courtesy of John Kerr Jr.)

Five

Natural Resources and Recreation

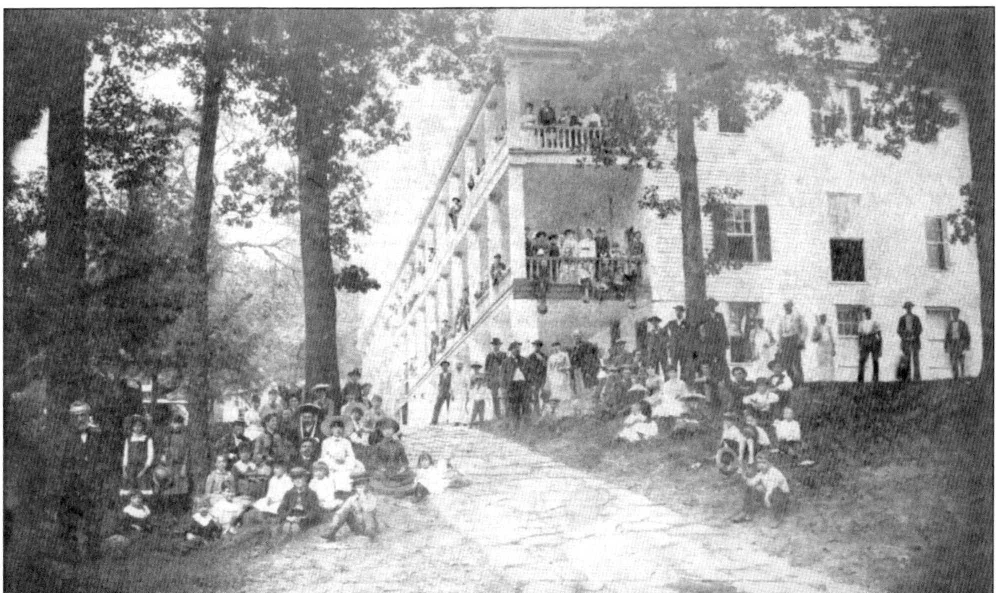

Daniel David Foute constructed the first Montvale Hotel, a massive log structure, in 1832. In 1850, Asa Watson bought the property and built the elaborate three-story Seven Gables Hotel, shown here in 1884 from the west end of the hotel. This hotel burned, and the Montvale Springs Hotel replaced it in 1901. The structure burned in 1933 and was not rebuilt. Montvale Springs was the largest and most popular of the "watering places" in Blount County, often referred to as the Saratoga of the South. (Courtesy of the Calvin M. McClung Historical Collection, Knox County Public Library.)

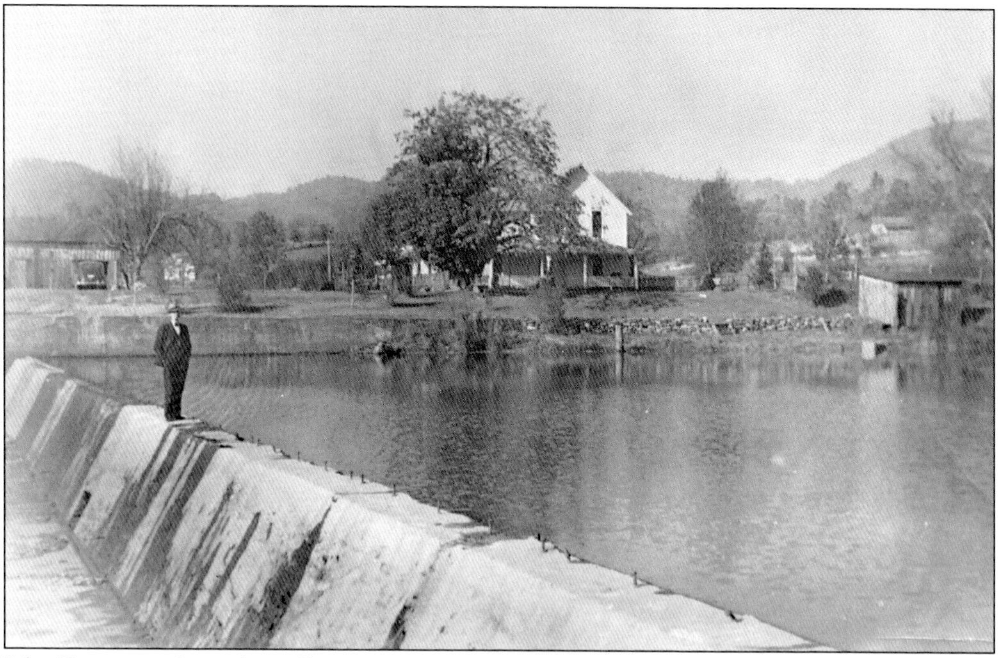

John Dunn stands on the spillway in Townsend in 1921. The dam was constructed by the Little River Lumber Company to produce hydroelectric power. The house in the background is the Dunn home. (Courtesy of the Blount County Public Library.)

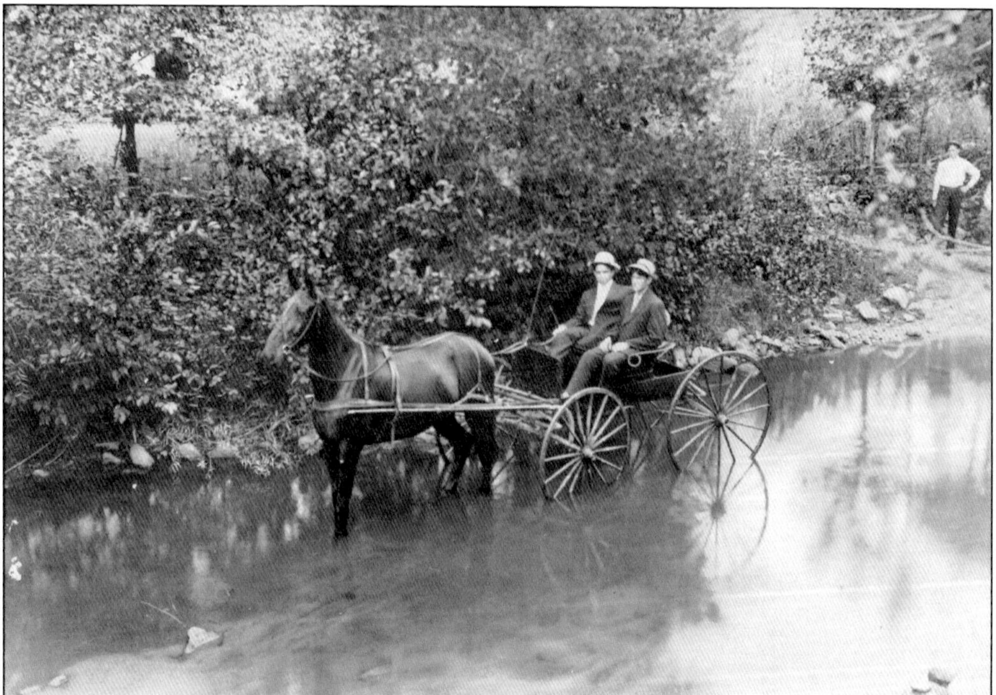

J. J. Myers (left) and a friend enjoyed riding through Little River at Walland around 1925. Little River continues to attract tourists, many of whom enjoy tubing down the river. (Courtesy of the Blount County Public Library.)

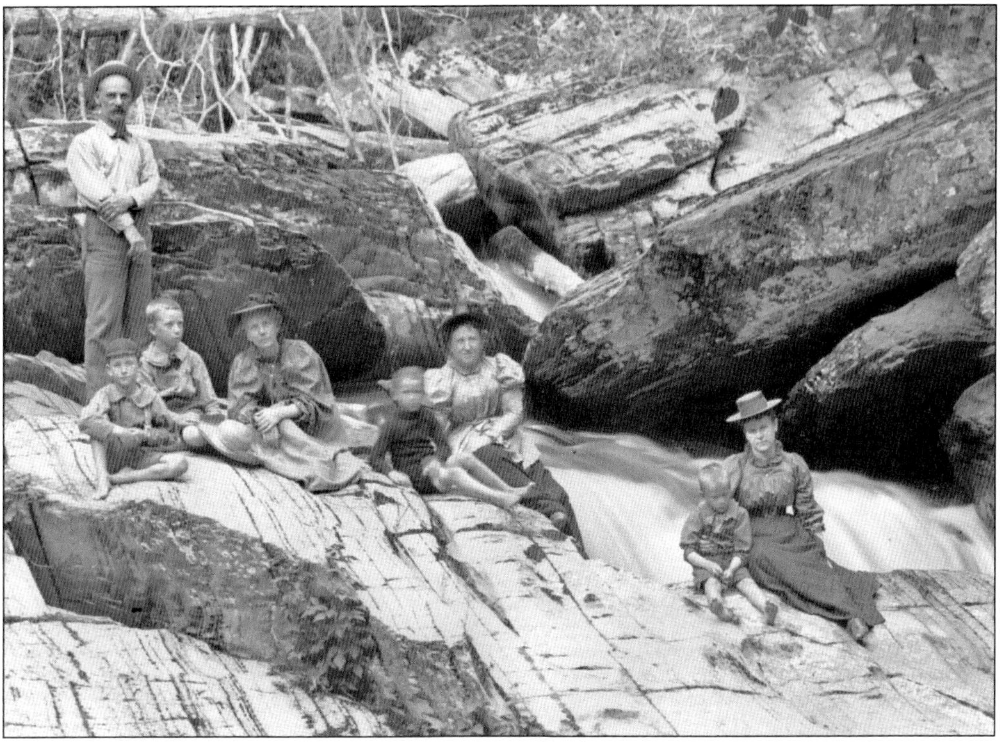

W. O. Garner's lens captured a camping trip taken by the Burger and Garner families at Maple Springs, a popular campsite in the late 1800s. Maple Springs was located at what is now Top o' the World. It was a favorite destination for extended camping trips by prominent Maryville citizens, including personnel from Maryville College and the two Quaker schools established after the Civil War. (Both, courtesy of the Blount County Public Library, W. O. Garner collection.)

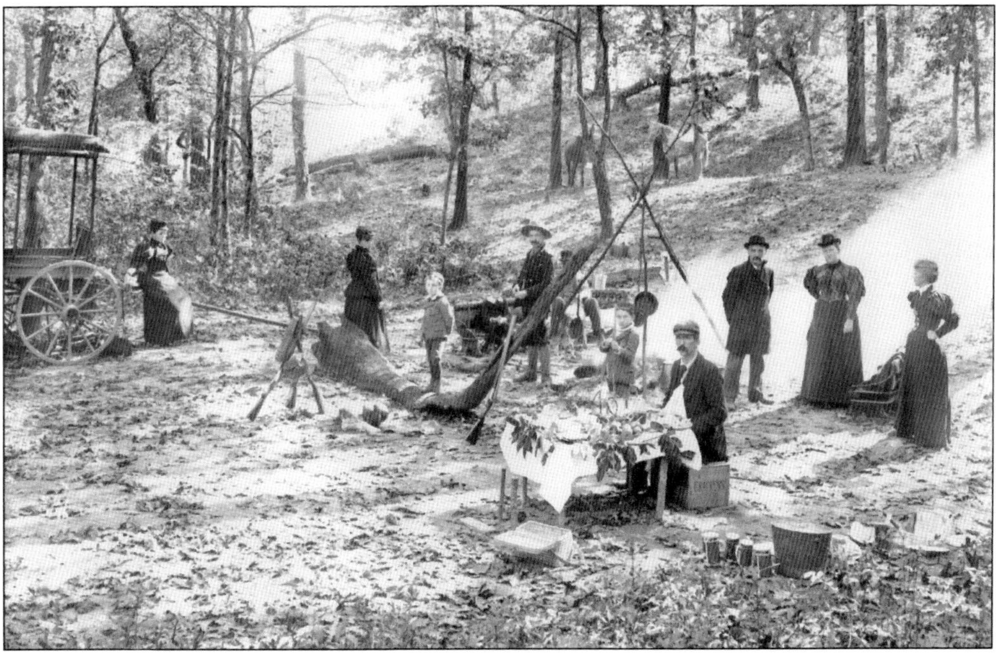

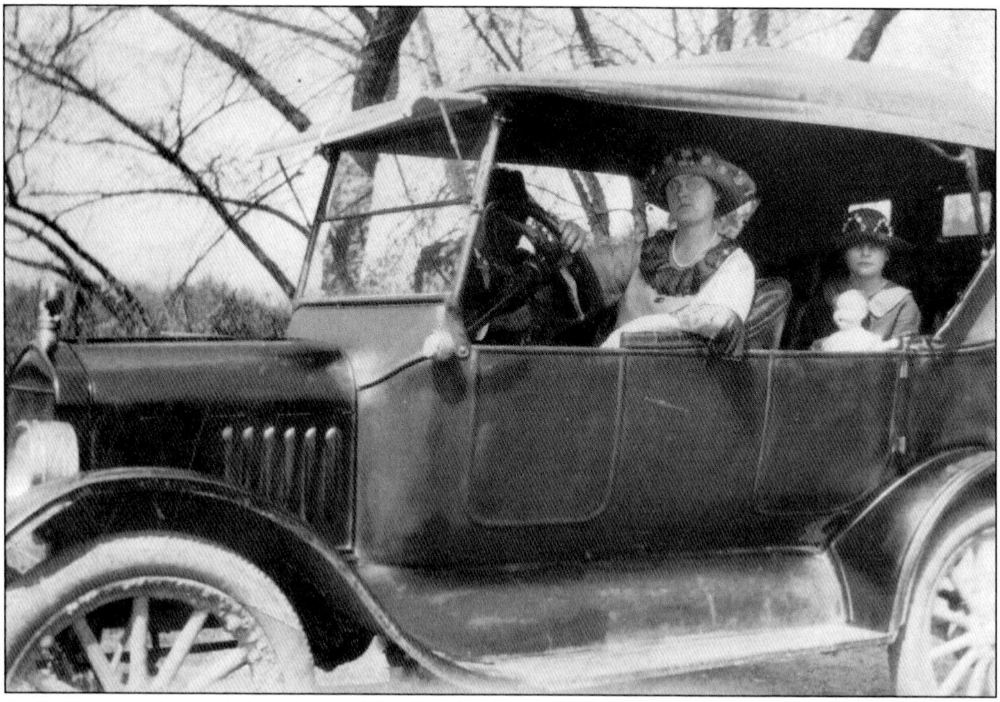

Della Parr gets behind the wheel of the family car in 1922 while her husband, Charles Parr, takes the passenger seat. Their daughter, Helen, looks out the window of the backseat with her china doll in her arms (Courtesy of Linda Braden Albert.)

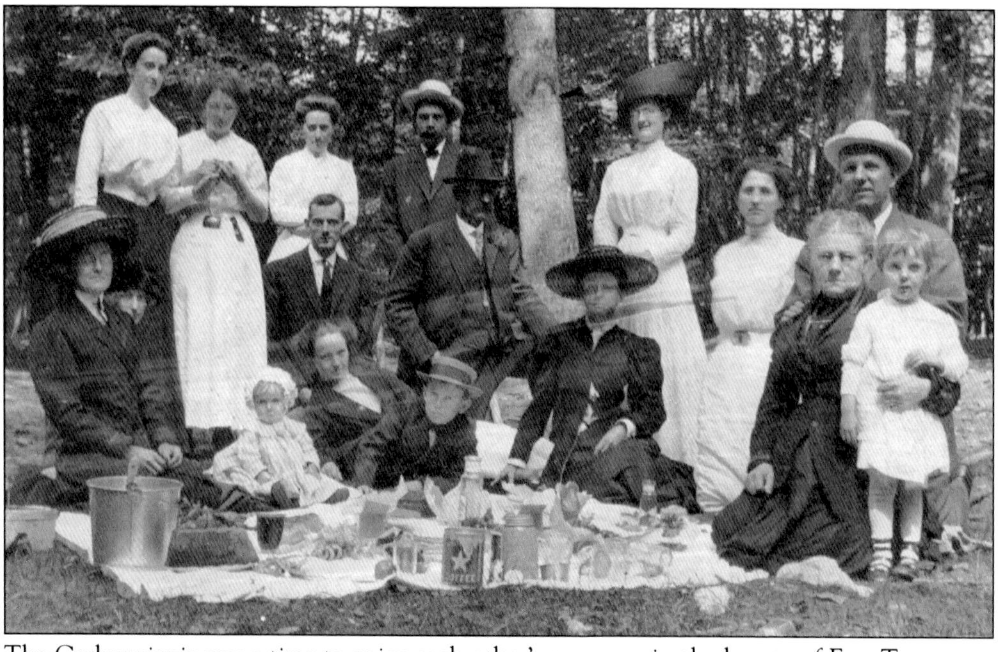

The Garber picnic was a time to enjoy each other's company in the beauty of East Tennessee. This photograph was taken around 1920. Martha Painter Garber is shown in the first row, second from right, and daughter Della Garber Parr is standing in back on the far right. (Courtesy of Linda Braden Albert.)

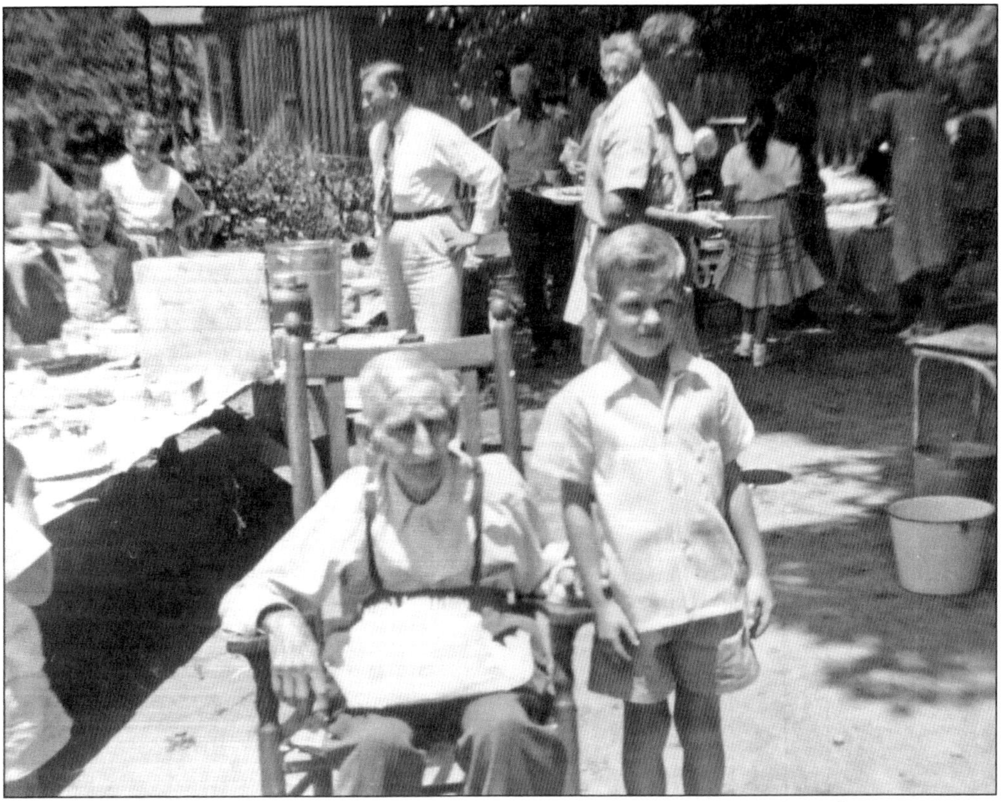

Will Braden (seated) and his great-grandson, Sammy, shared a June 8 birthday. They were guests of honor at a joint birthday party given by their family around 1954. Braden was born in 1872 and died in 1960. He is buried at Forest Hill Baptist Church. (Courtesy of Linda Braden Albert.)

Blount County had fun with the stereotypical hillbilly image by having a popular event called Hillbilly Homecoming annually in June from 1953 to 1978. Brian Bales dresses the part in this 1960s photograph. Since 2001, the city of Maryville has hosted its annual Foothills Fall Festival in mid-October, with craft booths, children's activities, food, and a concert series that has spotlighted stars such as 2009 headliner Alan Jackson. (Courtesy of Paul Bales.)

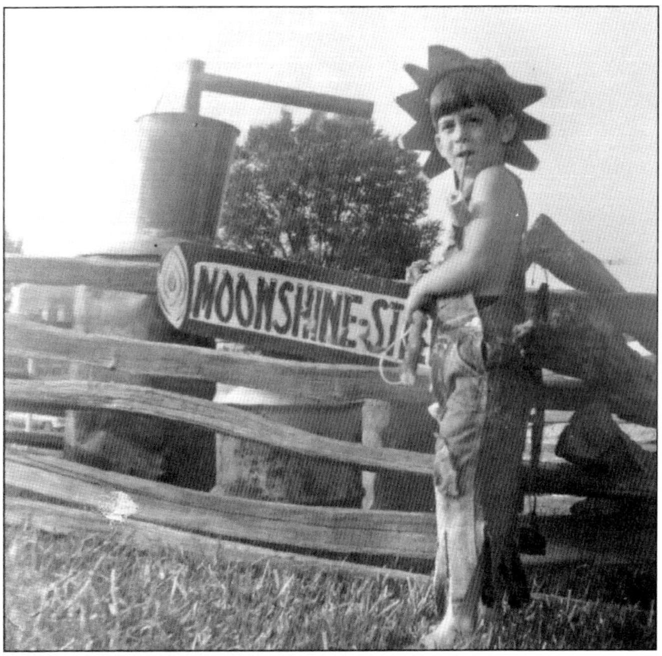

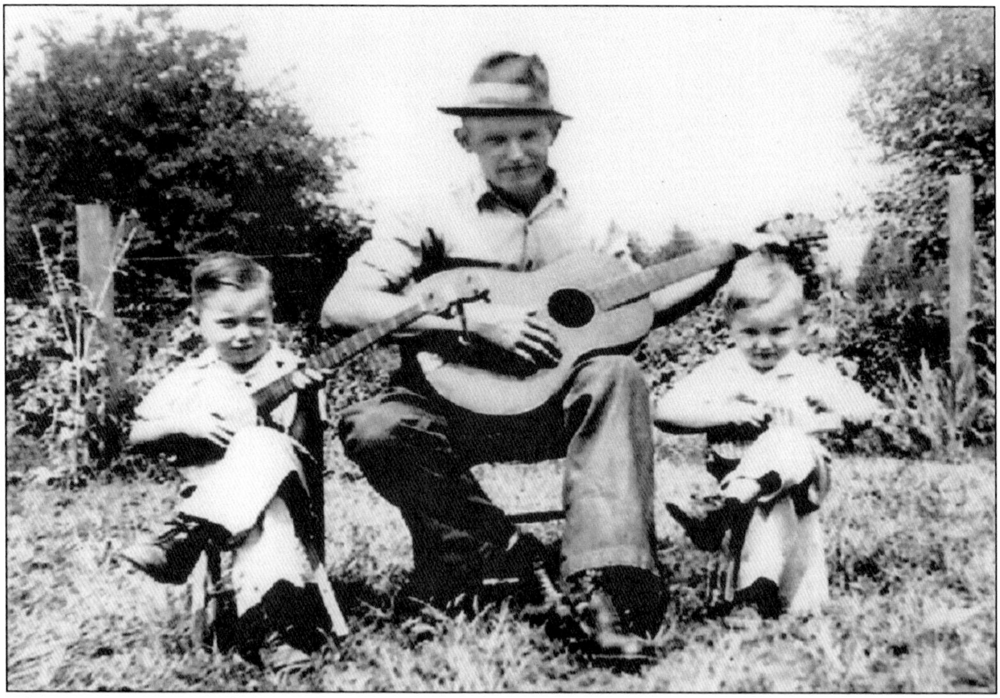

There is music in the hills and valleys of East Tennessee, as shown in this *c.* 1945 photograph of Clyde Sullivan (center) with the two oldest of his seven children, Will (left) and Bob. (Courtesy of Daryl Sullivan.)

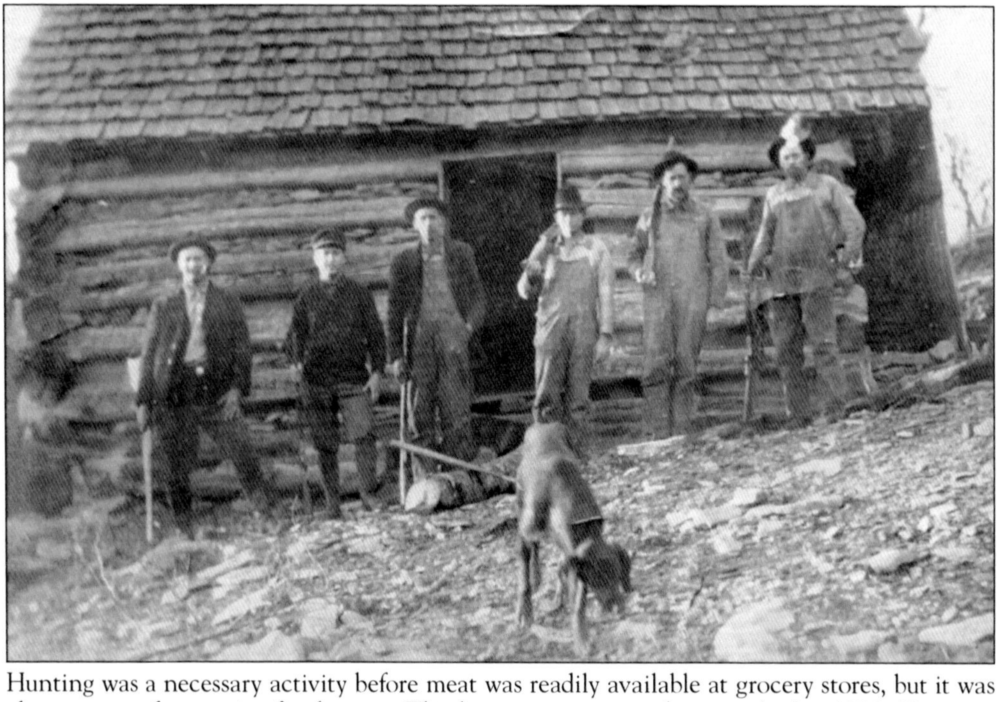

Hunting was a necessary activity before meat was readily available at grocery stores, but it was also a source of recreation for the men. This hunting party was photographed in 1926. (Courtesy of the *Daily Times*.)

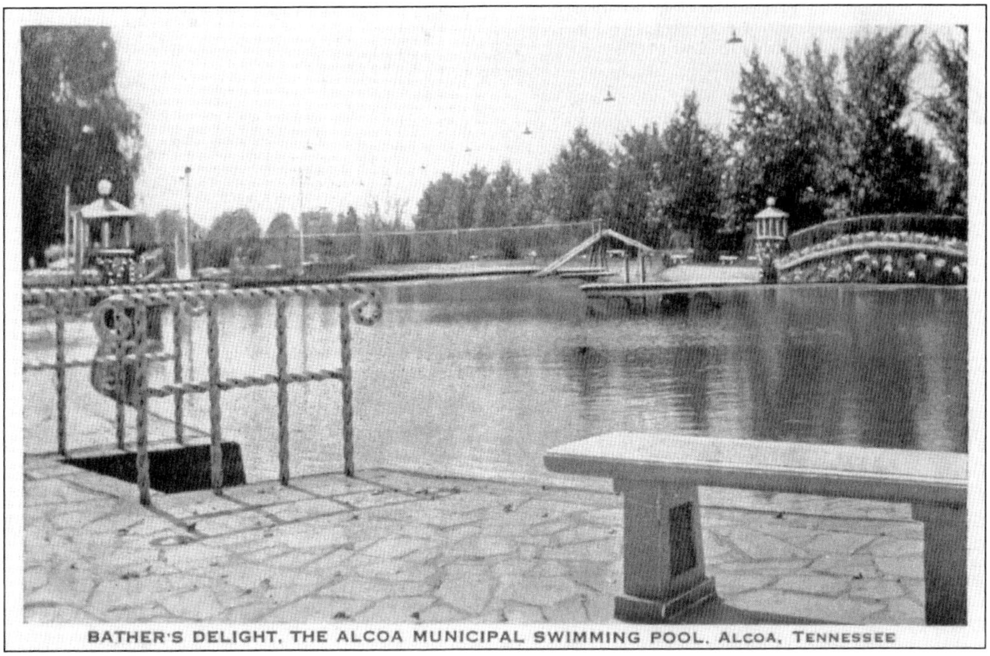

Cooling off in the Alcoa Municipal Swimming Pool continues to be a favorite pastime of Blount County residents. The pool is owned and operated by the City of Alcoa for the recreation and enjoyment of area residents. Large, tree-shaded facilities and playground areas surround the pool, which is 276 feet long, 80 feet wide, and holds 850,000 gallons of water. (Courtesy of B. Kenneth Cornett.)

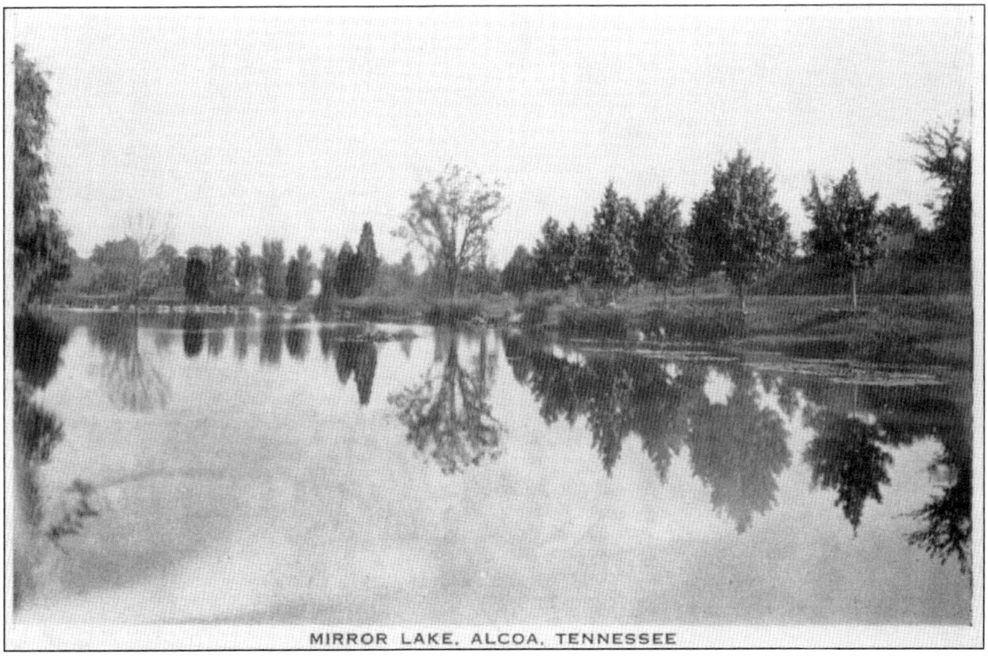

The Mirror Lake in Alcoa is now known as the Alcoa Duck Pond. Located adjacent to the Alcoa Municipal Swimming Pool, this lake is a favorite fishing area for young children. The photograph was taken around 1940. (Courtesy of B. Kenneth Cornett.)

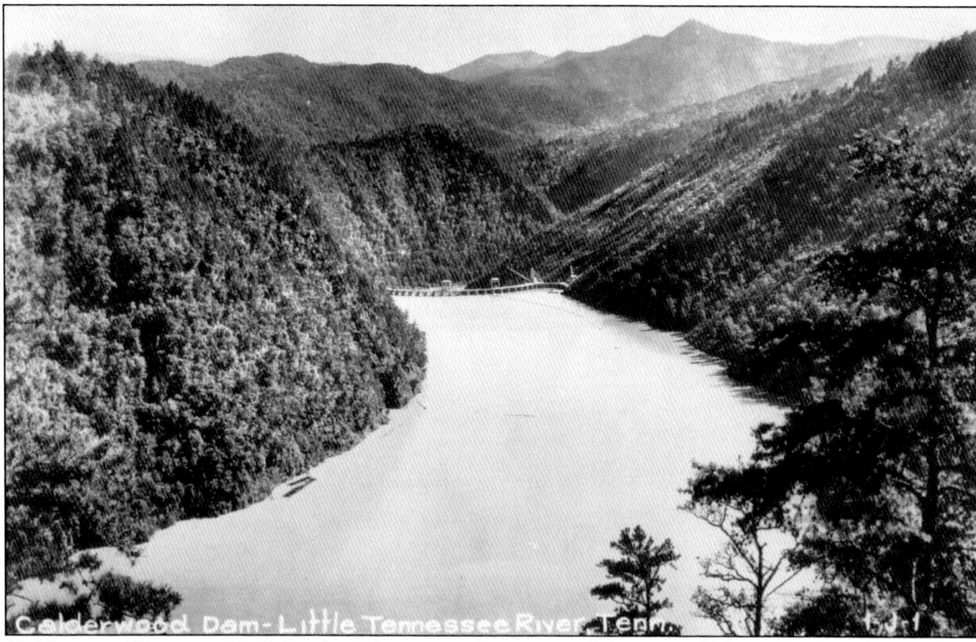

Calderwood Dam was built by the Aluminum Company of America (Alcoa, Inc.) in the 1940s on the Little Tennessee River to harness waterpower for its Tennessee operations. Today the lakes formed by dams built by both Alcoa, Inc., and the Tennessee Valley Authority provide recreational opportunities for residents and tourists alike. (Courtesy of B. Kenneth Comett.)

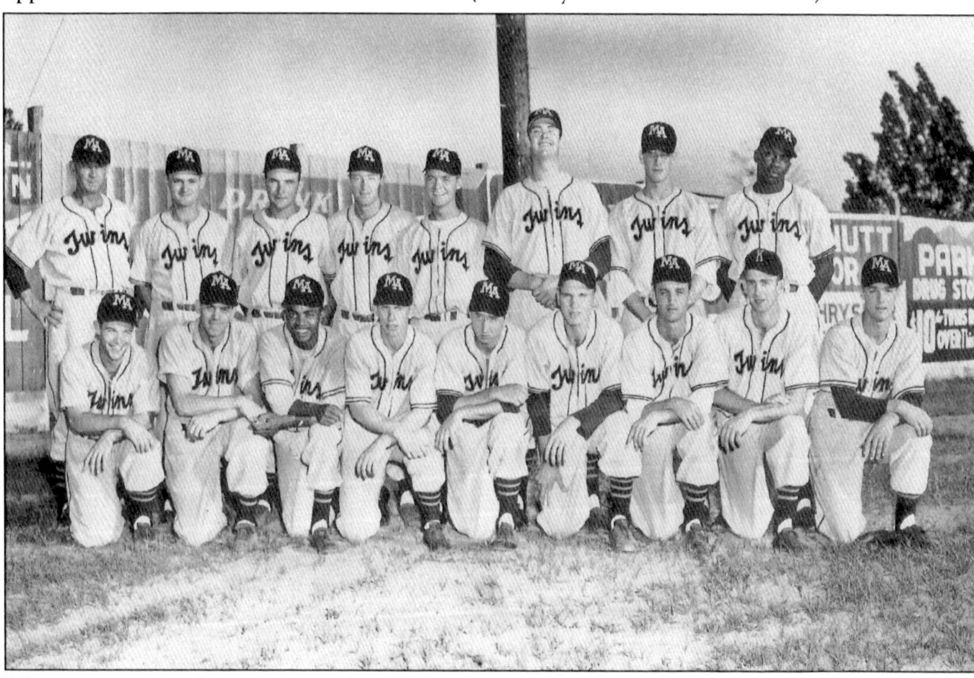

Blount County's only professional baseball team, the Maryville-Alcoa Twins, played the 1953–1954 season in Class D in the Mountain States League. The team practiced on Hunt Field in Alcoa. Pictured here are members of the team, including its star pitcher, Carl E. "Buster" McMillan, second row, third from left; he was also known as "Hound Dog." (Courtesy of Carl E. McMillan.)

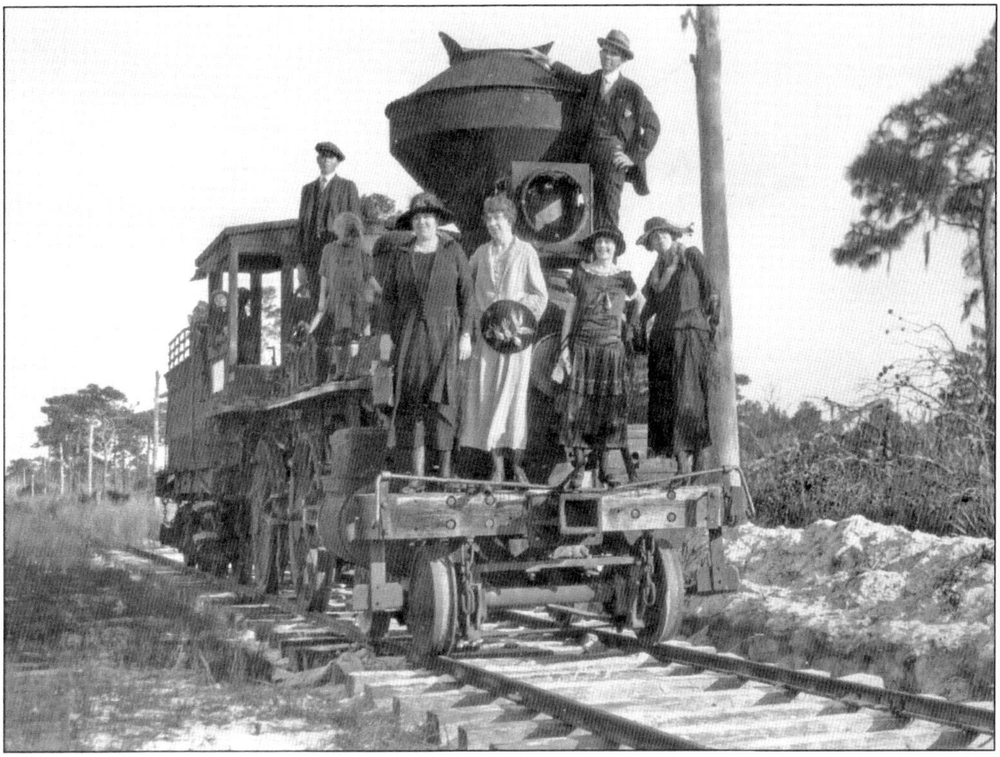

Riding the train was a favorite way to travel, as shown in this c. 1922 photograph taken at Louisville. Note how well dressed the ladies and gentlemen are for their outing. (Courtesy of Kathleen McCammon.)

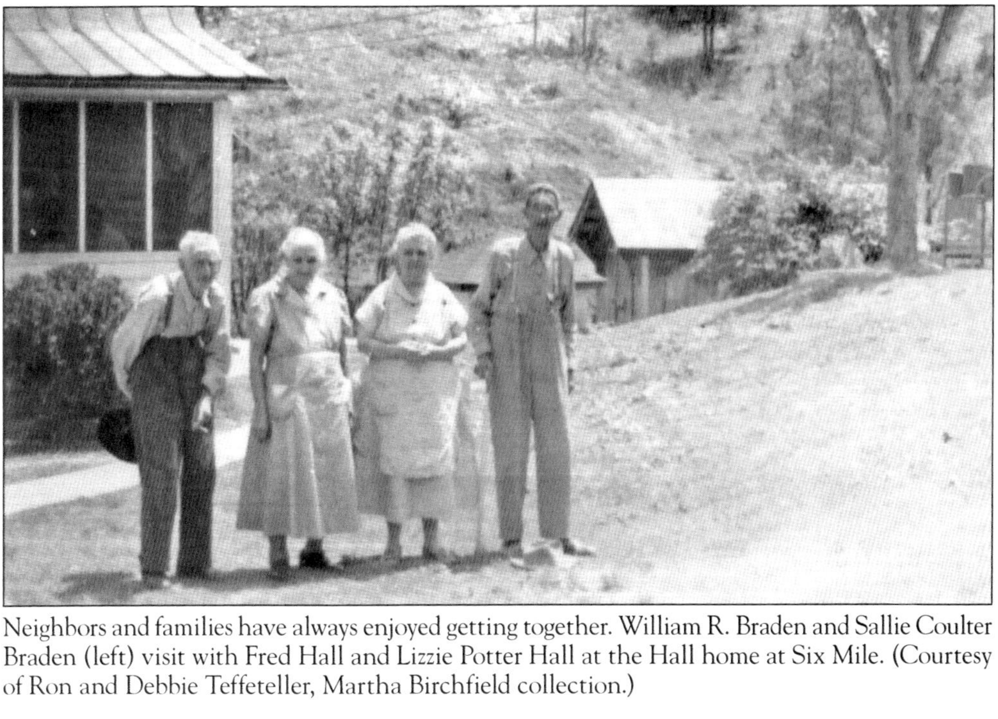

Neighbors and families have always enjoyed getting together. William R. Braden and Sallie Coulter Braden (left) visit with Fred Hall and Lizzie Potter Hall at the Hall home at Six Mile. (Courtesy of Ron and Debbie Teffeteller, Martha Birchfield collection.)

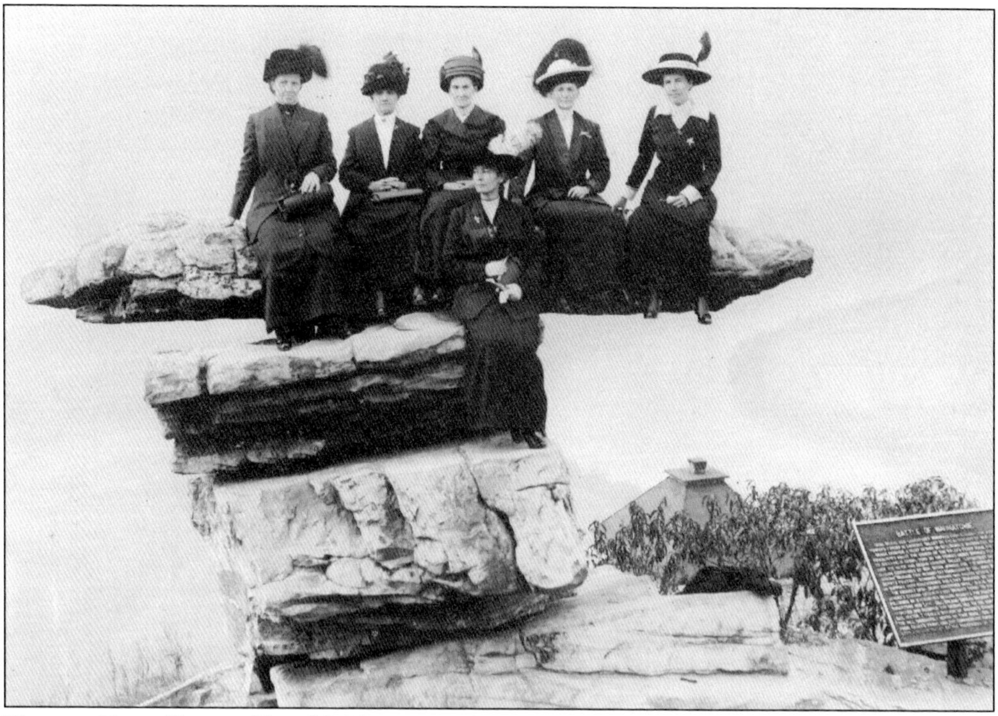

Pleasant Grove Baptist Church's Missionary Society went on an outing to Chattanooga in this 1915 photograph. Pictured are (first row) Rachel Williams Caldwell; (second row, from left to right) Lizzie Waters Gamble, Jennie Hitch Davis, Lou Gamble Hitch, Rachael Hitch, and Martha Massey Atchley. (Courtesy of Margaret Davis Coulter.)

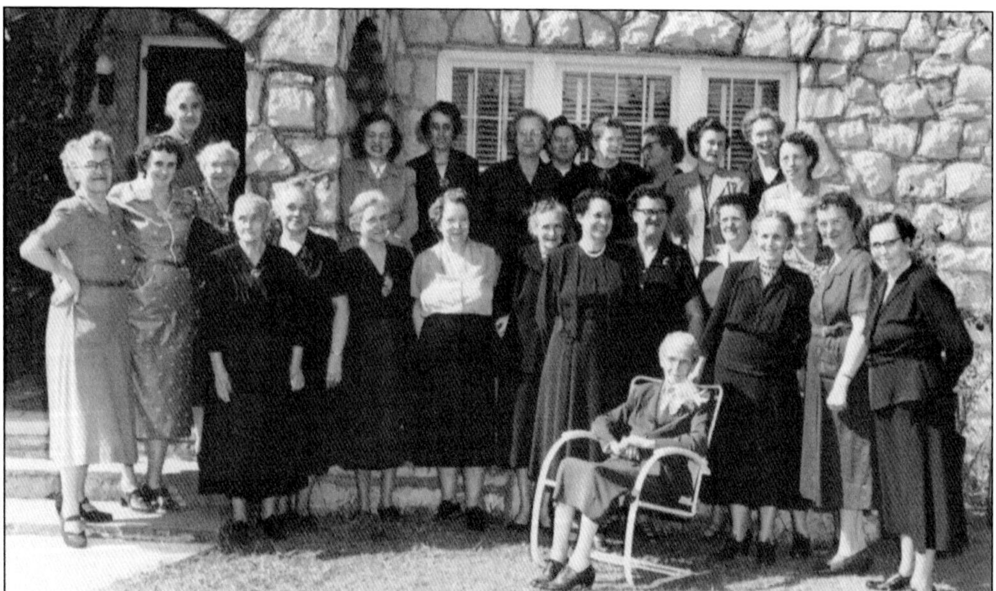

The Pleasant Grove Baptist Church's Women's Missionary Union (WMU) was organized in 1909, with Elizabeth "Lizzie" Gamble (seated) as president. Here the WMU members are celebrating Gamble's 90th birthday. (Courtesy of Margaret Davis Coulter.)

Six

The People of Blount County

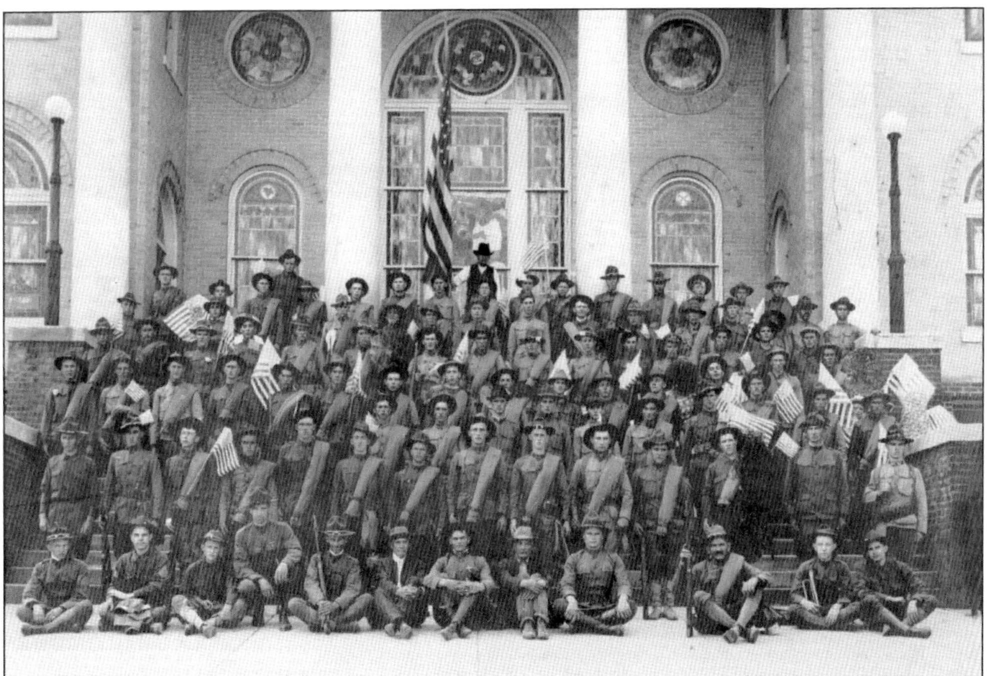

Company B, 3rd Regiment, Tennessee National Guard stands on the steps of the First Baptist Church Maryville in June 1916 before leaving for the Mexican border. They were mustered out on March 14, 1917. (Courtesy of the Blount County Public Library, Edwin Best collection.)

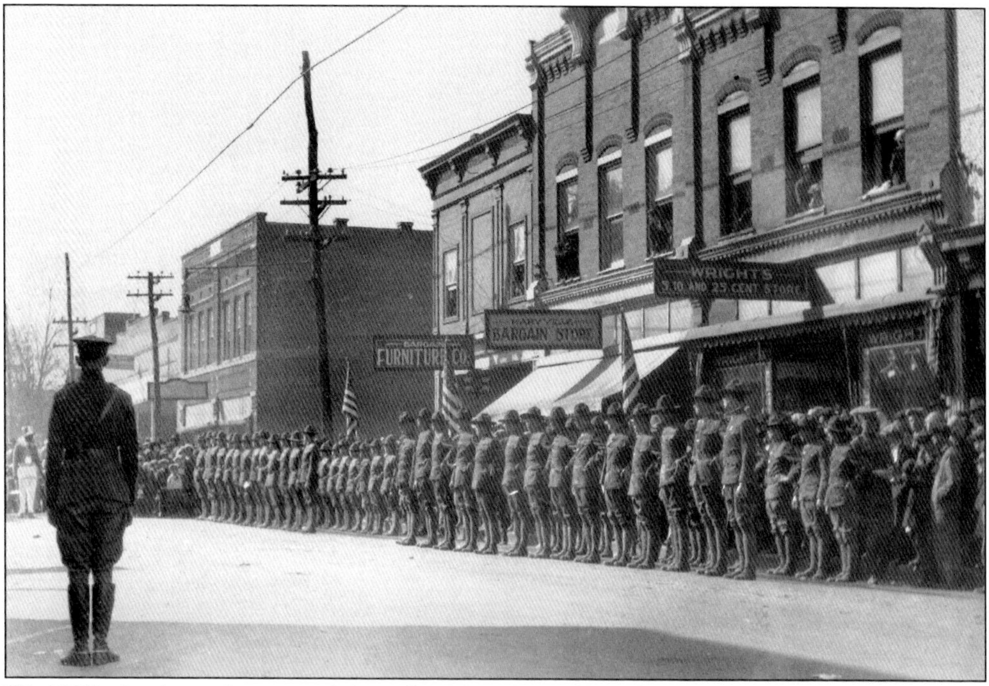

World War I enlistees line up on Maryville's Main Street (Broadway) around 1916. Blount County's citizens have always actively supported the armed forces. (Courtesy of B. Kenneth Cornett.)

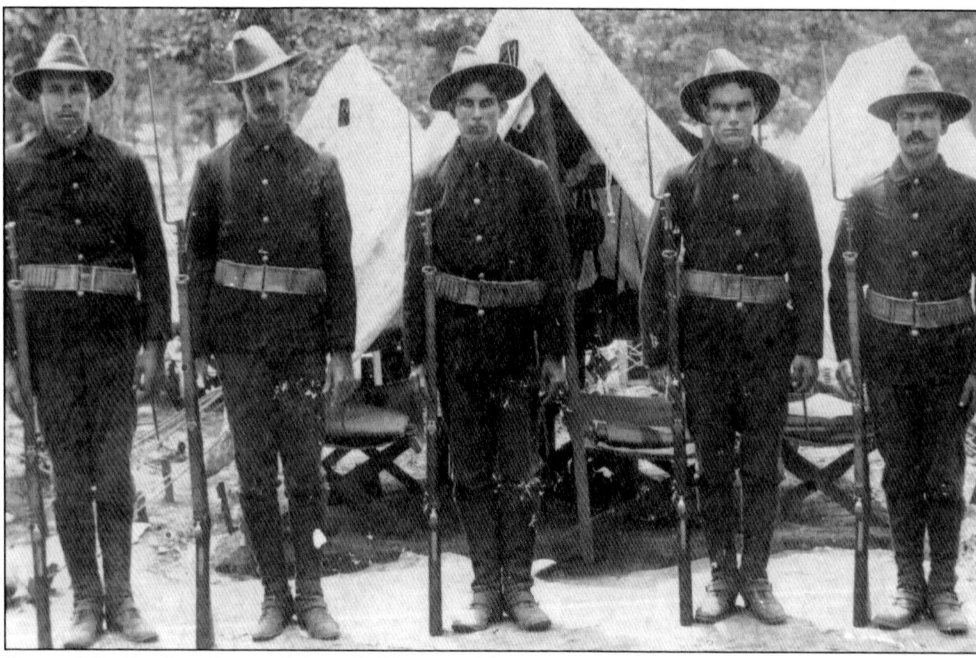

Samuel B. Braden (second from left) served his country in the Spanish-American War in the Philippines. Braden enlisted on June 17, 1898, in Knoxville in the Hospital Corps of the U.S. Army. He was discharged on January 31, 1899. He also served in the U.S. Infantry from May 1899 to November 1907 and in the Ordinance Detachment from 1908 to 1911. (Courtesy of Linda Braden Albert.)

Maj. Will A. McTeer (1843–1925) served in Company A, 3rd Regiment Tennessee Cavalry U.S. Volunteers during the Civil War. After the war, McTeer was a lawyer in Maryville, where he held many public offices and served one term in the Tennessee legislature. He was one of the organizers and president of the Bank of Maryville, treasurer of Maryville College, U.S. commissioner, and superintendent of the Sabbath School of New Providence Presbyterian Church. (Courtesy of the Blount County Public Library.)

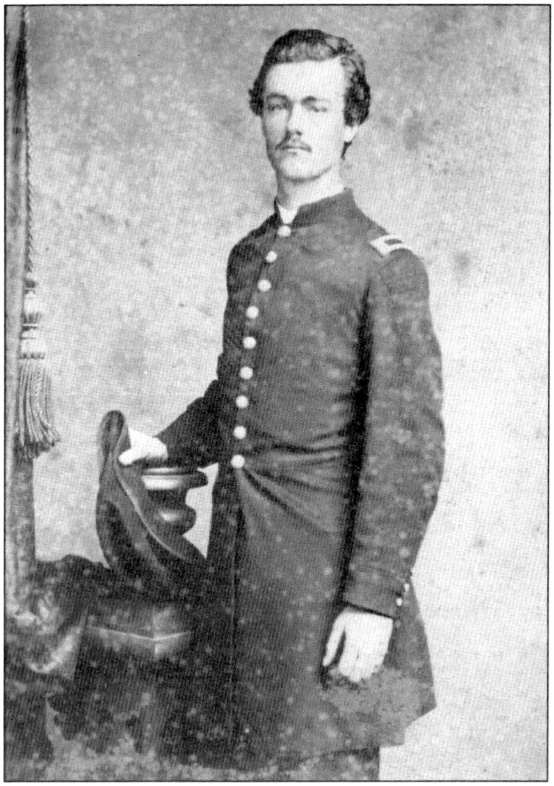

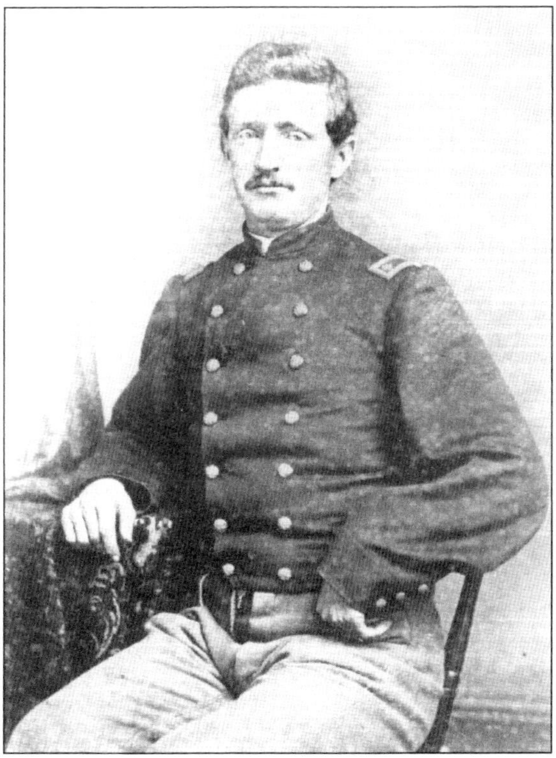

Maj. Ben Cunningham, a direct ancestor of Blount County mayor Jerry Cunningham, served in Company A, 3rd Regiment Tennessee Cavalry U.S. Volunteers during the Civil War. He served as Blount County court clerk for 22 years beginning in 1880 and as business manager and treasurer for Maryville College from 1885 until his death in 1914. (Courtesy of the Blount County Public Library.)

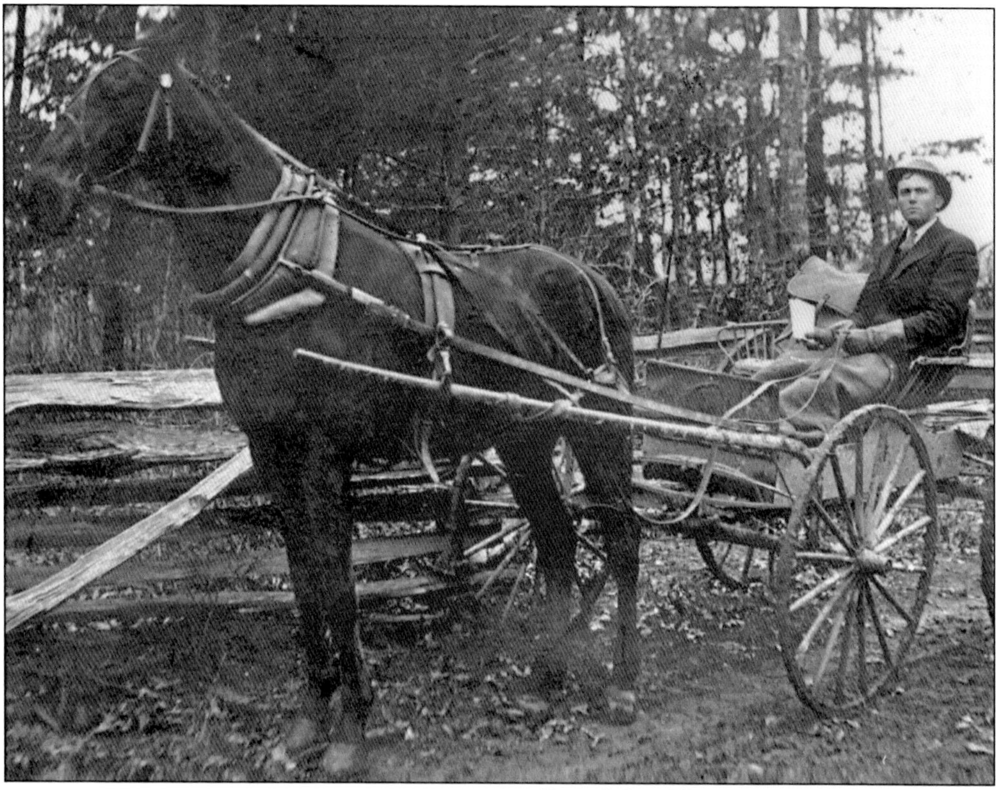

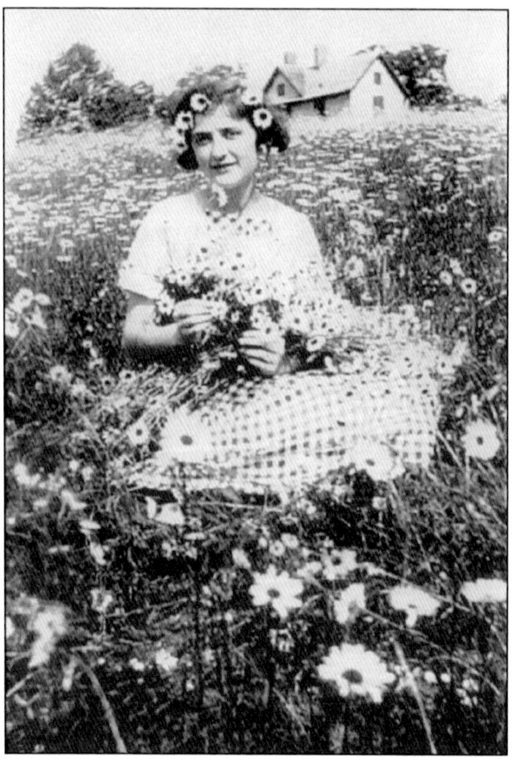

Daniel Otis Waters was a mail carrier for the Bank, Tennessee, post office. He is shown above on his appointed rounds about 1907. Rural mail carriers brought news and gossip along with the mail, gathering information along the route. The last person on the route got an earful, but the first one always caught up on the news the next time the mail was delivered. The Bank Post Office served the Wildwood community from 1880 to 1912. (Courtesy of Bob DeLozier, D. O. Waters collection.)

Helen Coulter (1908–1999), daughter of Charles R. and Nancy Millsaps Coulter, loved flowers. In this photograph, taken around 1928, she is surrounded by daisies in a field with the Coulter home place, off Tuckaleechee Road, visible in the background. Coulter and her brothers, Charles Jr. and Kenneth, operated Coulter Florists, which was founded by their father in 1896. (Courtesy of Linda Braden Albert, Helen Coulter collection.)

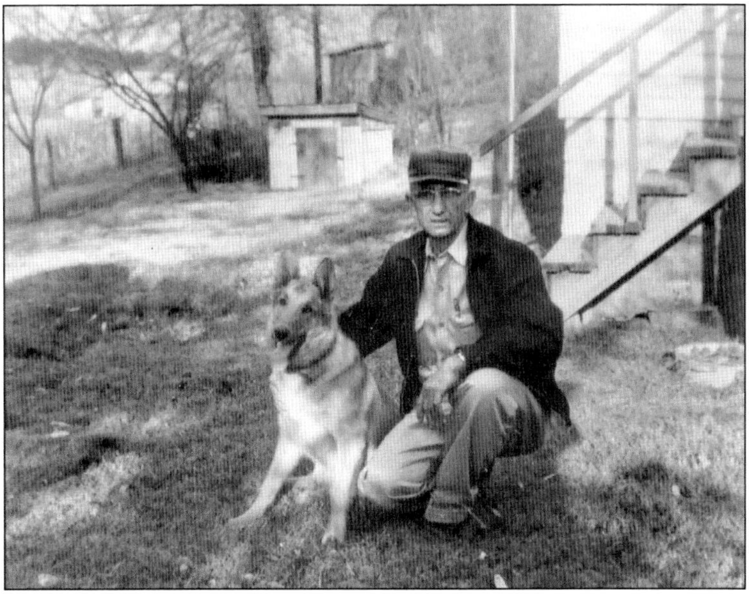

Hubert Braden and his dog, King, are shown in the front yard of the Braden home on Blockhouse Road in 1965. Note the well house and the outdoor toilet in the distance behind them. (Courtesy of Linda Braden Albert.)

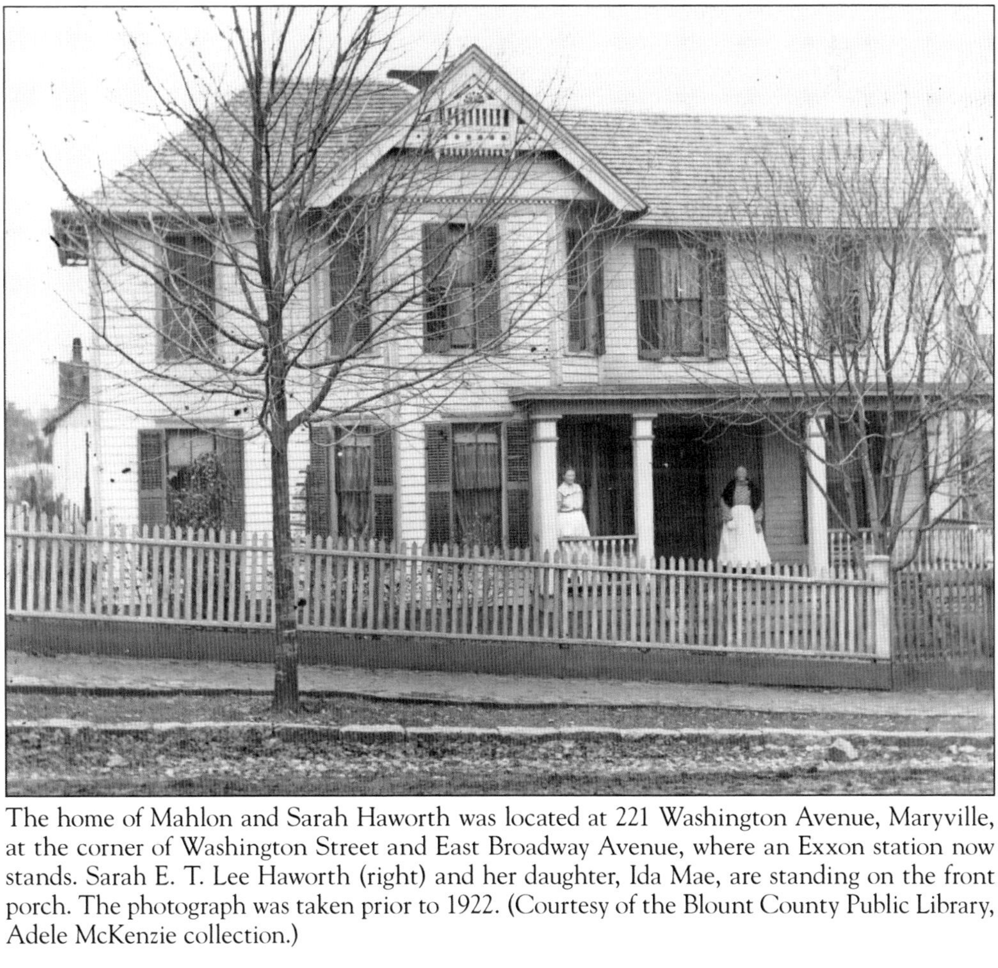

The home of Mahlon and Sarah Haworth was located at 221 Washington Avenue, Maryville, at the corner of Washington Street and East Broadway Avenue, where an Exxon station now stands. Sarah E. T. Lee Haworth (right) and her daughter, Ida Mae, are standing on the front porch. The photograph was taken prior to 1922. (Courtesy of the Blount County Public Library, Adele McKenzie collection.)

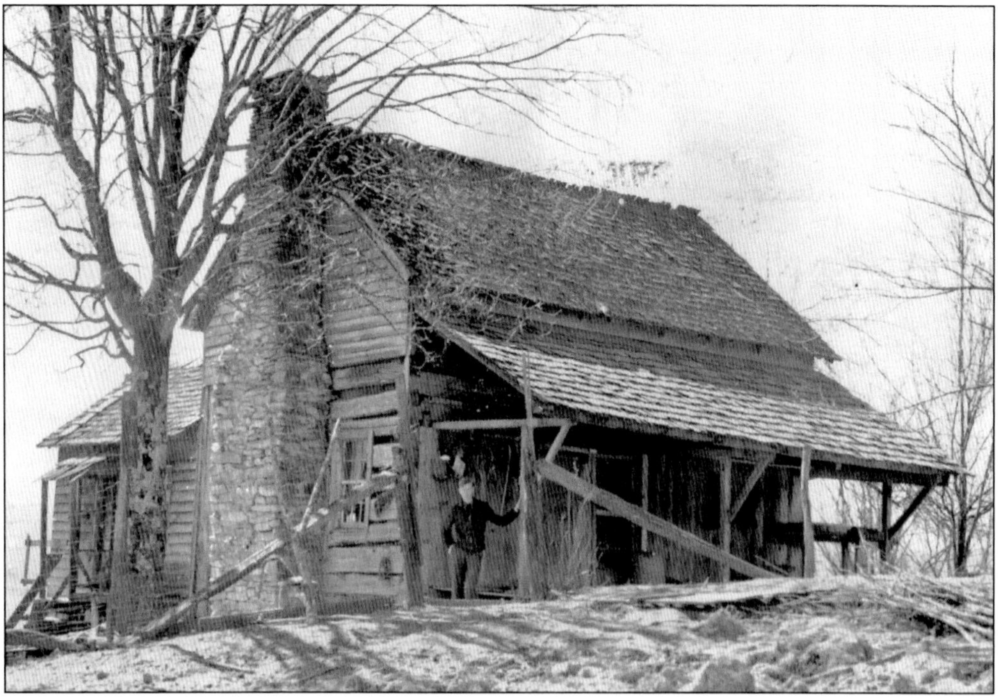

The log and frame home of Sherman Myers, shown here in 1937, was located on North Cove Road in Cades Cove. The home was dismantled by the Great Smoky Mountains National Park Service. (Courtesy of B. Kenneth Cornett.)

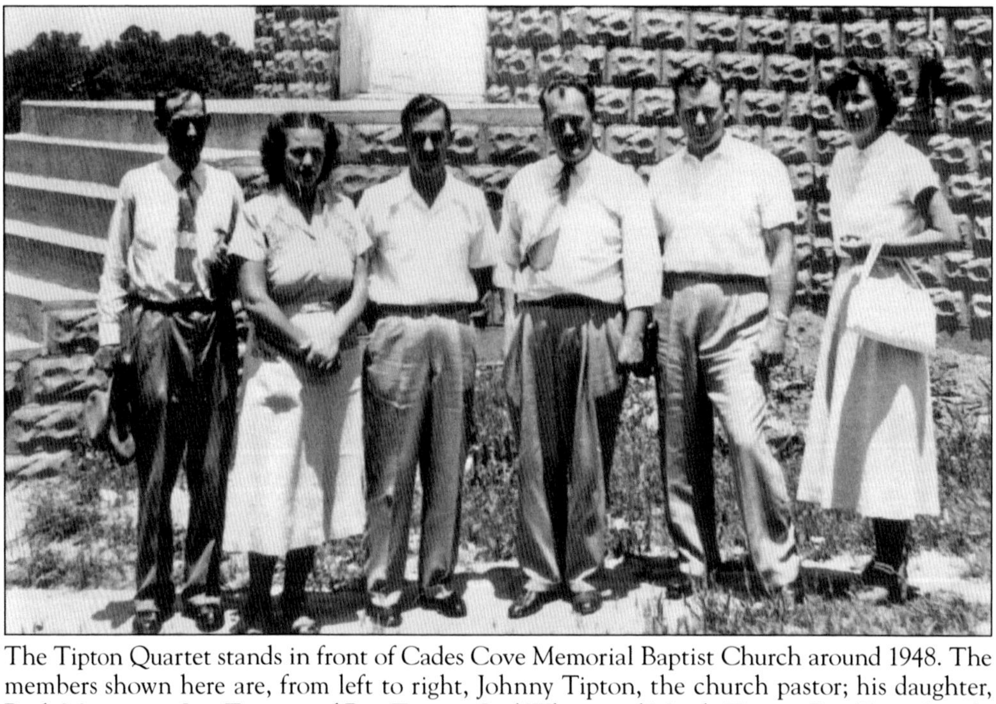

The Tipton Quartet stands in front of Cades Cove Memorial Baptist Church around 1948. The members shown here are, from left to right, Johnny Tipton, the church pastor; his daughter, Ruth Myers; sons Lee Tipton and Roy Tipton; Carl White; and Myrtle Tipton, Roy Tipton's wife. (Courtesy of Leon Myers.)

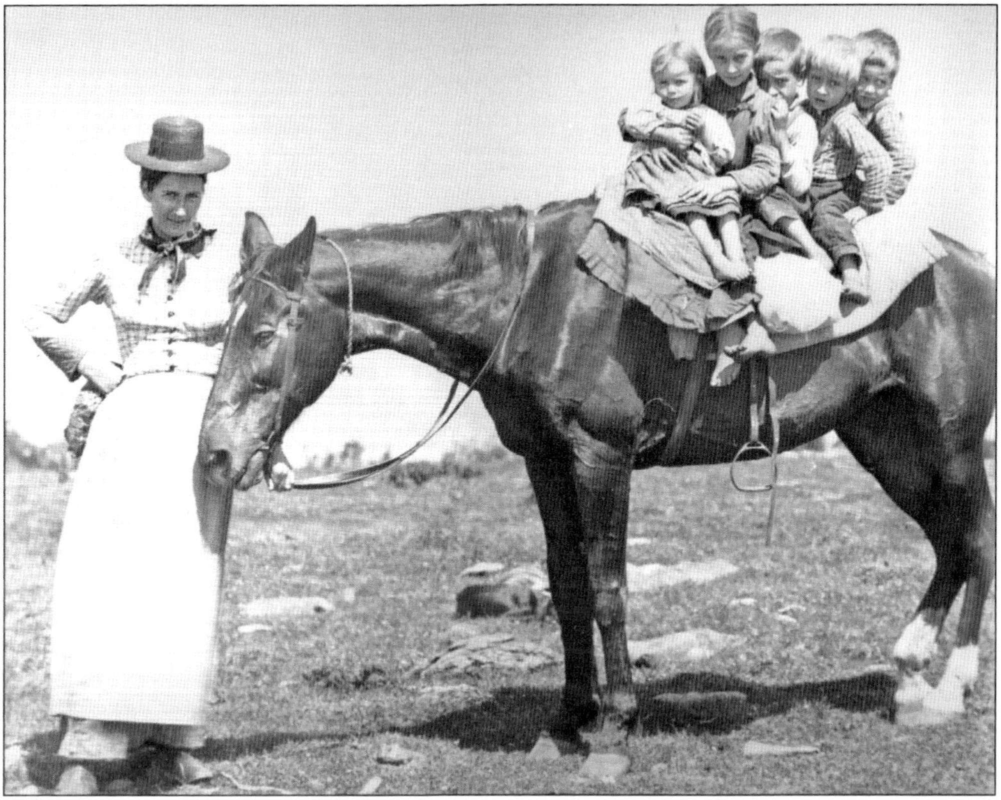

Jane Birchfield Tipton holds the reins of a horse carrying five children in this photograph, taken around 1900 by W. O. Garner. Garner's photographs of Blount County people and places give a glimpse into life at the beginning of the 20th century. (Courtesy of the Blount County Public Library, W. O. Garner collection.)

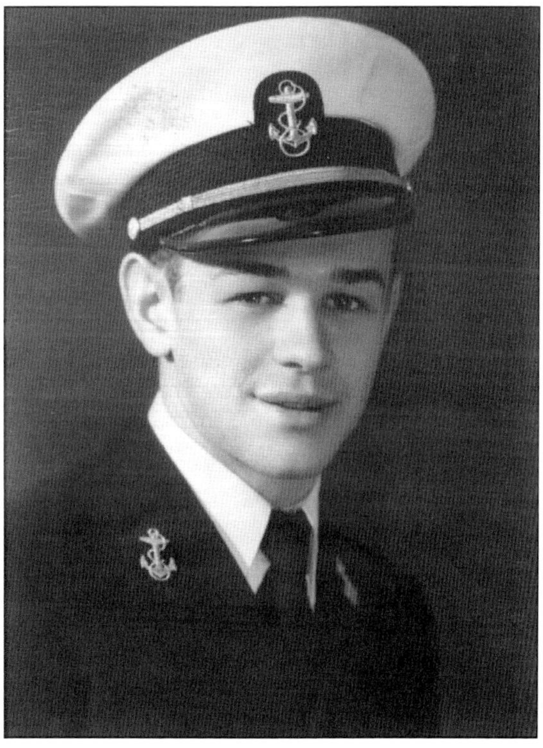

Donald Ray McCammon, born in 1926, enlisted in the U.S. Navy in 1944 and trained as a navy pilot. He was discharged in 1946 and returned to Blount County, where he completed his degree in business management at Maryville College in 1950. He worked for the Aluminum Company of America (Alcoa, Inc.), the Department of Energy, and Union Carbide Cooperation in Oak Ridge, where he retired in 1989. (Courtesy of Kathleen McCammon.)

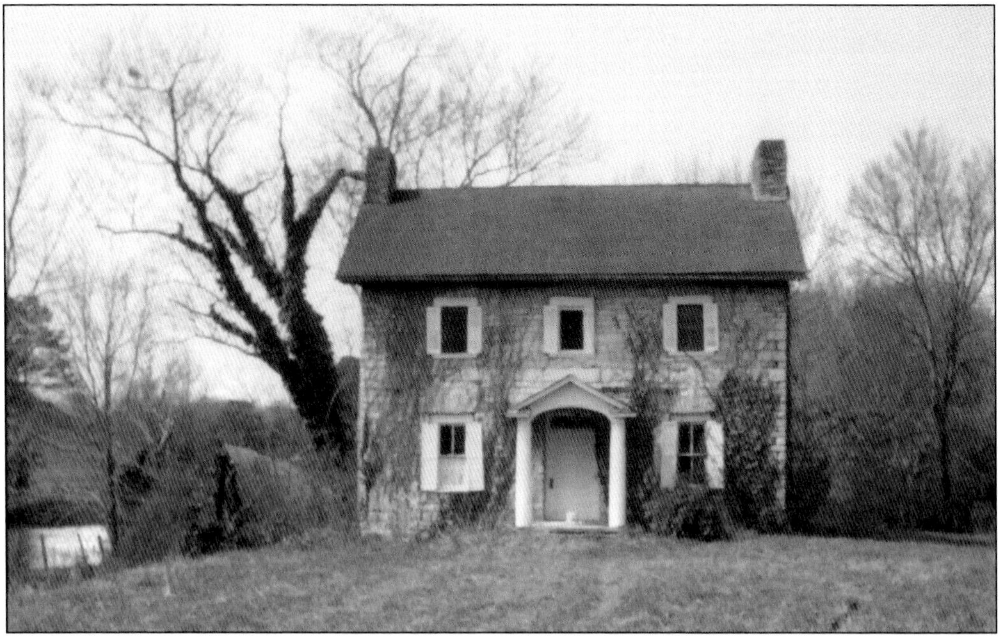

The house built at Lowe's Ferry in Louisville in 1802 by James Gillespie was constructed of quarried marble with walls that were 2-feet thick. The original home contained a sitting room, a parlor, and a dining room with the bedrooms upstairs. Early in the 20th century, a frame wing added a kitchen and porch on the ground level and a bedroom upstairs. The house had been unoccupied for some time when the above photograph was taken in 1999 and had deteriorated even more by the time the second photograph was taken in 2004. In 2008, the home was destroyed by fire. (Both, courtesy of Linda Braden Albert.)

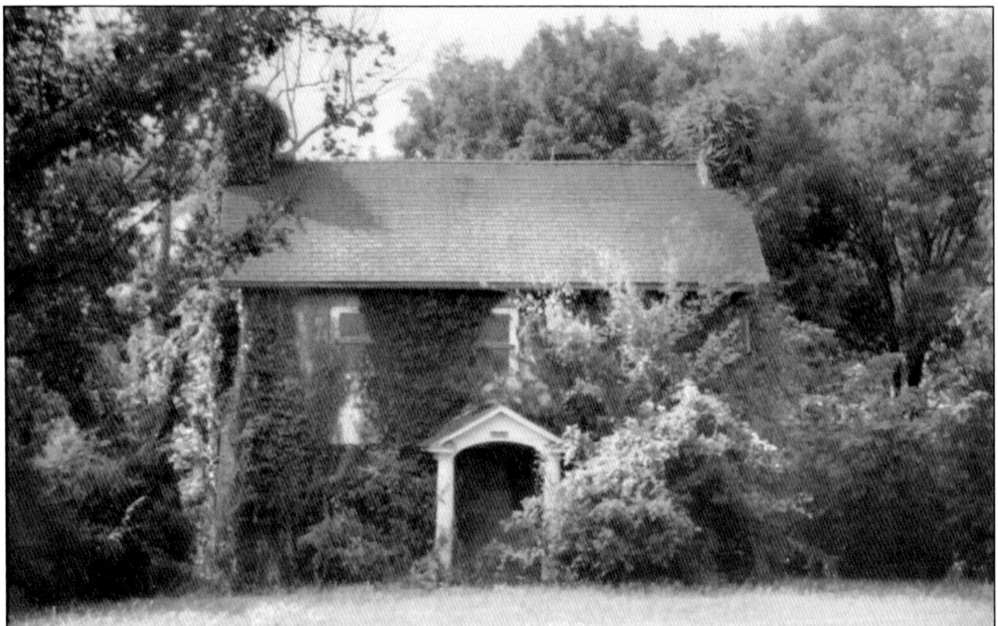

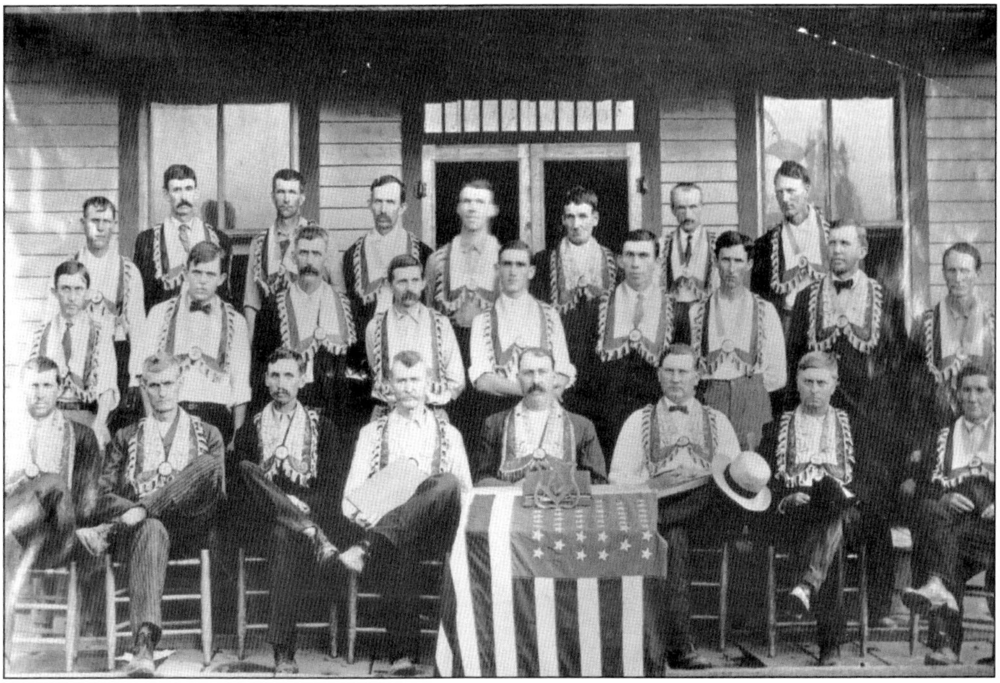

Lodge brothers pictured here around 1915 in Greenback are, from left to right, (first row) John D. Woods, ? Petty, Fate Murray, J. H. Scott, Martin McMillan, Ira E. Hammontree, W. P. Wampley, and George Griffith; (second row) R. M. Cook, Walter Anderson, unidentified, Edgar Wilson, John Hammontree, unidentified, William Kittrell, Will Woods, and unidentified; (third row) Sherman Guider, Quinn Carpenter, Willie Peterson, ? Carpenter, Floyd Hammontree, Peeler Anderson, Charlie Chapman, and Clay Greenway. (Courtesy of the Blount County Public Library, Edwin Best collection.)

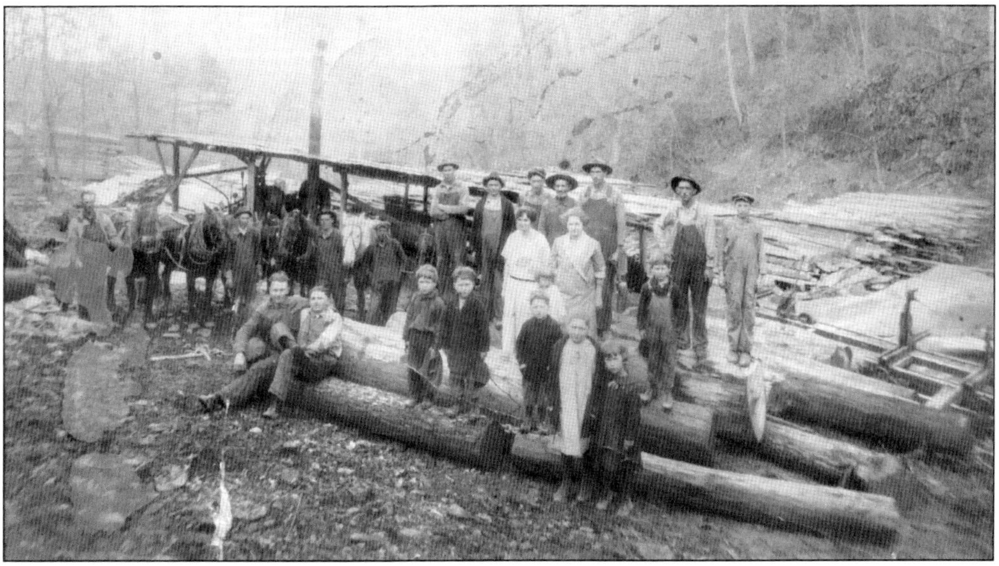

Working logging families gather for a photograph above their lumber mill. Note the teams of mules used to "snake leg" the logs into position for sawing. (Courtesy of the Blount County Public Library.)

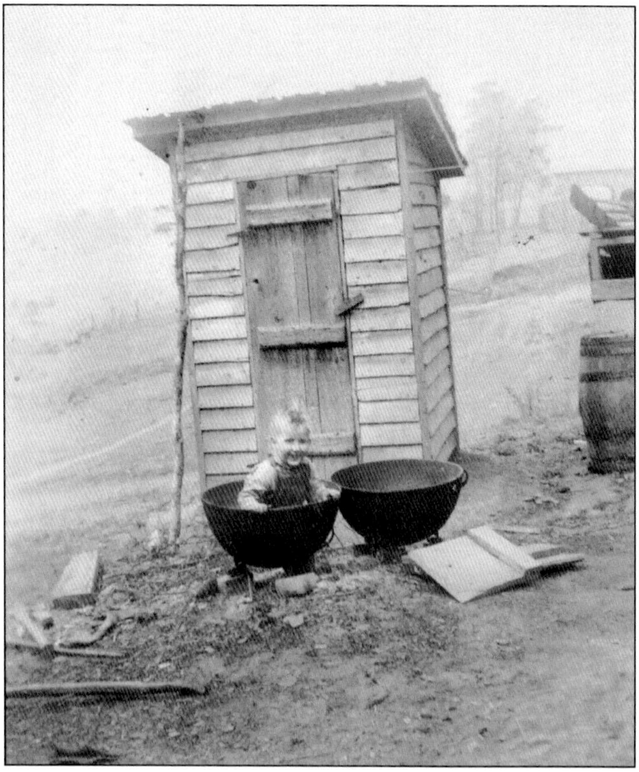

L. C. Tipton (1939–1981) sits in the family wash pot outside the outhouse in this photograph, taken around 1942. He is the son of Wiley and Pauline Everett Tipton from the Hubbard community. (Courtesy of Jackie Tipton Kitts.)

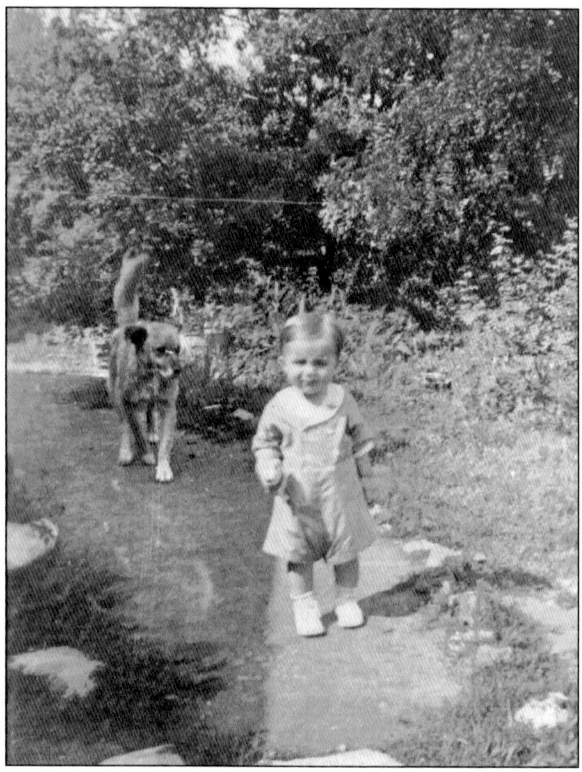

Harold Kitts plays with his dog in this c. 1933 photograph. Kitts (1936–1998) was a Knox County native who later lived in Blount County's Hubbard community with his wife, Jackie. (Courtesy of Jackie Tipton Kitts.)

Sam Tipton, son of George Tipton and Margaret Tuckaleechee Burchfield Tipton, was married to Nancy Abbott, daughter of John Abbott and Rhoda Lawson Abbott, on August 18, 1905, in Cades Cove. They had 10 children between 1906 and 1932. (Courtesy of Jackie Tipton Kitts.)

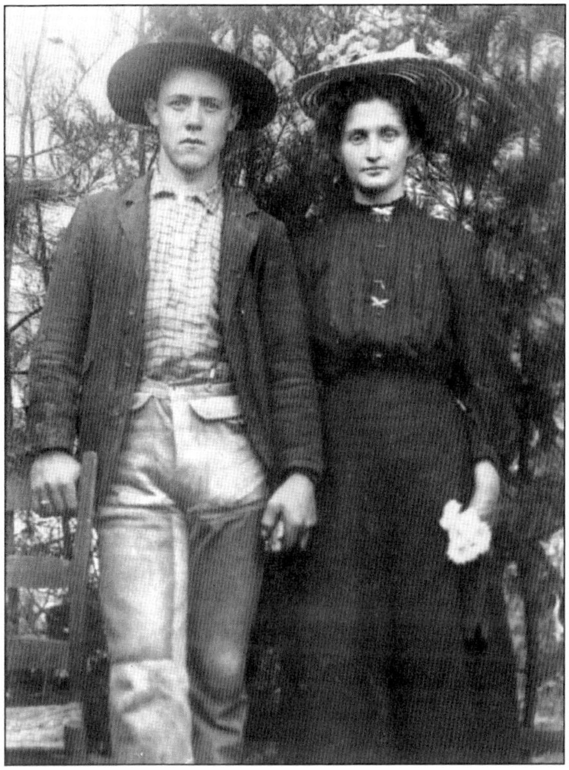

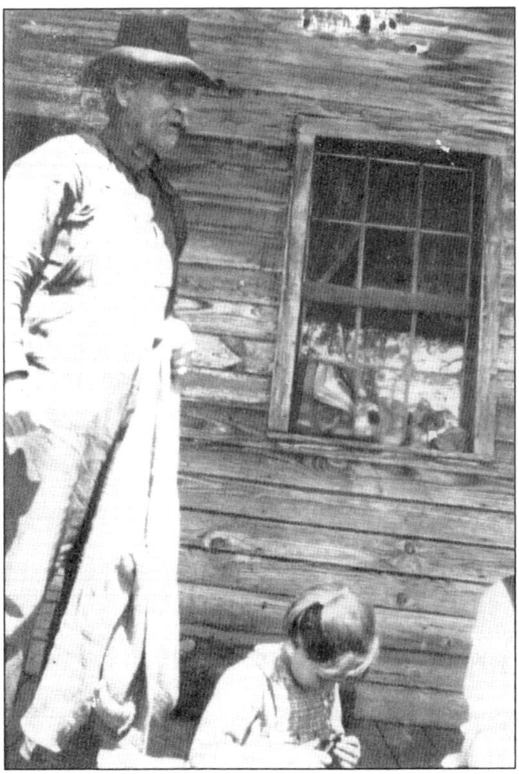

John Michael Garber (left) lived on Forest Hill Road with his wife, Martha Painter Garber. The Garbers donated a tract of land to Forest Hill Baptist Church on which the "new" cemetery is now located. With Garber at his home around 1920 is his granddaughter, Helen Parr Braden, who was about 7 years old. (Courtesy of Linda Braden Albert.)

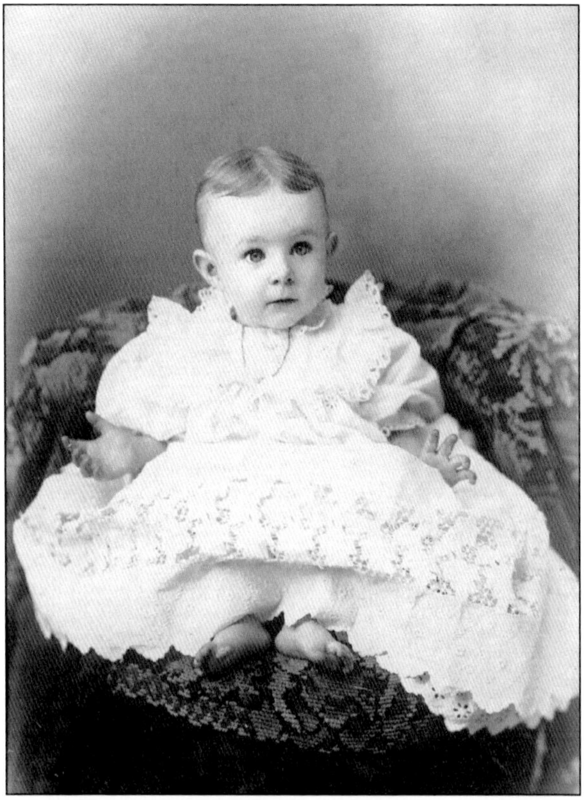

Cleo Ester Harper McCammon was born on September 15, 1901, to John and Annie Harper of Louisville. She was named Ester after a child born to family friends, the Kellers, who had died in infancy. Helen Keller, the famous blind and deaf educator, was the Kellers' niece. (Courtesy of Kathleen McCammon.)

Cleo Ester Harper McCammon (right) stands with her father, John Lonas Harper, near their Louisville home. (Courtesy of Kathleen McCammon.)

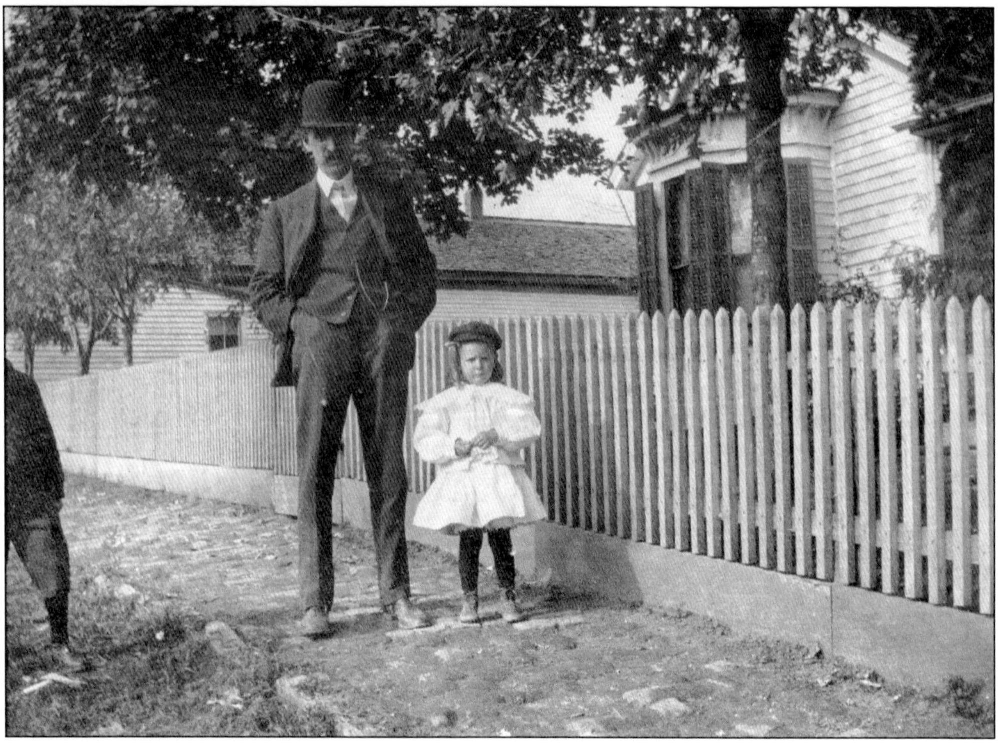

Andrew K. "A. K." Harper was one of three Harper brothers who moved to Blount County from Knox County in the late 1880s. He and his wife, Dora, lived in Maryville. The Harpers built the first library for the City of Maryville in honor of their son, Milton, who died in 1918 at the age of 31. The library was located on Church Street. The building housed the American Red Cross after a new library was constructed and is now the location of a retail business. (Courtesy of Kathleen McCammon.)

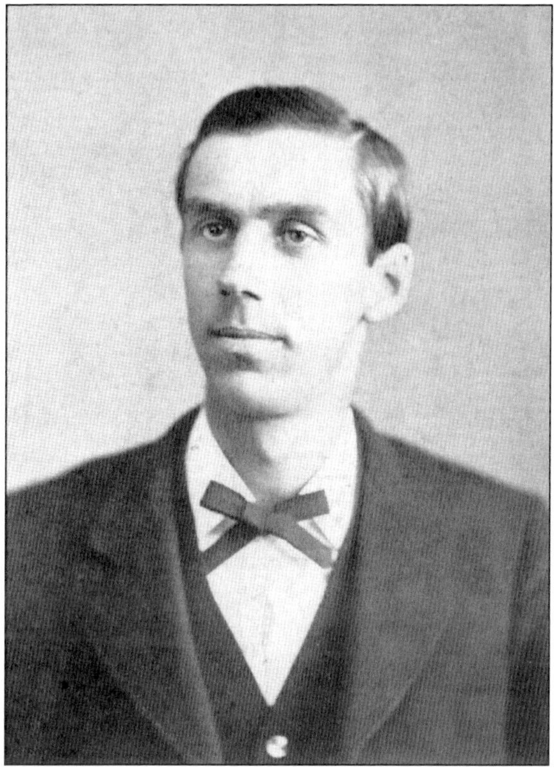

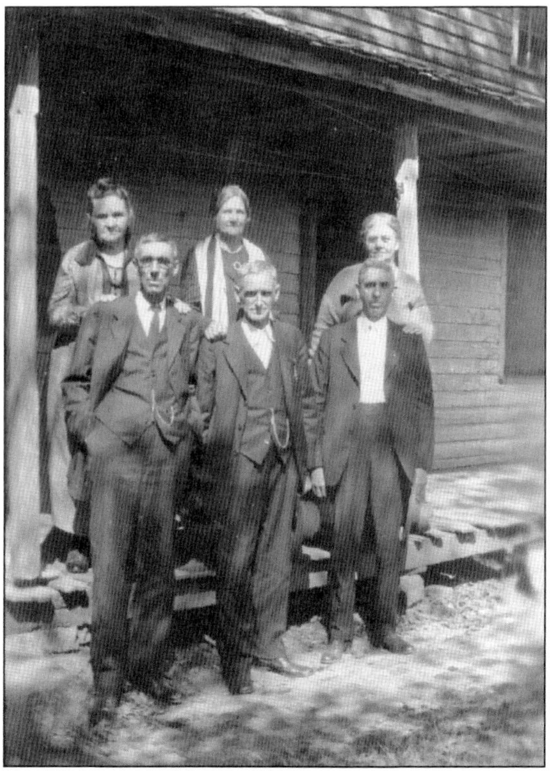

The Harper brothers, shown with their wives standing behind them, are, from left to right, Andrew K. and Dora; John L. and Annie; and Lafayette "Doc" and Mollie. The three brothers came to Blount County from Knox County in the late 1880s and became successful businessmen in Maryville and Louisville. (Courtesy of Kathleen McCammon.)

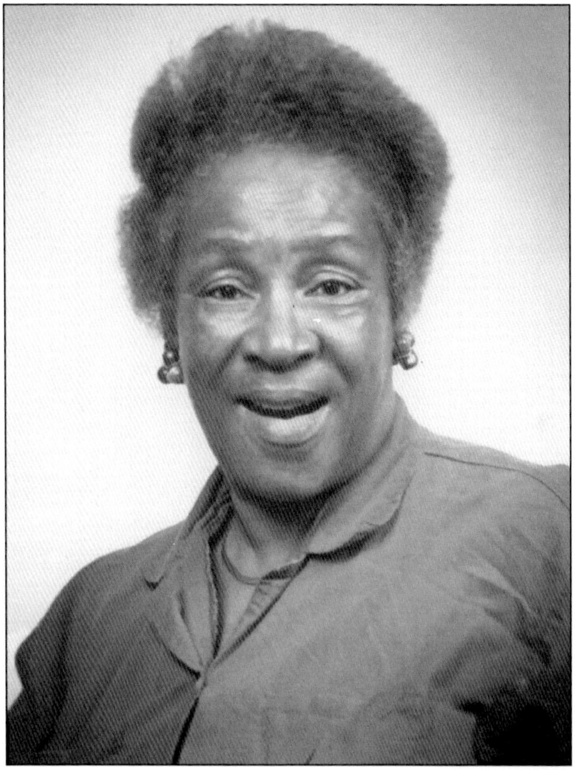

Folk artist Bessie Harvey, who lived in Alcoa, was born in 1929 in Dallas, Georgia, as the seventh of 13 children. She married at age 14, moved to Tennessee, and had 11 children for whom she struggled to provide. Harvey's creative outlet was to gather tree roots and branches and bring out the images she saw in them. She fashioned "dolls" in wood, often adding glitter, beads, even pieces of her own hair. The names of her pieces reflect her African American heritage. Harvey died in 1994, leaving a legacy of folk art that is exhibited in art galleries around the world. (Both, courtesy of Faye Dean.)

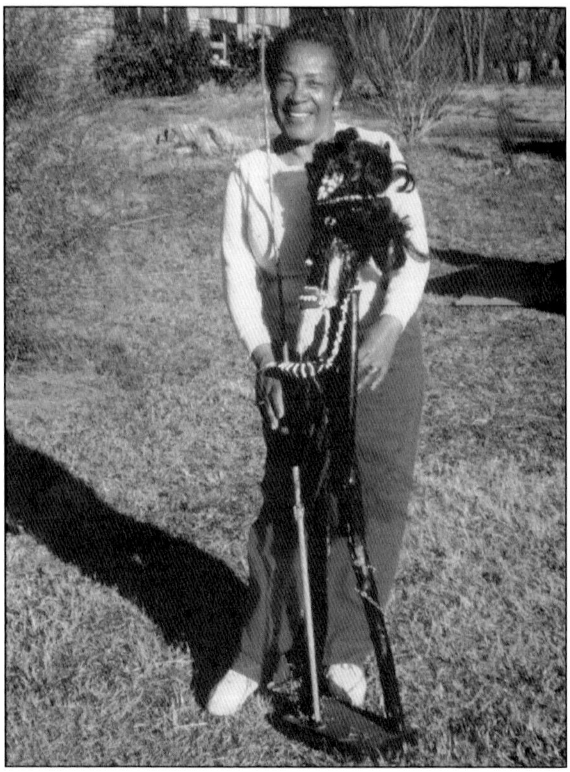

Fate and Mingie Bales are shown here on their wedding day. They lived in the Bales Hollow community of Friendsville. When Bales was called for military service in World War I, he caught the train at Friendsville and rode to Knoxville. Everyone was surprised when he soon returned home, but Bales explained the recruiters sent him home when they found out he had 10 children to support. When asked what he thought of the war, Bales said, "If it's farther than Knoxville, I don't want to go." (Courtesy of Paul Bales.)

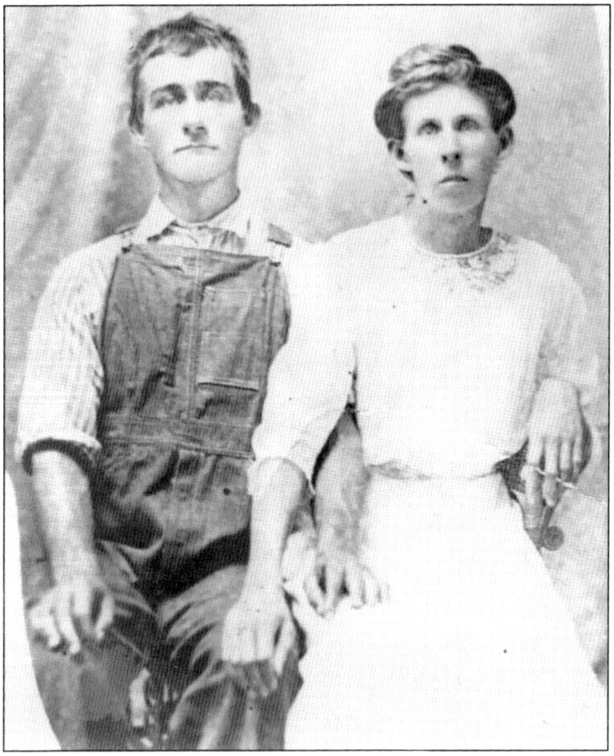

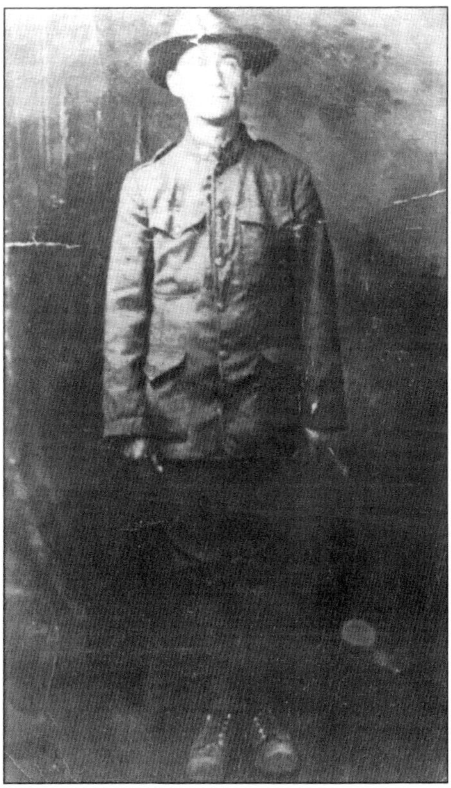

Fate Bales did not go to war during World War I, but he did have his photograph made at the recruiting office in uniform. He said the first thing new recruits did was to have a physical examination. If they passed, they were issued a uniform and were photographed, being told "You are now a soldier." However, Bales was dismissed from service due to his having a large family to support. (Courtesy of Paul Bales.)

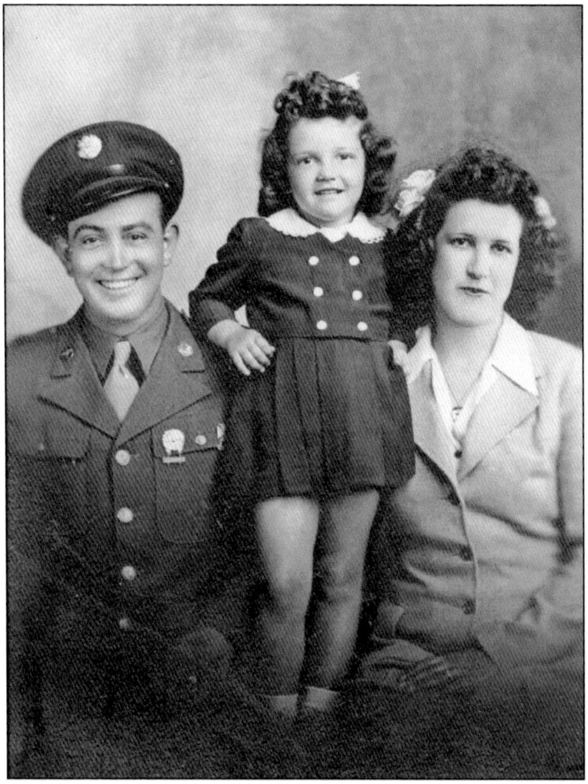

Shown here, from left to right, are Howard, Anita, and Pauline Wilson posing for a photograph. The Wilsons lived in the Forest Hill community and were active members at Forest Hill Baptist Church. (Courtesy of Paul Bales.)

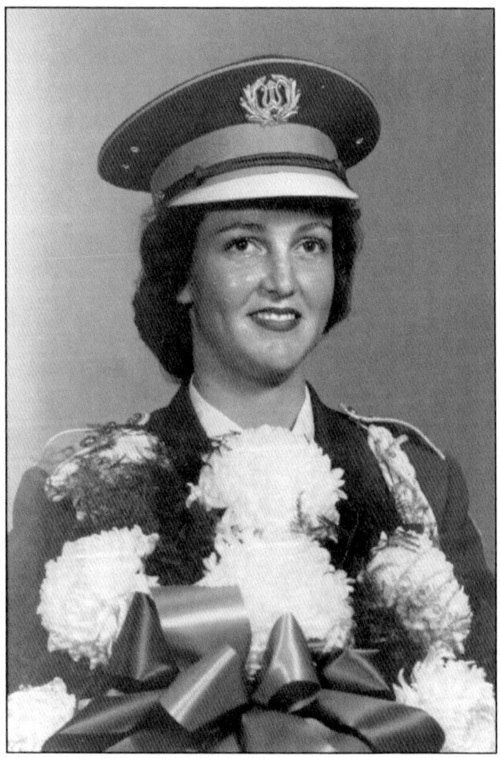

Anita Wilson Bales was the "band sponsor" at Everett High School during her senior year in 1959. The band sponsor walked with the drum major, leading the band. Ronnie Kerley was the drum major that year, Bales recalled. (Courtesy of Paul Bales.)

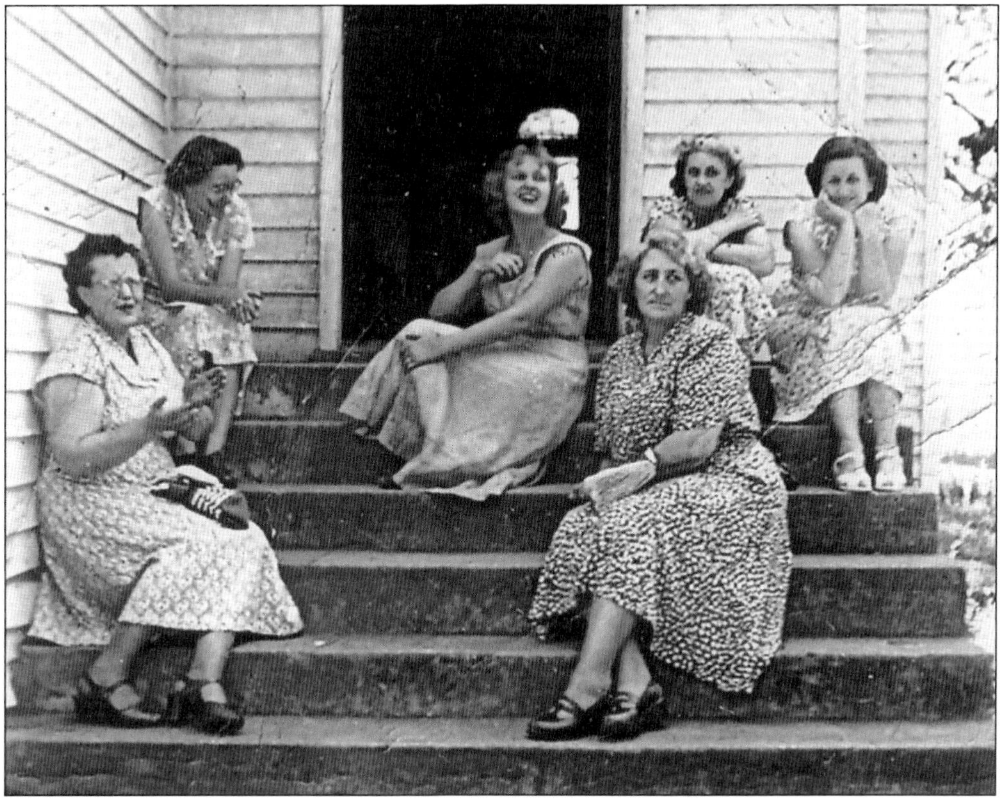

Friends enjoy visiting together around 1945. Clockwise from front left are Frankie Davis, Blanche Davis, unidentified, Nina Belle Coulter, Rita McNeilly, and Mamie West. (Courtesy of Margaret Davis Coulter.)

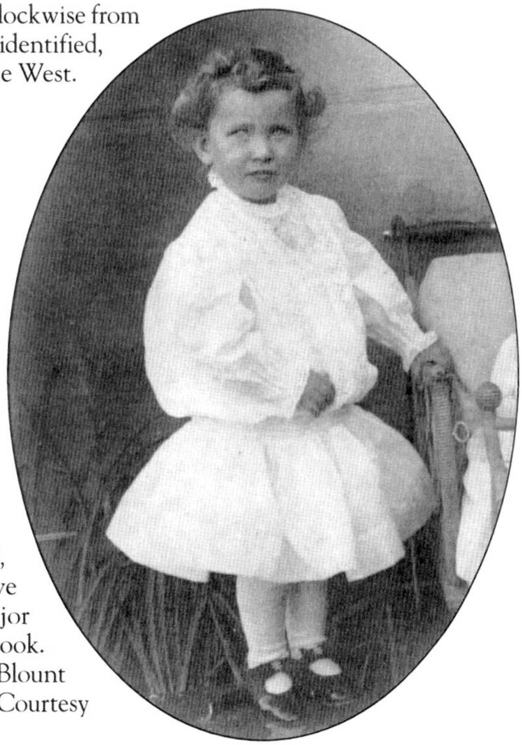

Inez Burns (1908–2004) is shown here as a baby. Burns had a passionate interest in history, later serving as the Blount County historian. Her book, *History of Blount County, Tennessee: From War Trail to Landing Strip, 1795–1955*, is considered one of the most comprehensive county histories in Tennessee and is a major source of the information included in this book. *History of Blount County* is available from the Blount County Genealogical and Historical Society. (Courtesy of Betty Boone Best.)

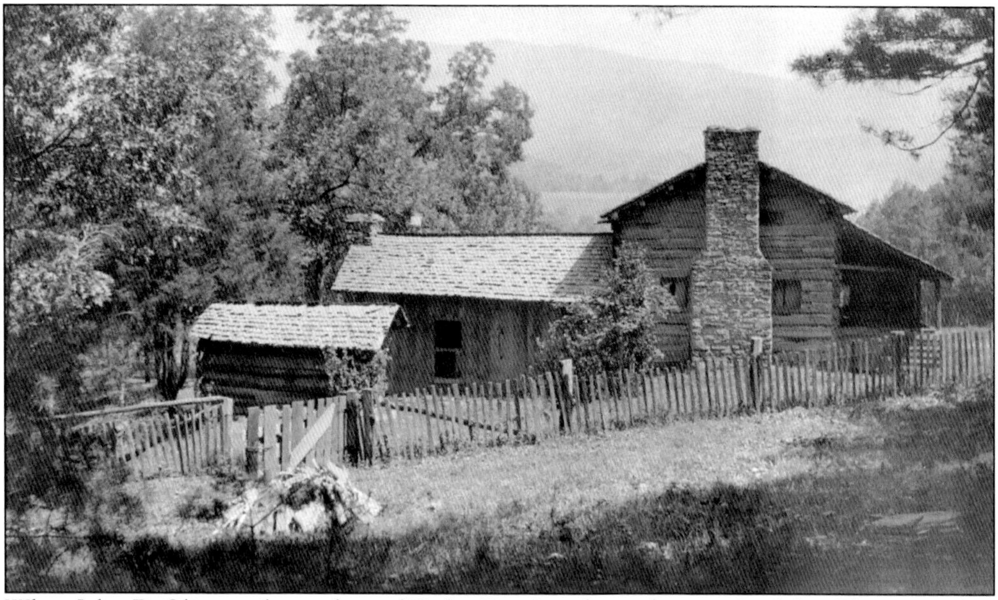

When John D. Oliver, a descendant of Cades Cove's earliest white settler, John Oliver, saw that Cades Cove people had lost the battle to save their homes from the creation of the Great Smoky Mountains National Park, he photographed many of the landmarks that would no longer be kept by the park service. One of those, which continues to be a tourist exhibit, was the Elijah Oliver home, shown here in 1934. (Courtesy of Stephen Weber.)

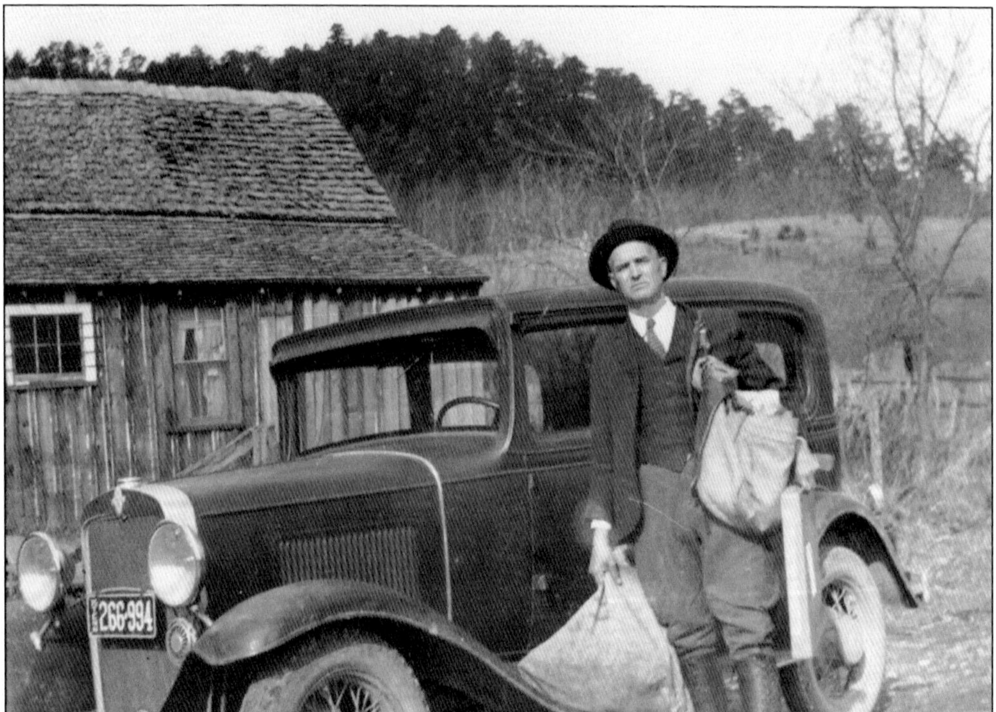

John D. Oliver delivered the mail in Cades Cove. He stands here with his mailbags, ready to run his route in the Cove. (Courtesy of Stephen Weber.)

Norma Singleton (Mrs. A. B. Smith) graduated in 1908 from Blount County High School, the only female in a graduating class of five. She was the commencement speaker, wearing this exquisite lace-trimmed dress that had been hand sewn by her mother. (Courtesy of Lorene Smith.)

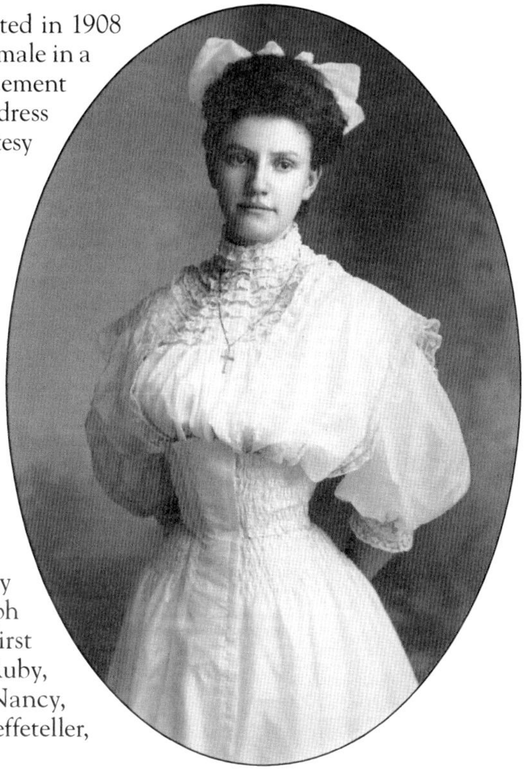

The family of Thomas Leonard and Nancy McDonell Teffeteller took time for a photograph around 1930. They are, from left to right, (first row) Gene, Cora Lee, Pauline, Thelma, Ruby, Annis, and Mary; (second row) Thomas, Nancy, and Harold. (Courtesy of Ron and Debbie Teffeteller, Martha Birchfield collection.)

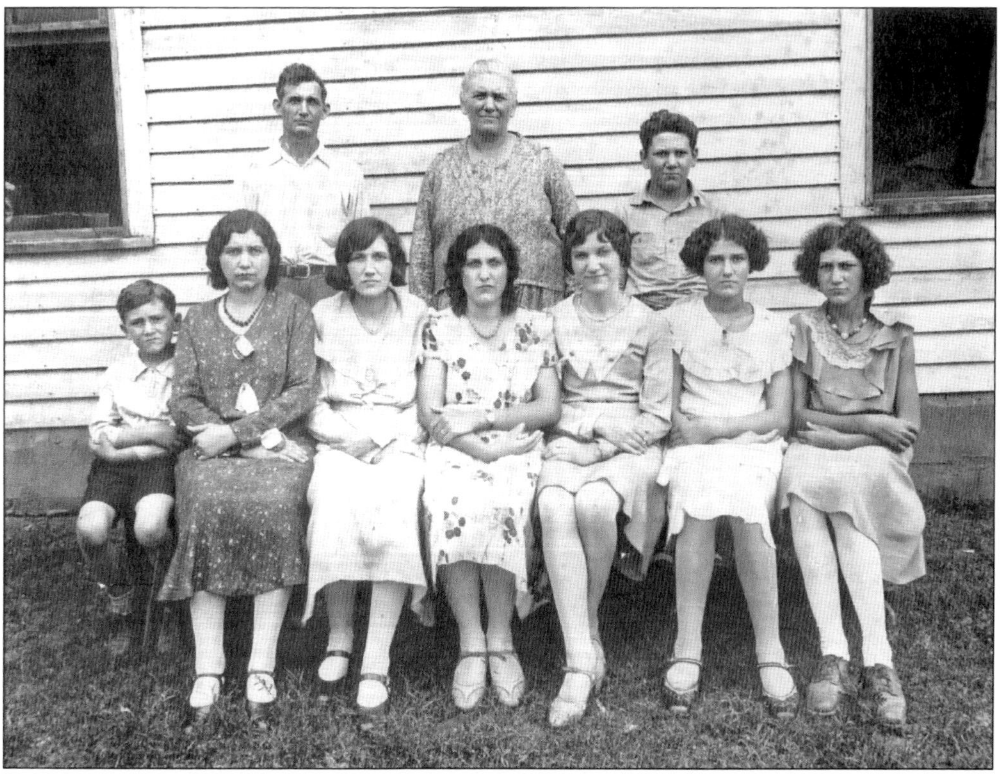

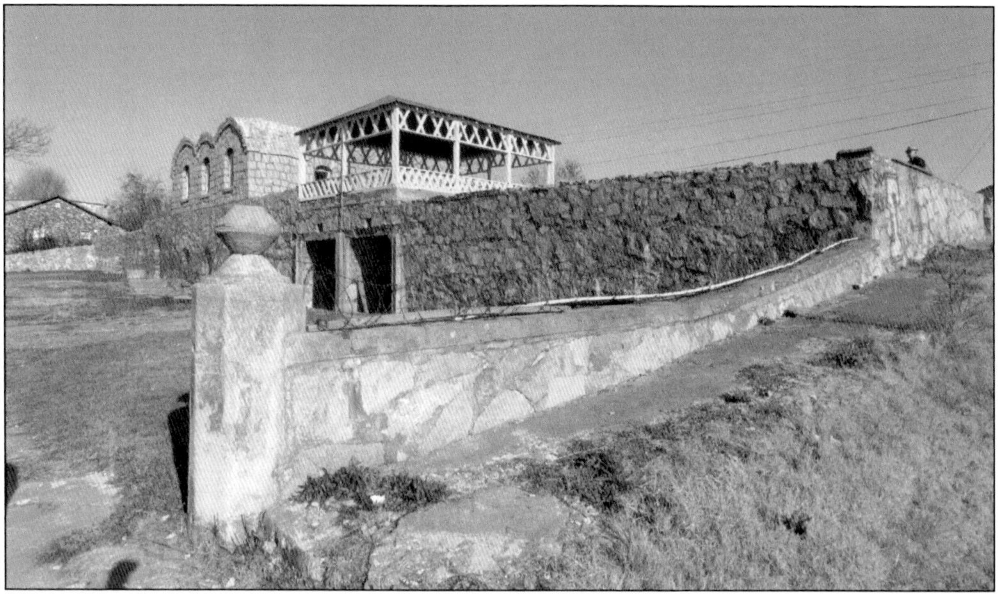

William Andrew and Fair Nicholson began building Stone Heaven, or Millennium Manor, in 1938 in Alcoa. No materials that could decay were used in construction other than the metal rods used to reinforce the stone and masonry because they thought the world would end in 1969 and 144,000 righteous would be left to witness the millennial reign of Christ. (Courtesy of the *Daily Times*.)

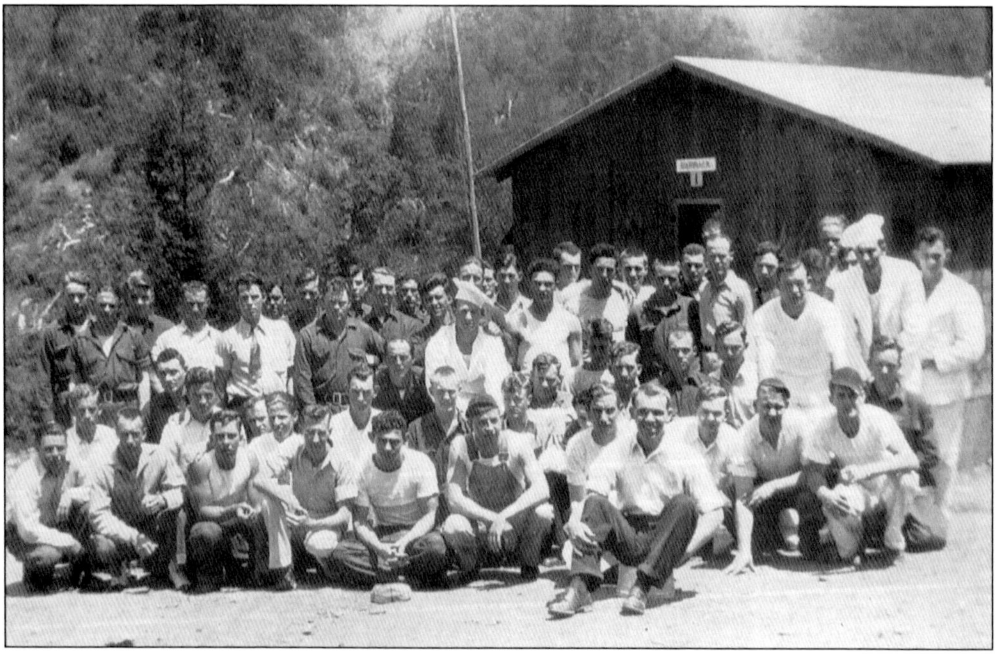

This group photograph of Civilian Conservation Corps (CCC) participants was taken at Tremont in 1933–1934. These young men built roads, bridges, trails, and facilities in the Great Smoky Mountains National Park. The Great Depression brought financial hardship, even disaster, to many families, and CCC provided work for many. CCC enrollees earned $30 monthly but received only $5 to spend; the rest was sent home to their families. (Courtesy of the Blount County Historical Museum.)

Anna Coltharp Irwin is shown here as a young reporter with the *Daily Times*, Maryville. The award-winning journalist gained the respect of her peers and the community at large with her fair and accurate reporting. Irwin served as a mentor to many young journalists and photographers, giving them valuable advice and encouragement as they progressed in their careers. She died in 2007. (Courtesy of the *Daily Times*.)

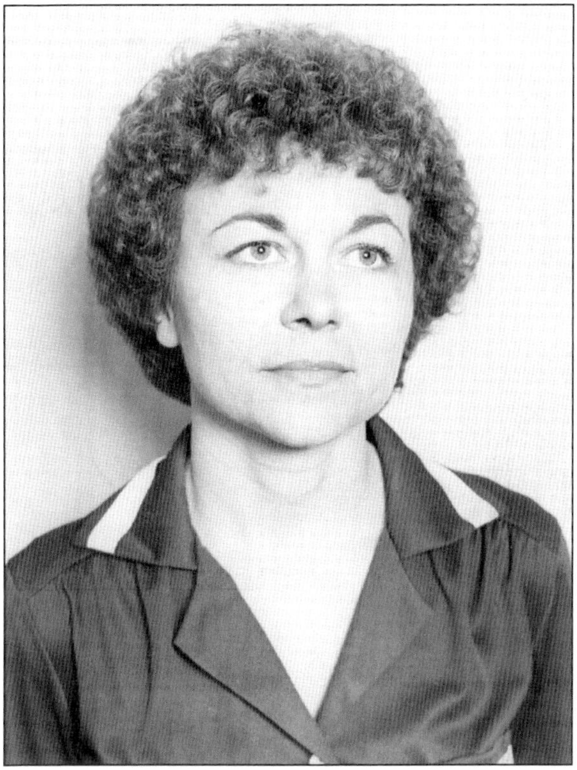

The wedding of Bob Huff and Irene Tedford was held at Fairview United Methodist Church in its original white-frame building. Attendants included the bride's sisters, Helen and Nancy. The Huff family continues to be active in the church. (Courtesy of Fairview United Methodist Church.)

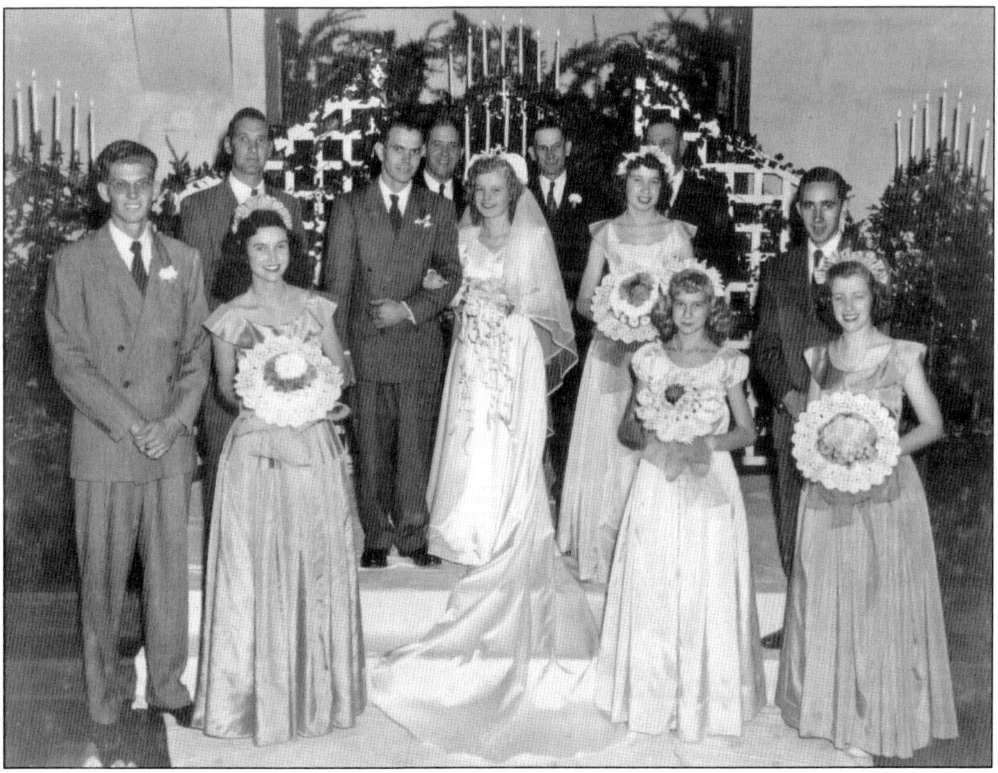

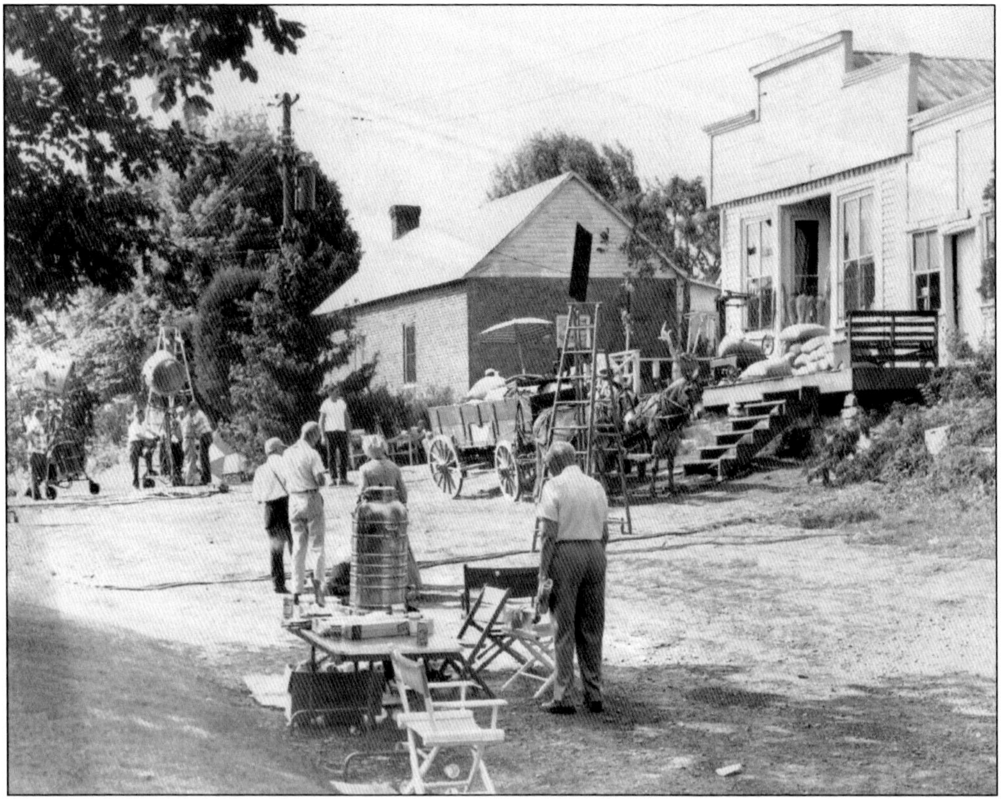

Blount County has been the location of several movies such as *The Fool Killer*, filmed at the Harper Brothers Store in Louisville. The movie, released in 1965, starred Anthony Perkins, of the famed *Psycho*, and young Edward Albert. (Courtesy of the *Daily Times*.)

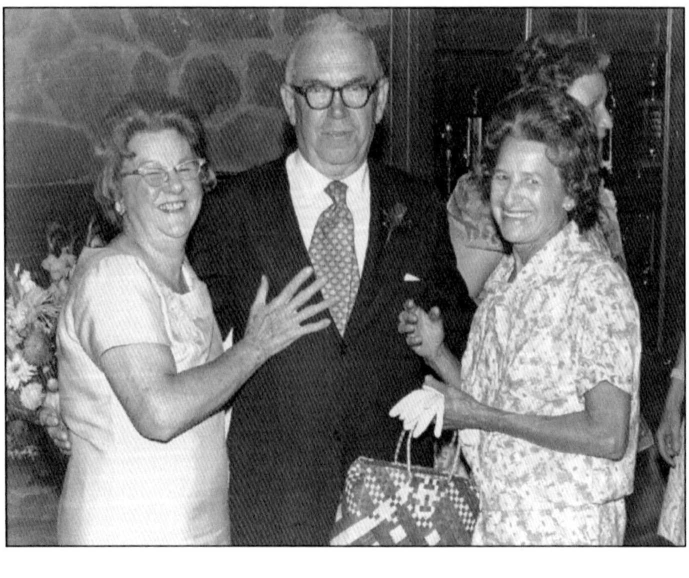

John Dixon Harper, a native of Louisville, began his lifelong career with the Aluminum Company of America (Alcoa, Inc.) in 1925. He rose through the ranks to head the corporation as president in 1963 and as chairman and chief executive officer in 1970. Harper is pictured here (center) with his two "favorite cousins," Irene Harper Haley (left) and Cleo Harper McCammon. (Courtesy of Kathleen McCammon.)

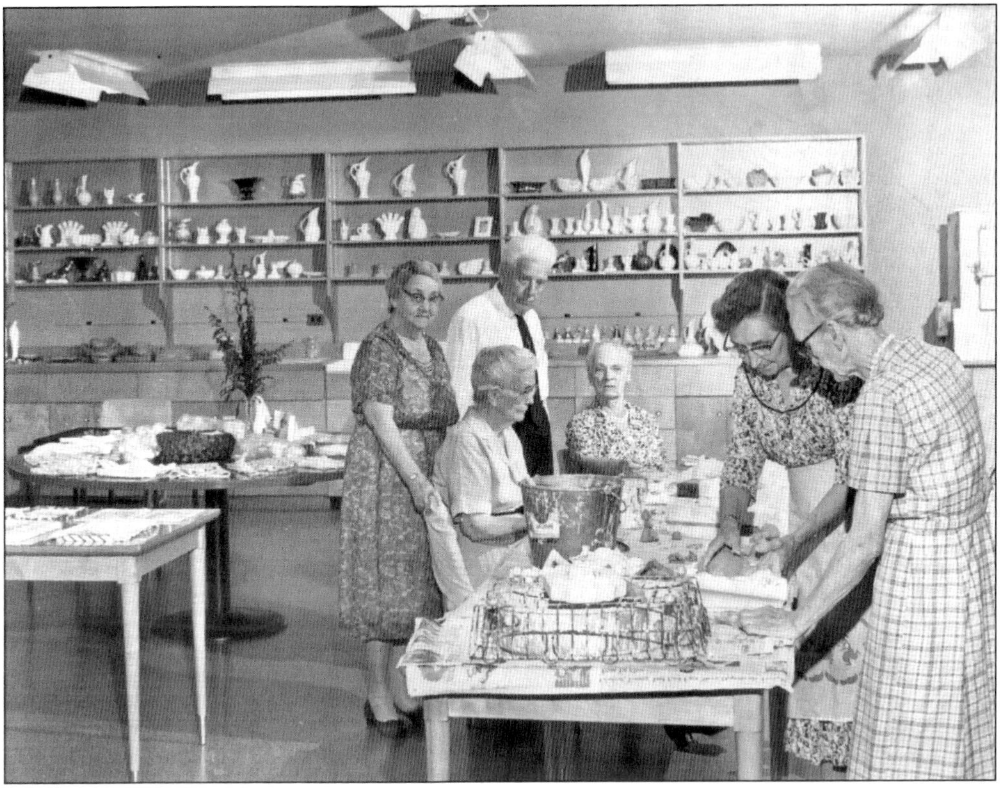

Residents of Asbury Acres, a retirement home built by the United Methodist Church on Sevierville Road, enjoy the craft room at the center in this 1962 photograph. Asbury Acres was formally opened in February 1960. It is now called Asbury Place. (Courtesy of the *Daily Times*.)

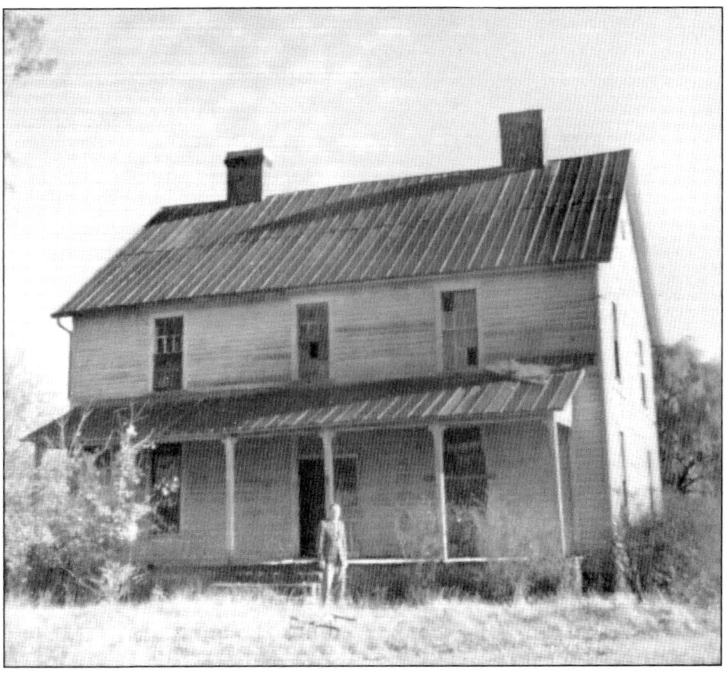

The Blount County Poor Farm, on County Farm Road in the Alnwick community, operated from about the time of the Civil War to 1955 and housed individuals who were unable to work and had no one to care for them. William Blount High School is now located on the site. (Courtesy of Paul Bales.)

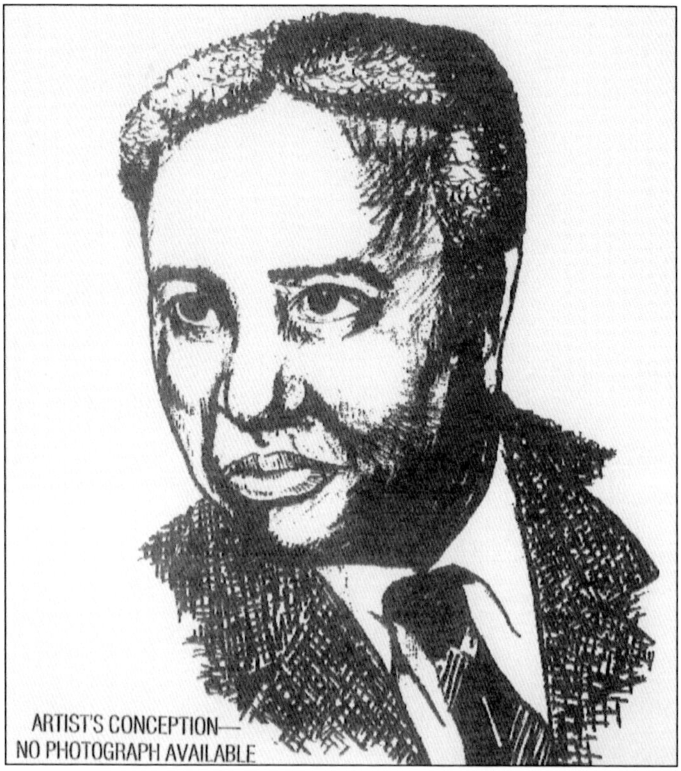

William B. Scott, born in 1821 in North Carolina, moved to Blount County in 1847 and established a saddle- and harness-making business in Friendsville. At the end of the Civil War, Scott and his son moved to Nashville and founded the *Colored Tennessean*, the first newspaper published by an African American in Tennessee. In 1868, they returned to Blount County and published the *Maryville Republican*. Scott was subsequently elected mayor of Maryville, the city's only black mayor to date. (Courtesy of the Blount County Historical Museum.)

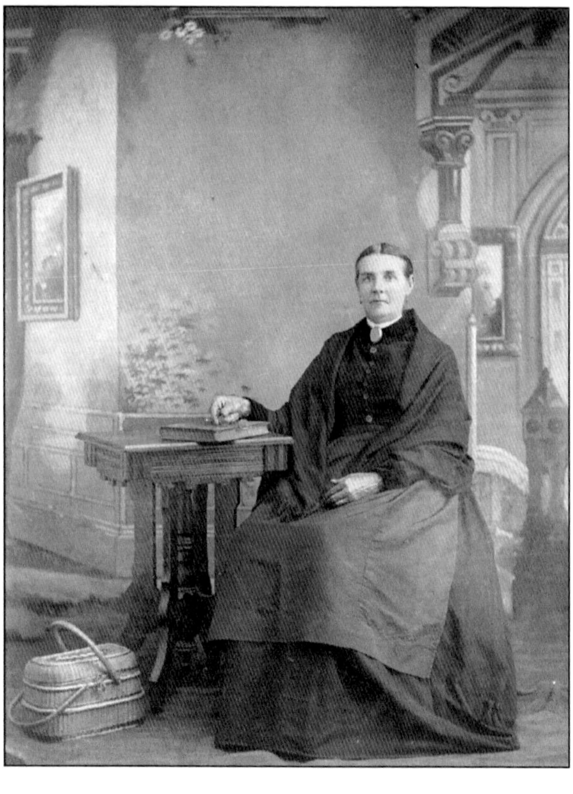

Dora Reagan Harper, wife of Andrew K. "A. K." Harper, is pictured at home on Main Street (Broadway) in Maryville. The home was located near the present-day Citizens Bank of Blount County. (Courtesy of Kathleen McCammon.)

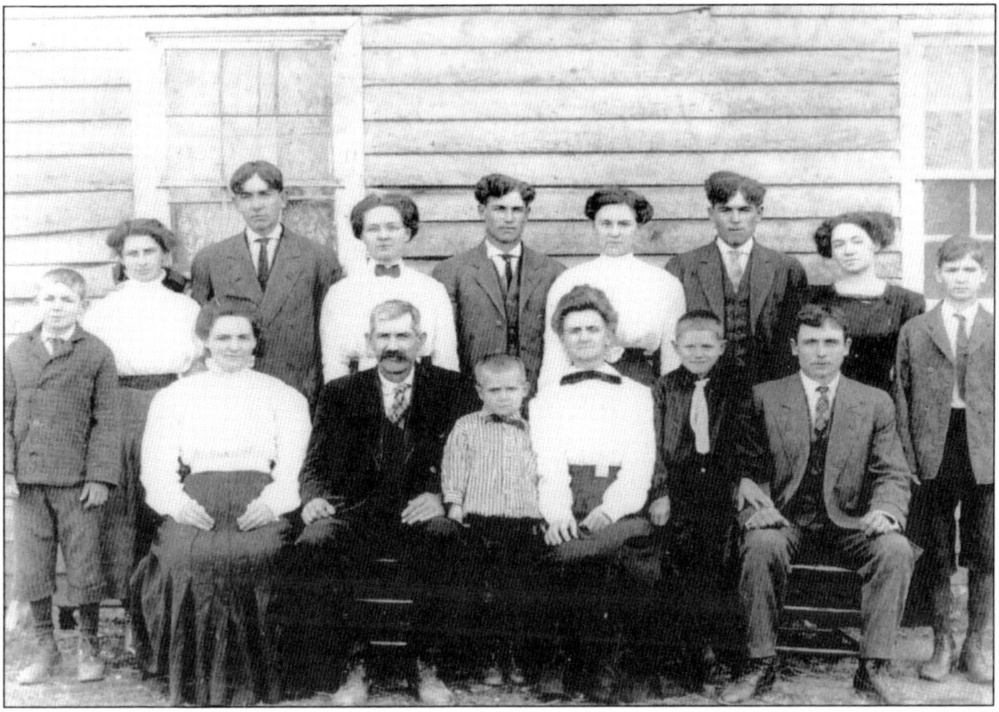

William Tolton Renfro and Lelia Clemens were married in 1879 and were the parents of 13 children. Shown in this *c.* 1908 photograph are, from left to right, (first row) Mamie Elizabeth, William Tolton, James Henry, Lelia, Paul, and Spence Clemens; (second row) Charlie, Margaret Luella, Samuel Robert, Alice Sarah, Homer Herman, Leila Mae, John Ross, Carrie Florence, and William. Six of the siblings died between 1912 and 1917. (Courtesy of Jack and Delores Renfro.)

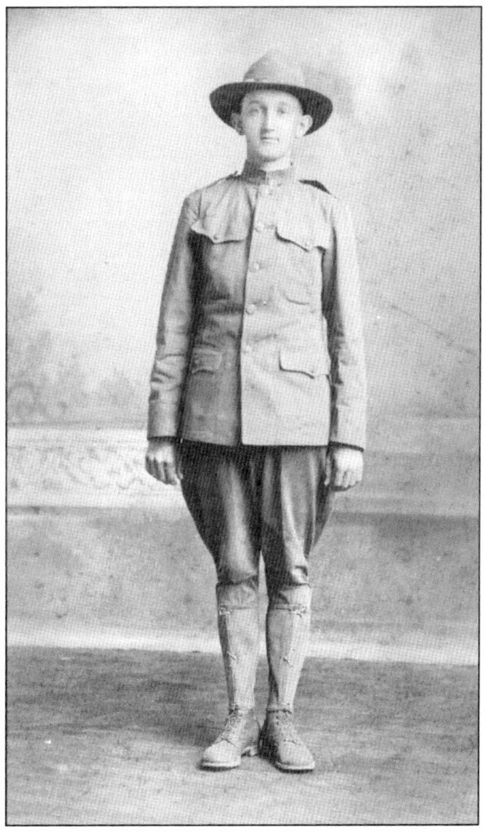

Ernest Avery "Abe" Braden stands in his uniform during World War I. Braden served in the National Guard. (Courtesy of Ron and Debbie Teffeteller, Martha Birchfield collection.)

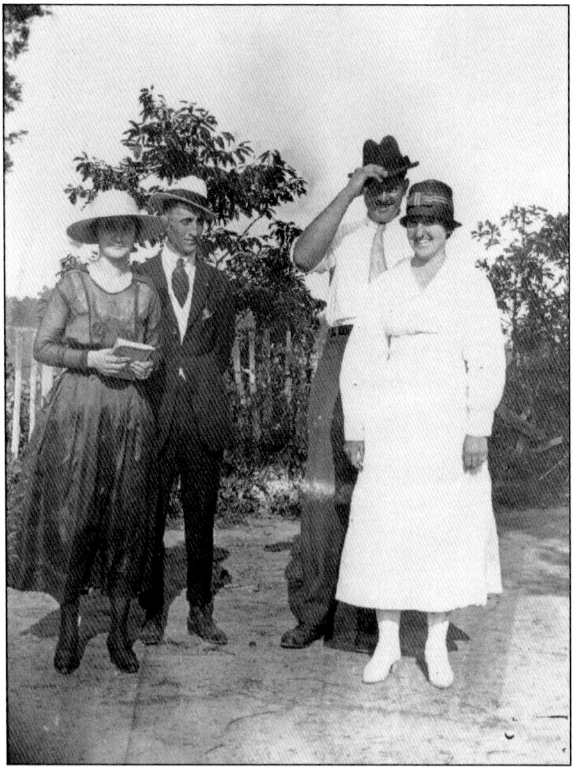

Shown here in the 1930s are, from left to right, Ruby Thompson LeQuire; her husband, Milton LeQuire; her brother, Ollie Thompson; and her sister-in-law, Johnnie Braden Thompson. (Courtesy of Ron and Debbie Teffeteller, Martha Birchfield collection.)

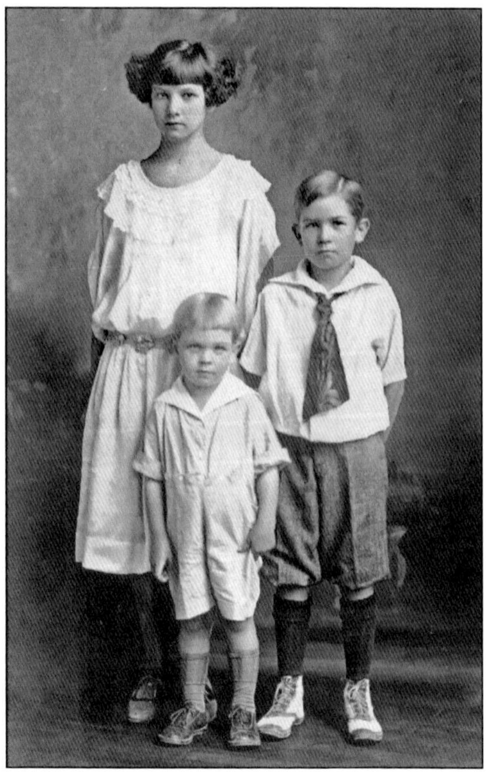

Siblings Mildred, Toll, and Charles "Shorty" Coulter, children of Jesse Tolton and Margaret Everett Coulter, appear clockwise from back left in this c. 1922 photograph. (Courtesy of Margaret Davis Coulter.)

The Davis children often visited the home of Andrew Coulter, who lived at Coulter's Bridge on Tuckaleechee Pike. Sisters, from left to right, Mary Lois, Nola, and Margaret Davis stand here on the one-lane bridge that was replaced in the 1990s with a two-lane road more suitable for modern travel. (Courtesy of Margaret Davis Coulter.)

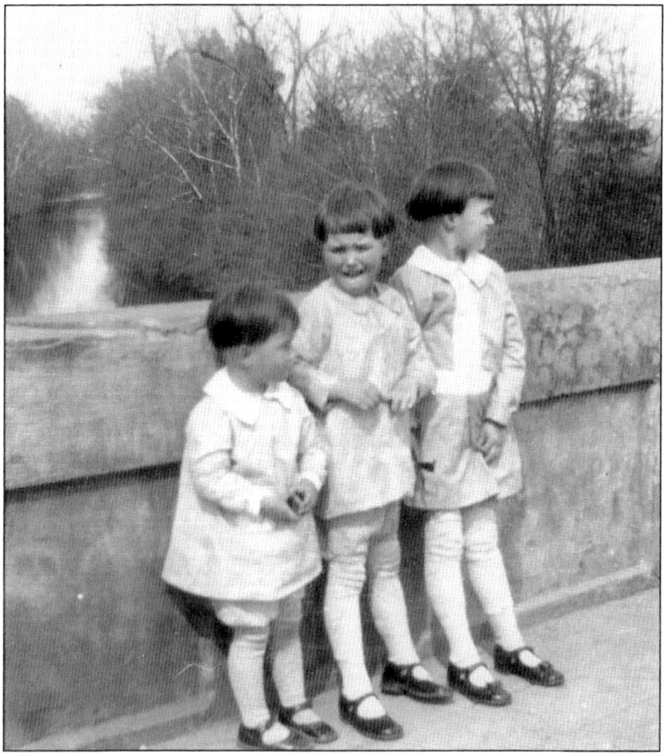

Christina Key Johnson (left) and John Wesley Johnson, a Civil War veteran, are pictured here at their home at Union Grove near Friendsville in 1914. The bicycle at left belonged to their son, Isaac Johnson. (Courtesy of Terry Huffstetler.)

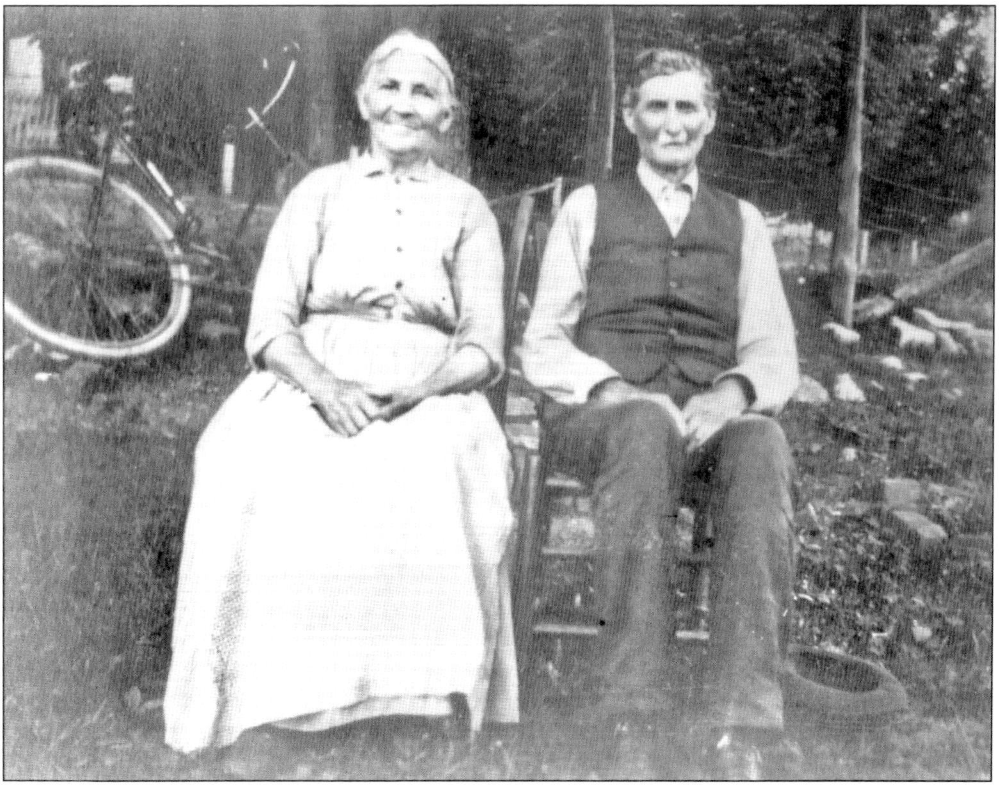

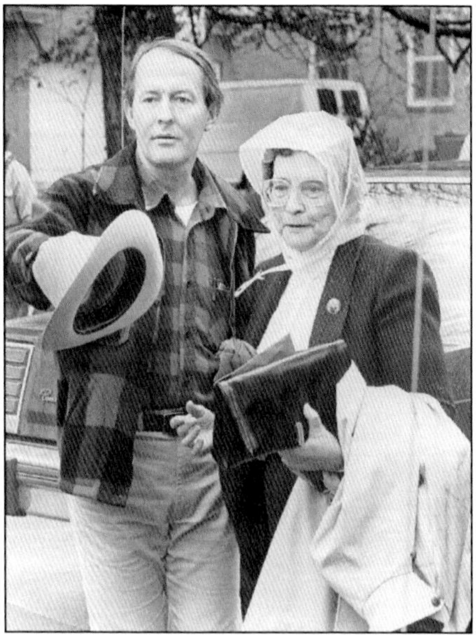

Lamar Alexander, a native of Maryville, is shown here in his famous red-checked shirt, his trademark during his run for governor of the State of Tennessee. He was elected governor in 1978 and reelected in 1982. With him is his mother, Flo Alexander, who started the first kindergarten in Maryville. Lamar Alexander was subsequently elected to the U.S. senate, where he continues to serve in 2009. (Courtesy of the *Daily Times.*)

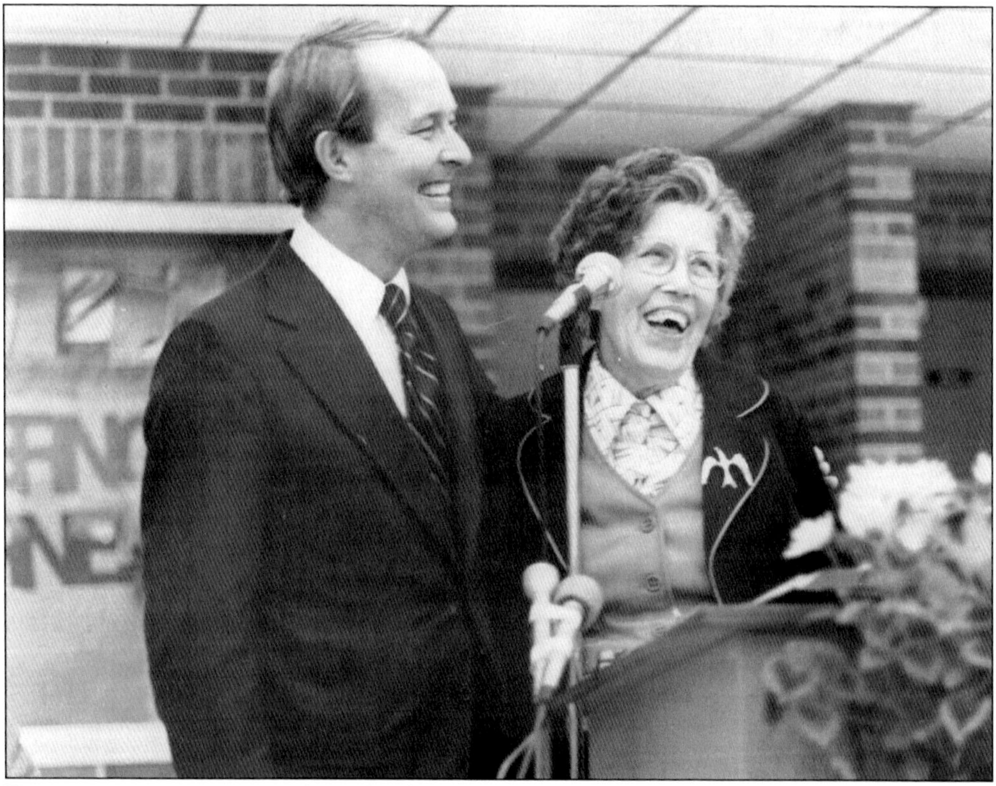

Tennessee governor Lamar Alexander shares a laugh with Elsie Burrell around 1978. "Miss Elsie" taught classes from first grade through college during her 44-year career. She came to Blount County in 1942 as an elementary school supervisor, retiring from the school system in 1969. She volunteered many hours to the Great Smoky Mountains National Park, including acting as a "school marm" at Little Greenbrier School and leading old-fashioned spelling bees attired in pioneer costume. She died in 2000. (Courtesy of the *Daily Times.)*

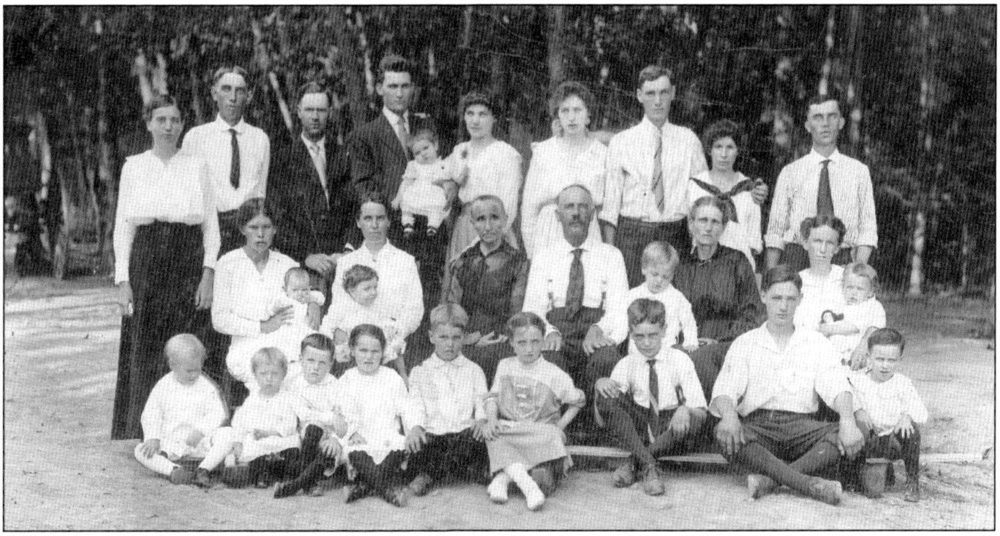

A family group poses for a photograph at their home. Let this be a lesson to all those interested in preserving history: Record names, dates, and a short description of the event on the backs of photographs. This unknown group photograph belonged to the late Rev. Bill Manning. (Courtesy of Javonna Manning.)

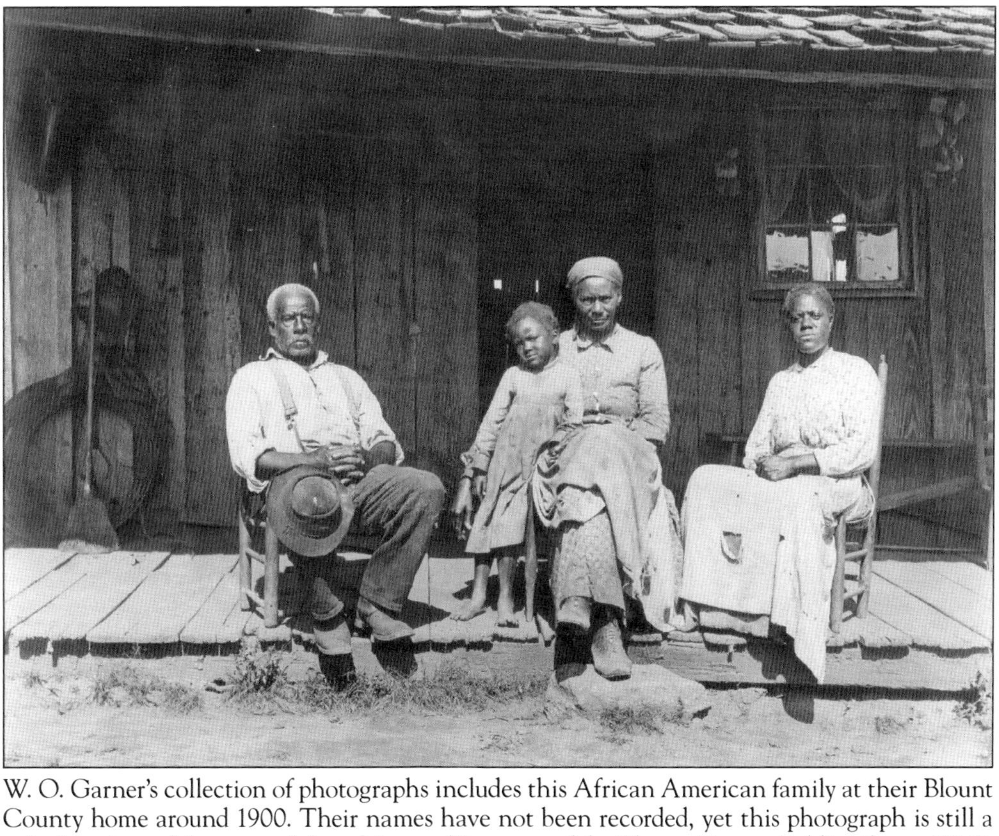

W. O. Garner's collection of photographs includes this African American family at their Blount County home around 1900. Their names have not been recorded, yet this photograph is still a valuable piece of the county's long history. (Courtesy of the Blount County Public Library, W. O. Garner collection.)

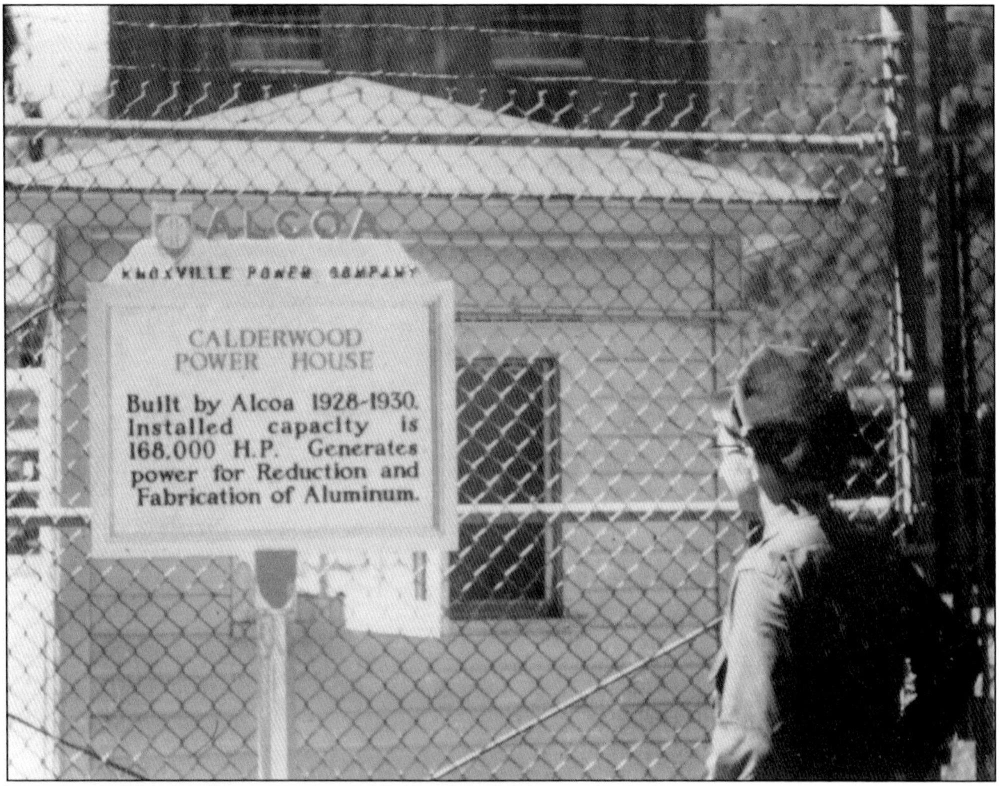

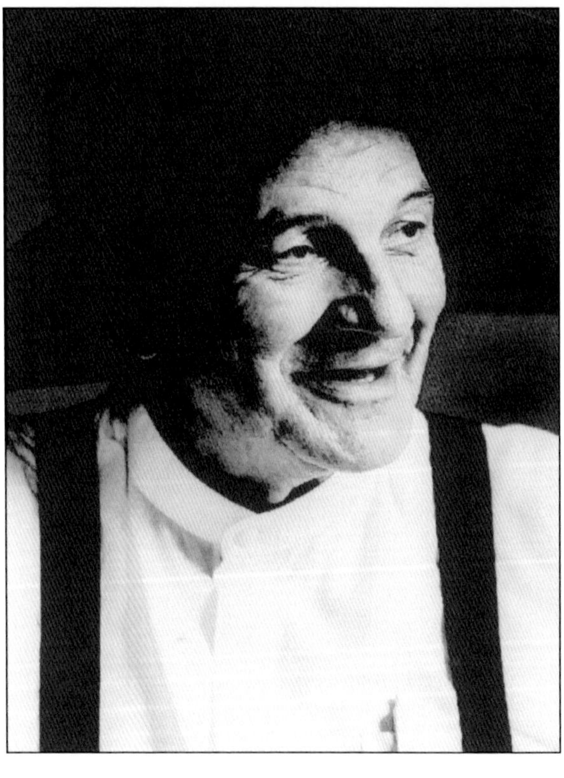

Calderwood Dam was built by the Aluminum Company of America from 1928 to 1930. Water flowed from the dam through a tunnel of solid rock into the power plant, with turbines sending power over high-tension lines to the aluminum plants in Alcoa. Hubert "Doc" Braden, shown above, served as a guard at the power plant around 1940. (Courtesy of Linda Braden Albert.)

George Henry, Friendsville historian, and his wife, Betty, dress as members of the Society of Friends (Quakers) to present programs on Friendsville's history. They are members of the Friendsville Friends Meeting. (Courtesy of the *Daily Times*.)

Seven

SPOTLIGHT ON HISTORY

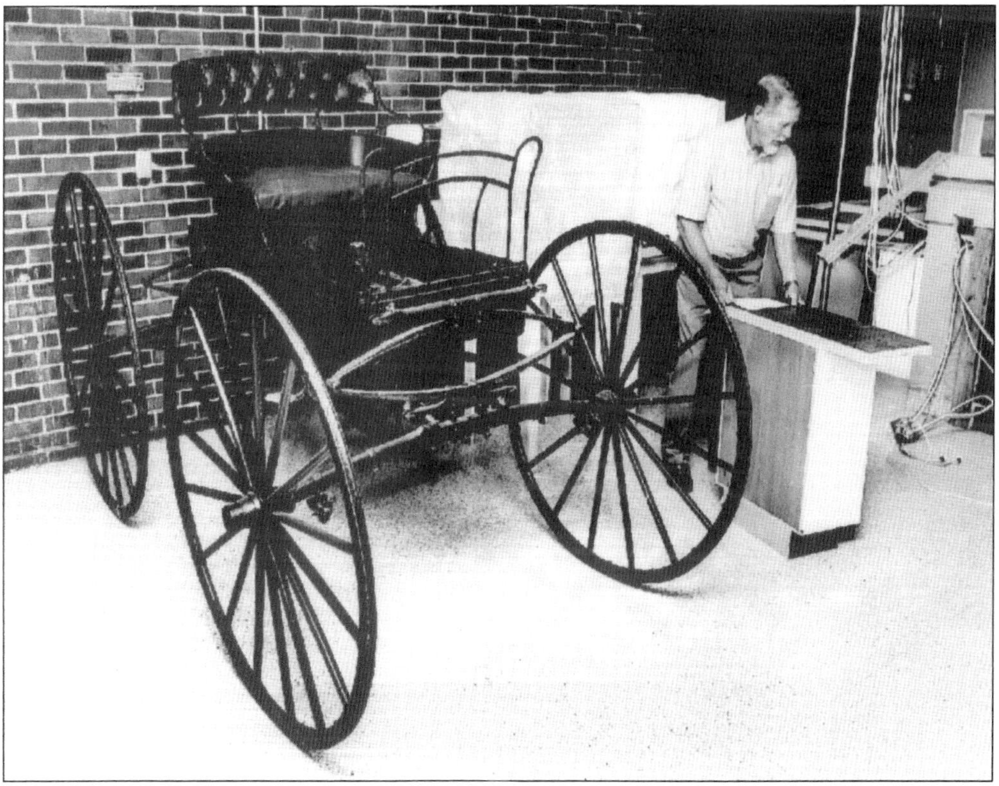

B. Kenneth Cornett works on an exhibit at the Blount County Historical Museum, located at 1004 East Lamar Alexander Parkway, Maryville. The buggy was donated to the museum by Herman and Betty Boone Best. The museum will benefit from the sale of this book. (Courtesy of the *Daily Times*; photograph by Daryl Sullivan.)

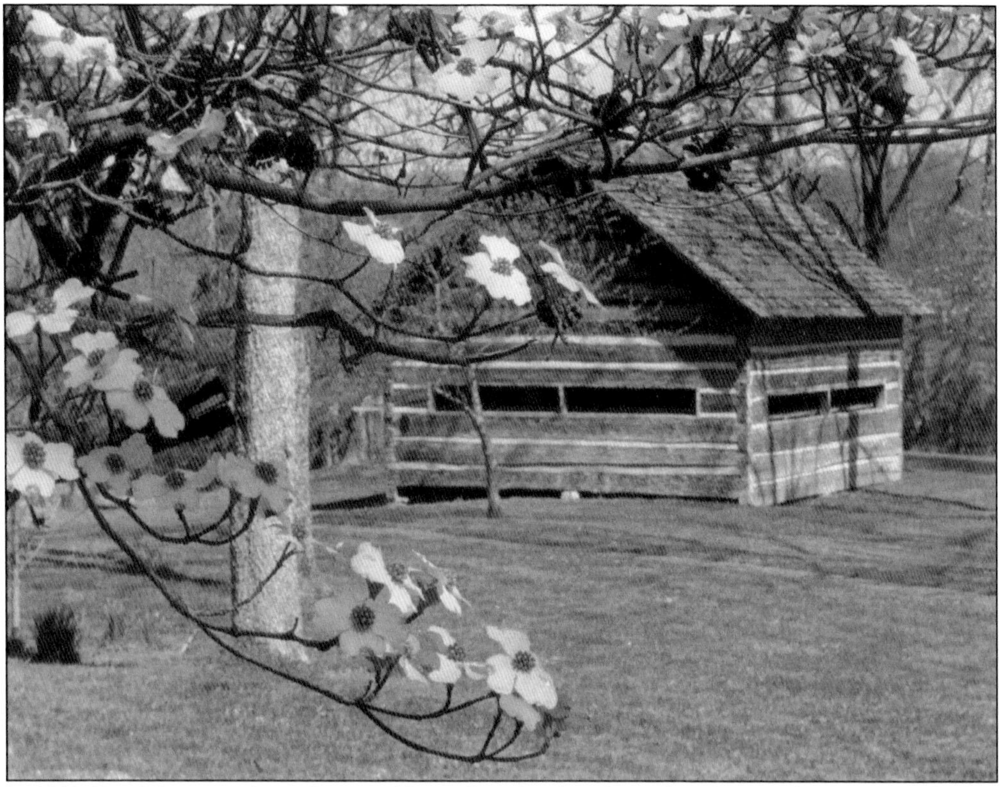

In 1812, Sam Houston, then 19 years old, taught school in this cabin that was built in 1794, before Tennessee became the 16th state added to the Union. Tuition was $8 per term, with payment accepted in corn, calico, and cash. The schoolhouse, shown above in 1995, is now one of Blount County's historic treasures. (Courtesy of the *Daily Times*.)

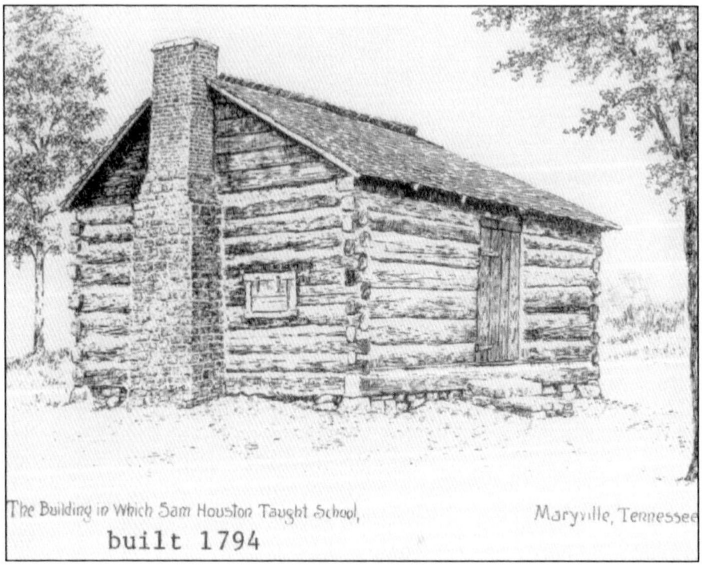

This drawing of the Sam Houston Schoolhouse shows how it looked in its early days. The school was built by the Kennedy and McCullough families to educate the children of the Wildwood community. (Courtesy of the Sam Houston Schoolhouse Association.)

Sam Houston's portrait hangs in the museum at the Blount County site that bears his name. After spending his youth and young adulthood in Blount County, Houston was governor and U.S. congressman for Tennessee, president and general of the Army of the Republic of Texas, and governor and U.S. senator for the State of Texas. (Courtesy of the Sam Houston Schoolhouse Association.)

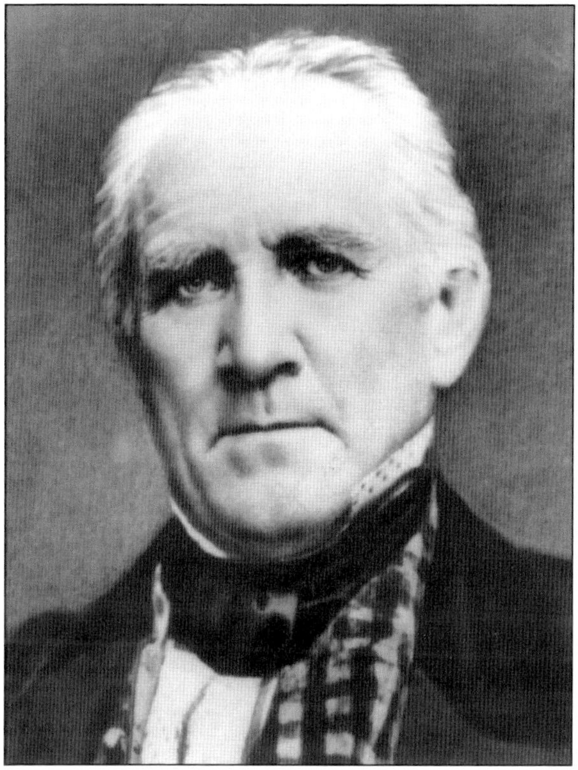

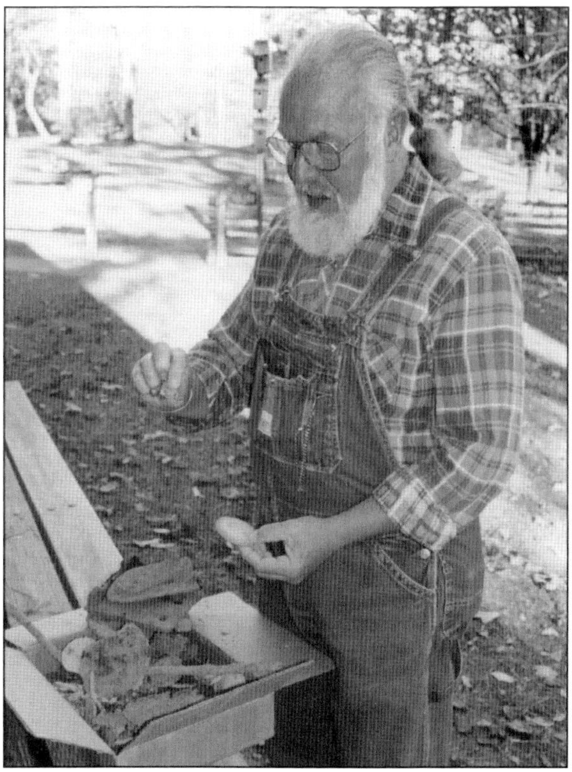

The Sam Houston Historic Schoolhouse was fortunate to have Ralph Grindstaff as its resident manager for several years until illness forced him to retire in 2007. Grindstaff often dressed as Sam Houston would have done in his days of living with the Cherokee and presented programs on the grounds to schoolchildren and others. He died in 2008, leaving the grounds in the capable hands of Mary Lynn and Bob Bell. (Courtesy of Linda Braden Albert.)

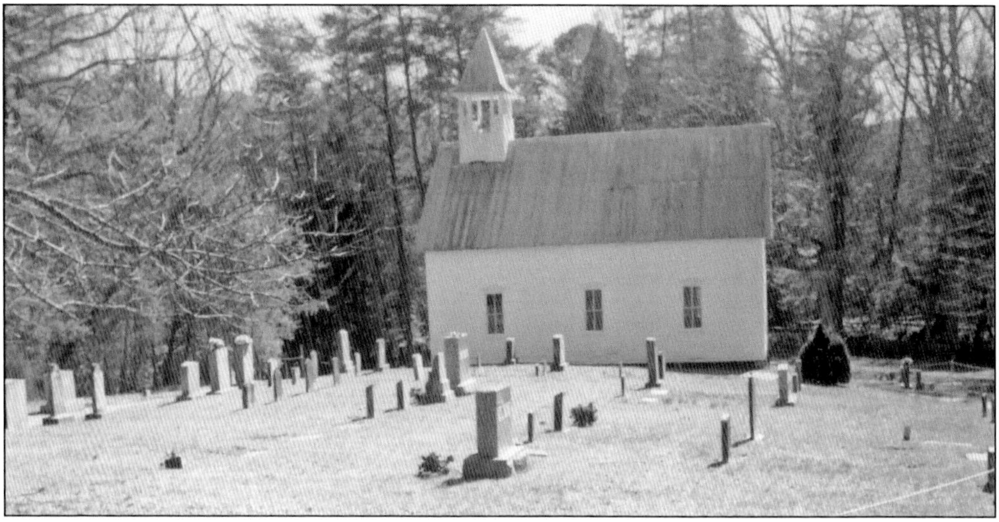

The Methodist church in Cades Cove and its adjoining cemetery benefit from the efforts of Cades Cove Preservation Association (CCPA). In partnership with the Great Smoky Mountains National Park Service, CCPA volunteers keep the churches clean and maintain the cemeteries to preserve the heritage of the mountain community that draws millions of visitors annually. Members present programs to the community and display relics from the cove in the Cades Cove/Thompson-Brown House Museum, Maryville. CCPA will also benefit from the sale of this book. (Courtesy of Linda Braden Albert.)

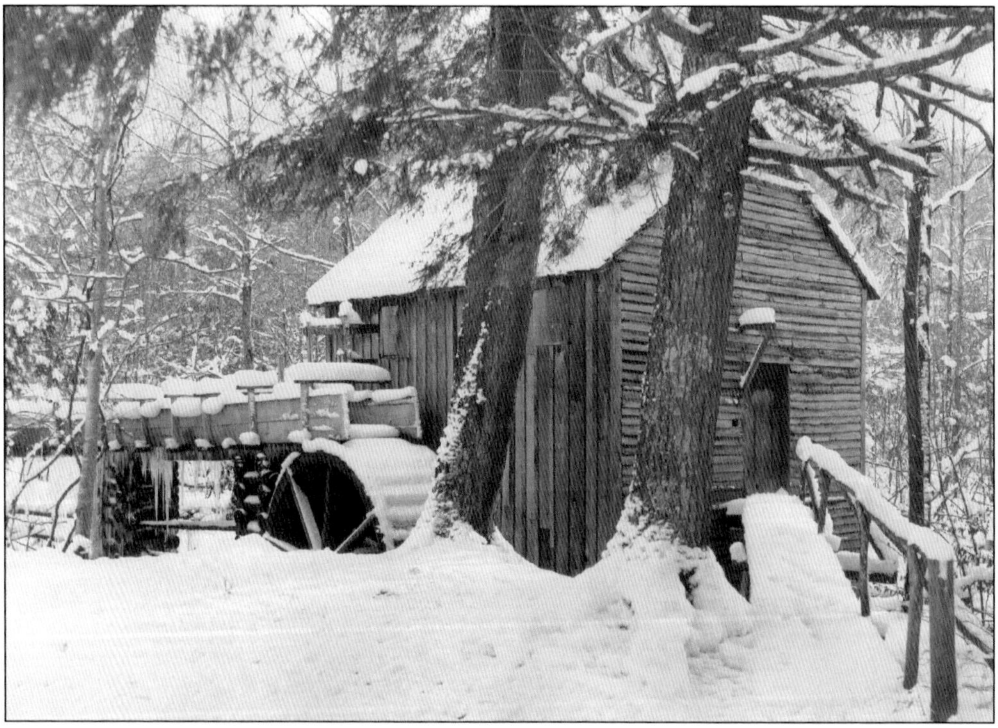

Shown here around 1995, the Cable Mill in Cades Cove was owned by the Cable family before the Great Smoky Mountains National Park was formed. The gristmill harnessed the waters of Mill Creek to grind flour and corn meal for the citizens of the cove. (Courtesy of the *Daily Times*.)

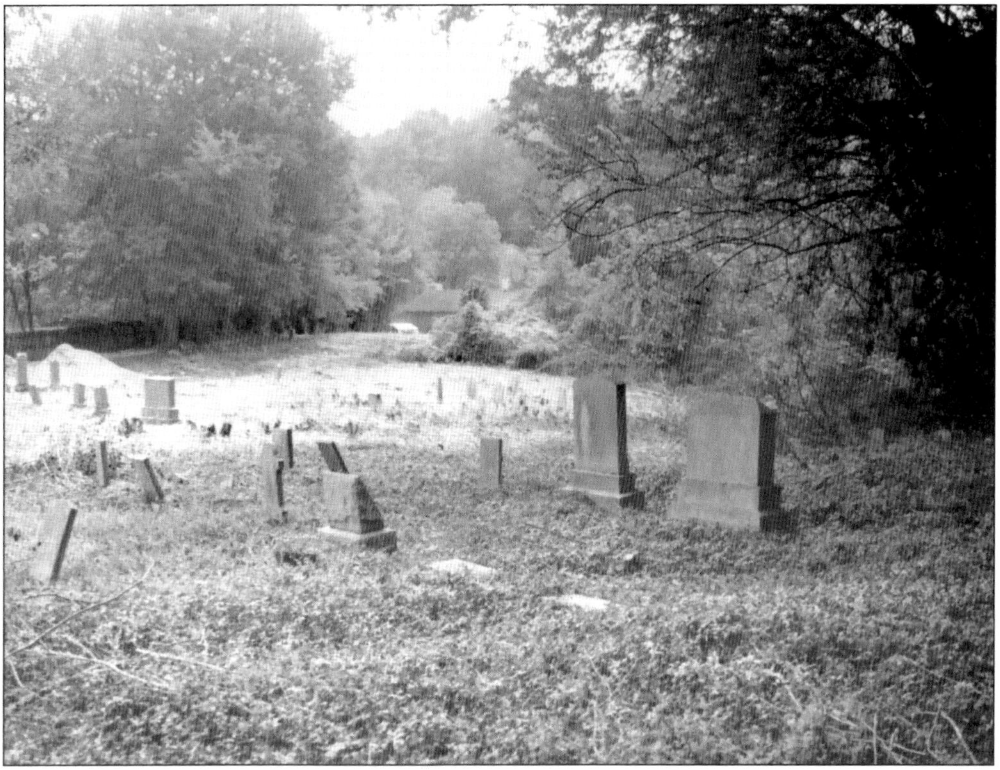

Mt. Moriah Cemetery in Louisville was almost completely lost until volunteers, led by B. Kenneth Cornett, began clearing brush, cutting trees, filling depressions, and finding and repairing tombstones that had fallen into disrepair. The undergrowth at the right of the photograph, taken in 2004, is how the entire cemetery looked before work began. Cornett was recognized for his efforts by the East Tennessee Historical Society in 2005. (Courtesy of Linda Braden Albert.)

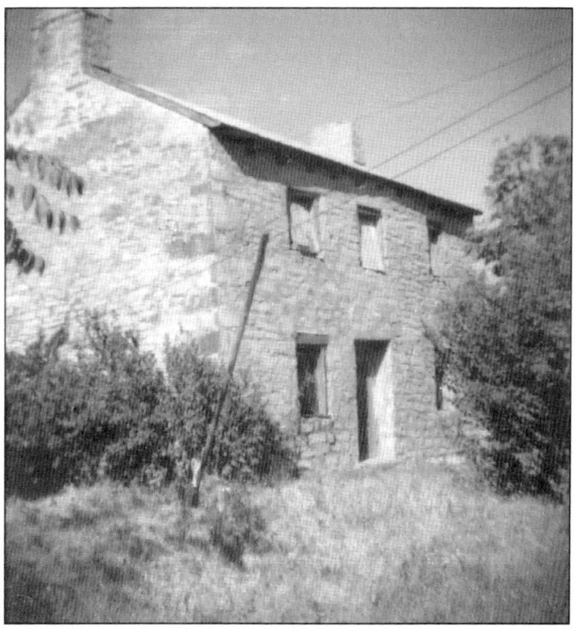

"The Old Stone House" on Big Springs Road between Greenback and Friendsville is shown here in 1956. The house, built by Samuel Frazier around 1772 of hand-quarried marble, is the oldest house still standing in Blount County and is said to have stood in three states—North Carolina, the State of Franklin, and Tennessee—without having been moved. It has been restored by current owners Anne and Frank Landers. (Courtesy of Alleen Powlus.)

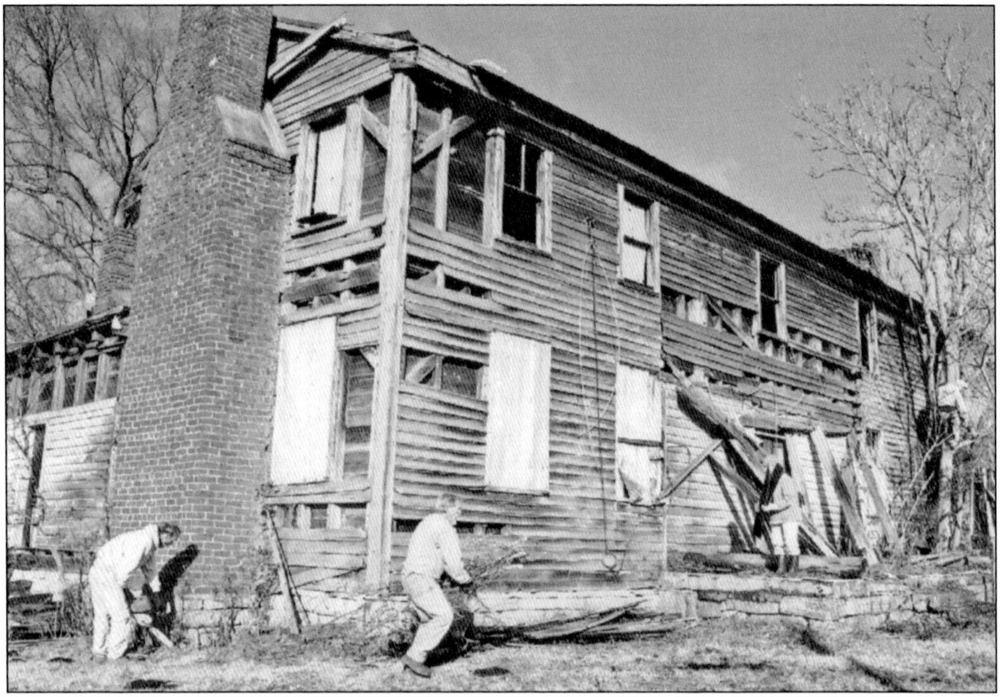

Construction on the Warner Martin Mansion in the Wildwood community began in 1793 and was completed by 1800. The entire house, framing and weatherboarding, were slash sawed from heart of pine found on the property. Efforts to save the historic structure are currently underway as a project of Blount County Historic Trust. Above, volunteers work to clear trees and brush encroaching on the house in 2008. The photograph below shows one of the fireplaces in the home. (Both, courtesy of the *Daily Times*; photographs by Mark A. Large.)

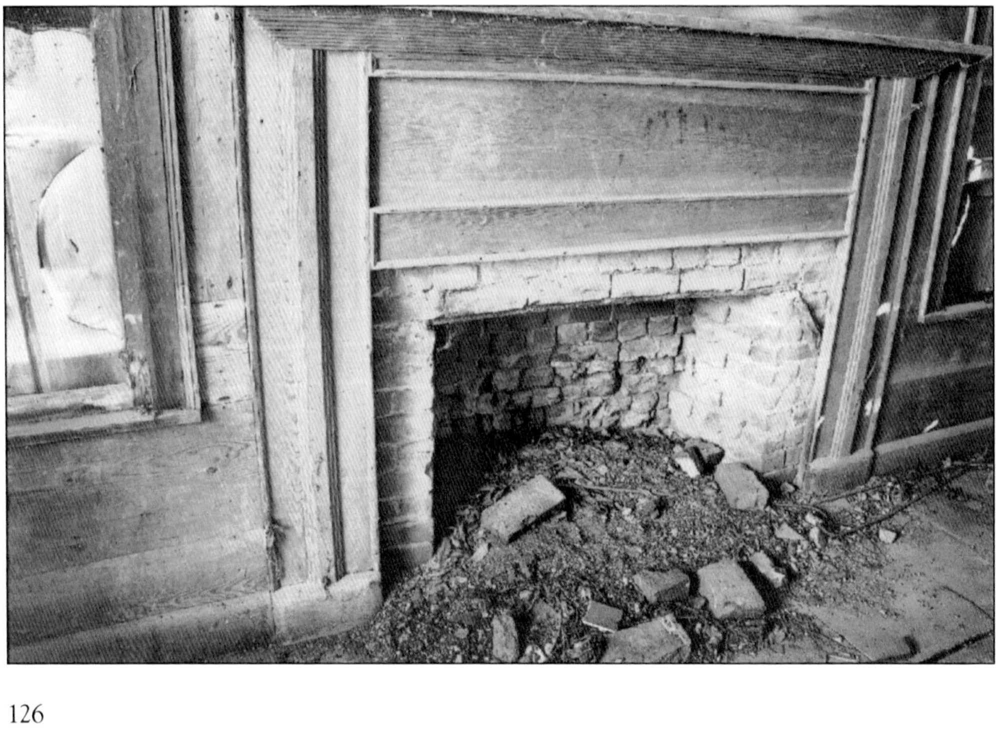

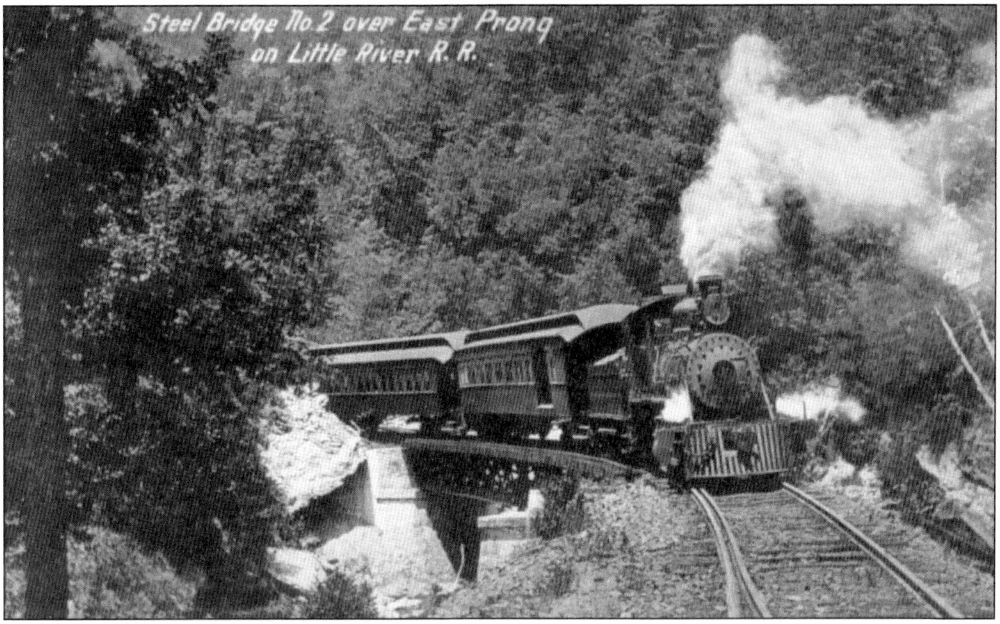

The Little River Lumber Company was chartered in February 1901, operating a logging operation based in Tuckaleechee Cove. The town that sprang up around the camp was named Townsend in honor of Col. W. B. Townsend, superintendent of the logging operations. Little River Railroad was chartered nine months later and was built along Little River to facilitate getting the cut timber out of the mountains. In 1926, Townsend sold almost 80,000 acres to the State of Tennessee to become part of the Great Smoky Mountains National Park, with the company retaining some cutting rights. The Townsend sawmill officially closed in 1938, and the railroad abandoned the line in 1939. The present road between Townsend and Elkmont is built on the old railroad bed. Learn more about this at the Little River Railroad and Lumber Company Museum in Townsend. (Both, courtesy of B. Kenneth Cornett.)

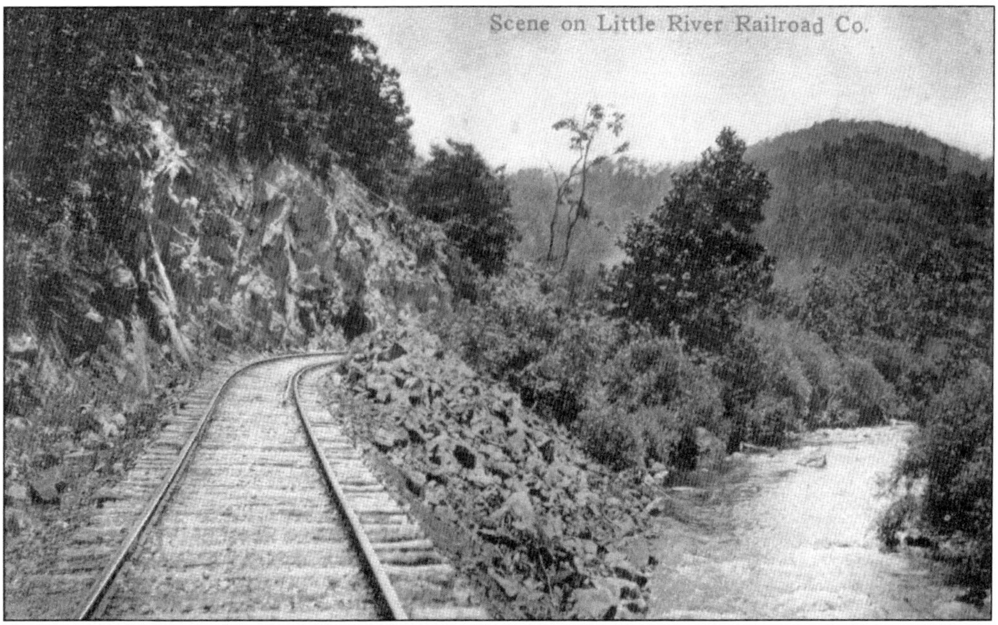